MY FIRST
500 KOREAN WORDS
BOOK 1

MY FIRST 500 KOREAN WORDS • BOOK 1

이야기로 배우는 **한국어 500 단어 ①**

1판 1쇄 · 1st Edition published	2017. 5. 15.
2판 3쇄 · 3rd Edition published	2024. 2. 26.
지은이 · Written by	Talk To Me In Korean
책임편집 · Edited by	선경화 Kyung-hwa Sun, 스테파니 베이츠 Stephanie Bates, 에밀리 프리즈러키 Emily Przylucki
디자인 · Designed by	한보람 Boram Han, 이은정 Eunjeong Lee
녹음 · Voice Recordings by	Talk To Me In Korean
펴낸곳 · Published by	롱테일북스 Longtail Books
펴낸이 · Publisher	이수영 Su Young Lee
편집 · Copy-edited by	김보경 Florence Kim
주소 · Address	04033 서울특별시 마포구 양화로 113, 3층(서교동, 순흥빌딩) 3rd Floor, 113 Yanghwa-ro, Mapo-gu, Seoul, KOREA
이메일 · E-mail	TTMIK@longtailbooks.co.kr
ISBN	979-11-86701-61-4 13710

TTMIK - TALK TO ME IN KOREAN

MY FIRST 500 KOREAN WORDS

BOOK 1

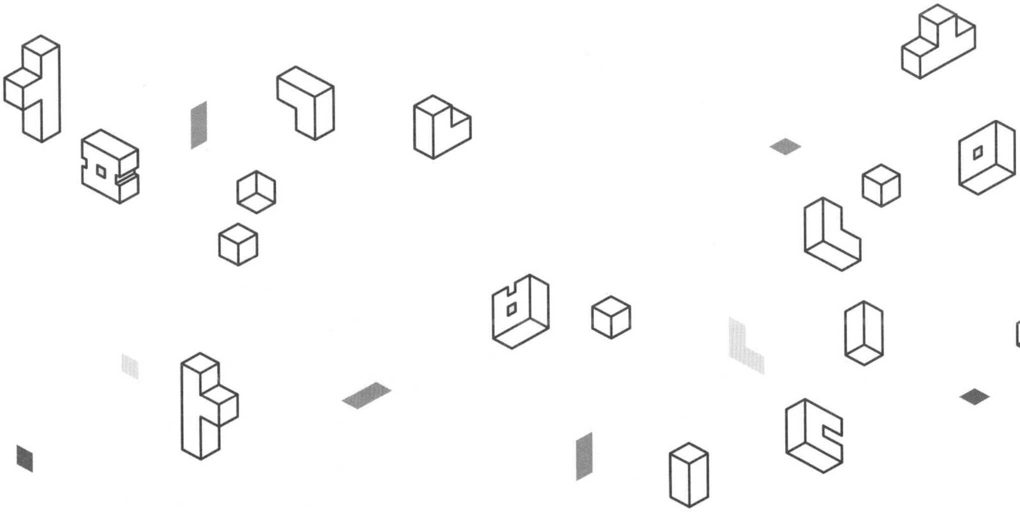

CONTENTS

PREFACE

My First 500 Korean Words · Book 1 is a vocabulary book designed for beginner learners of the Korean language. This book introduces 500 essential Korean words in context to make them more meaningful for you and easier to memorize. Learning vocabulary in this fashion provides you with an opportunity to substantially increase your ability to understand, retain, and use Korean words without having to solely rely on the standard rote memorization method.

Along with the 500 words in this book which are used on a daily basis by native speakers, related words and expressions are included to give you access to a broader understanding of the Korean language. Each chapter also provides you with some creative opportunities to review what you have learned through word matching, crossword puzzles, and fill-in-the-blank questions. It is recommended that you study one chapter per day in this book, but if you are busy and need to take two or three days to complete one chapter, the results will be great as long as you stay consistent and don't give up!

If you are ready to learn,
let's get started!

HOW TO USE THIS BOOK

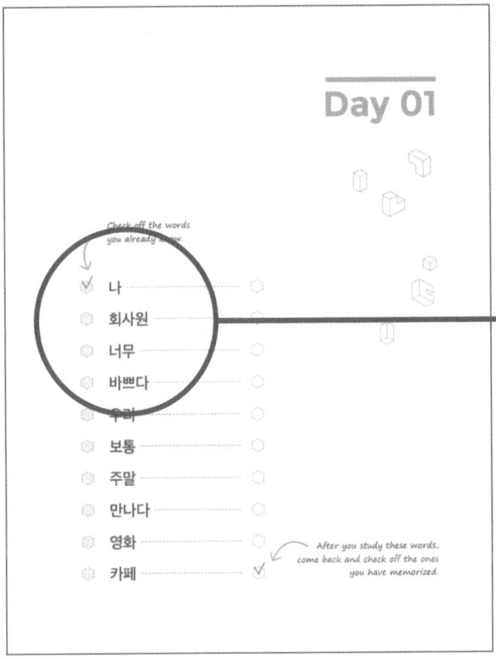

Each "Day" introduces 10 words. Place a check next to the words you already knew prior to this chapter, and then come back to this page to see how many words you memorized at the end of the Day.

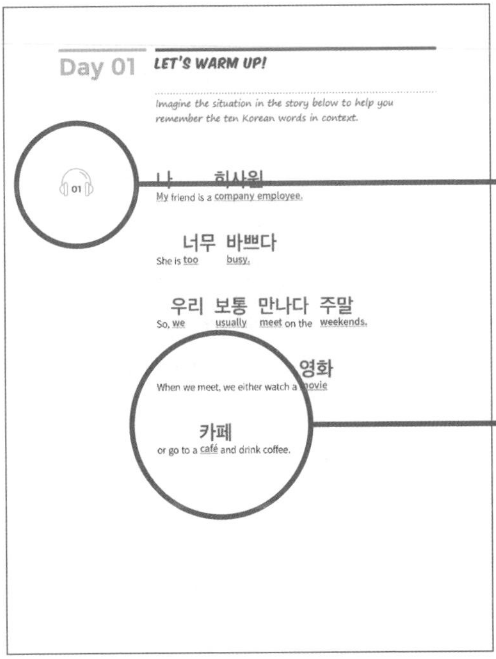

Listen to the words of the "Day" pronounced by native Korean speakers by downloading the MP3 audio files at **https://talktomeinkorean.com/audio.**

Before diving into the vocabulary, read the short story in English with the Korean translation of the 10 words written above. This will help put the words, which will be introduced on the following pages, into context.

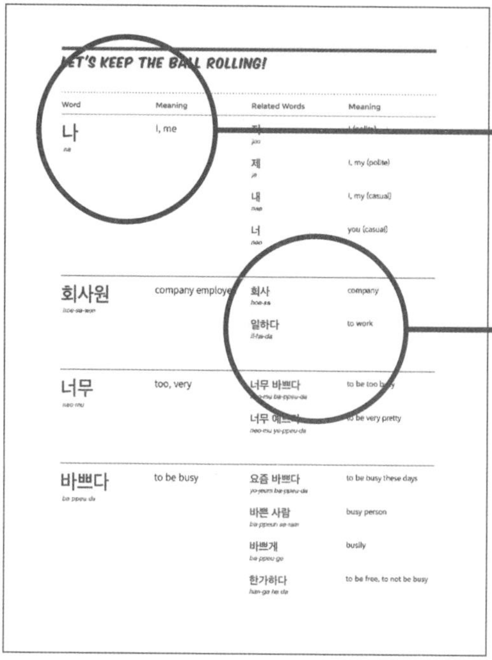

The main words are listed here with their meaning in English.

Words in this section are related to the main vocabulary word. You can find plural forms, synonyms, antonyms, common collocations, conjugated forms, derivative forms, or casual/honorific forms.

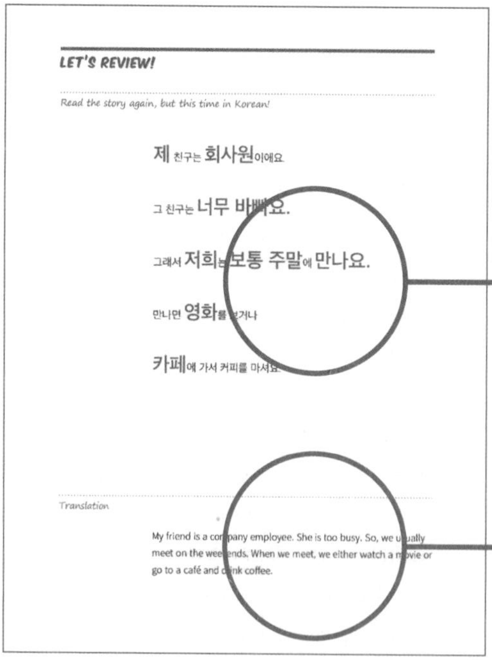

After committing the 10 words to memory, read the same story from Section 1, only this time entirely in Korean.

Check your understanding of the story with this English translation.

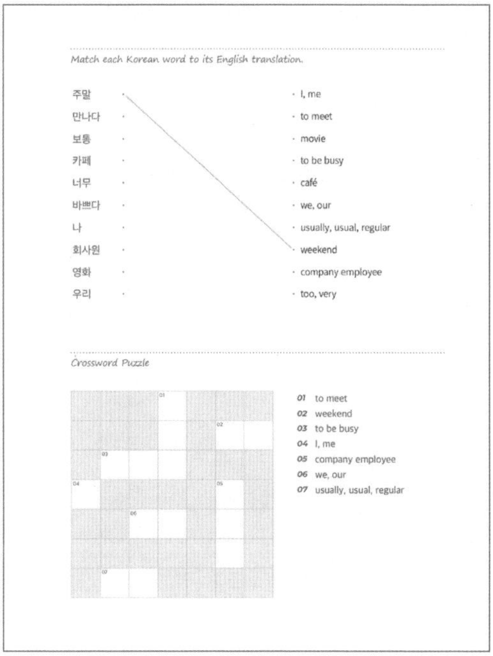

Match each Korean word to its English translation.

주말	I, me
만나다	to meet
보통	movie
카페	to be busy
너무	café
바쁘다	we, our
나	usually, usual, regular
회사원	weekend
영화	company employee
우리	too, very

Crossword Puzzle

01 to meet
02 weekend
03 to be busy
04 I, me
05 company employee
06 we, our
07 usually, usual, regular

Review what you have studied with a few exercises.

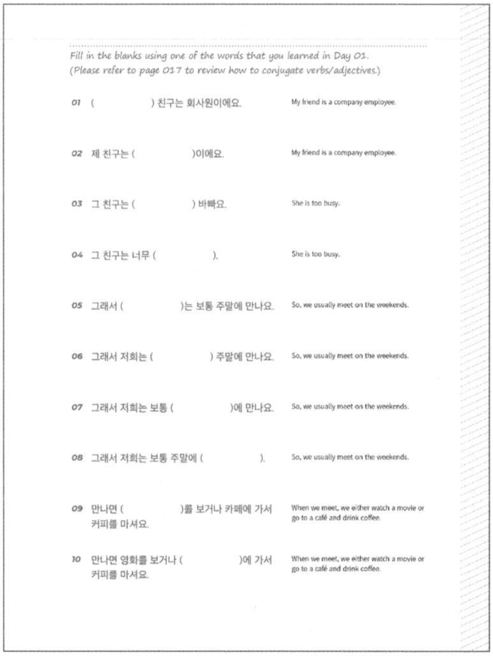

Fill in the blanks using one of the words that you learned in Day 01.
(Please refer to page 017 to review how to conjugate verbs/adjectives.)

01 (　　　) 친구는 회사원이에요. My friend is a company employee.

02 제 친구는 (　　　)이에요. My friend is a company employee.

03 그 친구는 (　　　) 바빠요. She is too busy.

04 그 친구는 너무 (　　　). She is too busy.

05 그래서 (　　　)는 보통 주말에 만나요. So, we usually meet on the weekends.

06 그래서 저희는 (　　　) 주말에 만나요. So, we usually meet on the weekends.

07 그래서 저희는 보통 (　　　)에 만나요. So, we usually meet on the weekends.

08 그래서 저희는 보통 주말에 (　　　). So, we usually meet on the weekends.

09 만나면 (　　　)를 보거나 카페에 가서 커피를 마셔요. When we meet, we either watch a movie or go to a café and drink coffee.

10 만나면 영화를 보거나 (　　　)에 가서 커피를 마셔요. When we meet, we either watch a movie or go to a café and drink coffee.

Complete the story by filling in each blank with a word you have learned, but in its correct conjugated form.

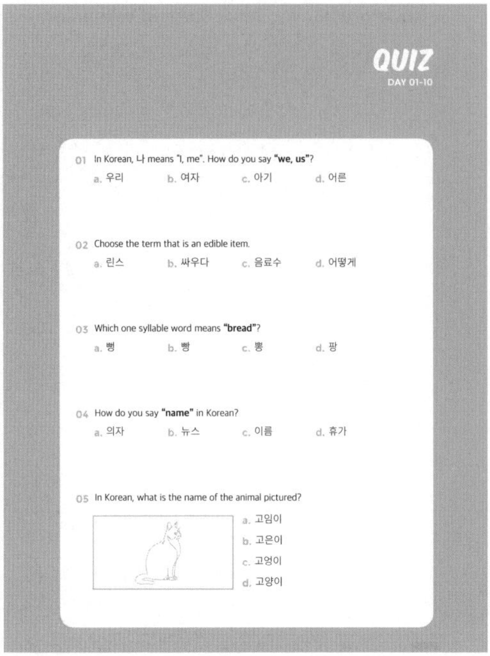
QUIZ
DAY 01-10

01 In Korean, 나 means "I, me". How do you say **"we, us"**?
a. 우리 b. 여자 c. 아기 d. 어른

02 Choose the term that is an edible item.
a. 린스 b. 싸우다 c. 음료수 d. 어떻게

03 Which one syllable word means **"bread"**?
a. 뻥 b. 빵 c. 뽕 d. 팡

04 How do you say **"name"** in Korean?
a. 의자 b. 뉴스 c. 이름 d. 휴가

05 In Korean, what is the name of the animal pictured?
a. 고임이
b. 고은이
c. 고엉이
d. 고양이

After studying 10 "Days" worth of words (or 100 words), there is a multiple choice quiz covering all of the vocabulary so that you can check your progress and create new goals.

Honorific Speech in Korean

In Korean, the relationship between the speaker/writer and the audience or listener is reflected in speech to or about someone. There are three main honorific speech types in Korean: subject, object, and relative.

Relative-honorific speech is most commonly known as “speech levels,” where a speaker uses either high or low forms of speech to the person being spoken to, regardless of the topic being discussed. The level of relative-honorific speech is usually determined based on the age of the speaker versus the listener. This explains why Korean people will often ask you about your age when first meeting you - they want to know what level of speech to use. Subject-honorific speech uses honorifics toward the subject of a sentence (not directly speaking to someone, but rather ABOUT someone who is older or in a higher position), while object-honorific speech is speaking to the object of a sentence using honorifics.

As a beginner level learner, you will focus mainly on relative-honorific speech.

When it comes to relative-honorific speech, there are two main speech levels: formal and informal.

Formal sublevels	Informal sublevels
합쇼체	해요체
하오체	해체
하게체	
해라체	

합쇼체 and 해요체 are polite forms which are used to speak to someone who is older or in a higher position than you, and these forms belong to a category of polite language called 존댓말 (존대 means "to treat with respect"). Even when speaking to someone who is younger or in a lower position than you, it is polite to use 존댓말 until you get permission to use casual language from him/her.

Casual forms such as 해라체 and 해체 belong to the 반말, or casual language, category. You can use 반말 to someone who is much younger or in a lower position than you. Between adults, 반말 is not used right away, even after finding out each other's ages, as the younger person may feel offended. Instead, 반말 is generally used between close friends and with children.

In contemporary Korean language, typically only the following four sublevels are used: 합쇼체, 해라체, 해요체, and 해체.

Endings used for each sublevel in declarative sentences:

합쇼체: -(스)ㅂ니다
해라체: -(ㄴ)다
해요체: -아/어/여요
해체: -아/어/여

If conjugating these endings with a verb, the ending changes slightly based on the verb stem. The verb 가다 (to go) is used in the following example:

합쇼체: 가다 + -(스)ㅂ니다 = 갑니다
해라체: 가다 + -(ㄴ)다 = 간다
해요체: 가다 + -아/어/여요 = 가요
해체: 가다 + -아/어/여 = 가

Since 합쇼체 is too formal to use every day, only 해요체 is used in this book.

Aside from endings, speakers sometimes use lower forms of certain words to sound humble or polite when speaking to someone in a higher position. For example, "I" is 나 in Korean, but 저 is the lower form of 나 in 존댓말. "We" is 우리, but 저희 is used to express humility or politeness.

Conjugation of Regular Verbs

The infinitive form (also known as "dictionary form") of Korean verbs always ends with -다, but for most verb conjugations in Korean, you use the "verb stem" of a verb and add various endings to it. The verb stem is formed by simply dropping the -다 from the infinitive form of a verb. All verbs in Korean end with -다 (e.g. 가다, 보다, 하다, etc.), so if you remove -다 from the end, you are left with the verb stem (e.g. 가, 보, 하, etc.).

Present Tense = -아/어/여요

Present tense verbs in Korean cover a wider range of tenses than in English; therefore, a sentence in the present tense in Korean can be translated to many different things in English. For example, 가요 can be translated as "I go", "I'm going", "I'm going to go", or even "I will go".

To create a present tense sentence, add -아요, -어요, or -여요 after the verb stem. If the verb stem's last vowel is ㅏ or ㅗ, it is followed by -아요. If the last vowel is NOT ㅏ or ㅗ, it is followed by -어요. Only one verb stem, 하, is followed by -여요. However, 하여요 is always shortened to 해요.

Examples

만나다 = to meet

만나 + -아요 → 만나아요 → 만나요. (I meet. / I'm meeting. / etc.)

- When ㅏ meets -아요, 아 is omitted to become 만나요, not 만나아요.

마시다 = to drink

마시 + -어요 → 마시어요 → 마셔요. (I drink. / I'm drinking. / etc.)

- When ㅣ and -어 are combined, it becomes ㅕ.

보내다 = to send

보내 + -어요 → 보내어요 → 보내요. (I send. / I'm sending. / etc.)

- When ㅐ meets -어요, 어 is omitted to become 보내요, not 보내어요.

시작하다 = to start, to begin

시작하 + -여요 → 시작하여요 → 시작해요. (I start. / I will start. / etc.)

- When 하 and -여 are combined, 하여 is always shortened to 해.

Past Tense
= -았/었/였어요

Add -았어요, -었어요, or -였어요 after the verb stem to form a past tense statement. If the last vowel of the verb stem is ㅏ or ㅗ, it is followed by -았어요. If the last vowel is NOT ㅏ or ㅗ, it is followed by -었어요. Only one verb stem, 하, is followed by -였어요. However, 하였어요 is usually shortened to 했어요.

Examples

만나다 = to meet

만나 + -았어요 = 만났어요. (I met.)

- When ㅏ meets -았, 아 is omitted to become 만났어요, not 만나았어요.

마시다 = to drink

마시 + -었어요 = 마셨어요. (I drank.)

- When ㅣ and -어 are combined, it becomes ㅕ.

보내다 = to send

보내 + -었어요 → 보내었어요 → 보냈어요. (I sent.)

- When ㅐ meets -었, 어 is omitted to become 보냈어요, not 보내었어요.

시작하다 = to start, to begin

시작하 + -였어요 = 시작했어요. (I started.)

- When 하 and -였 are combined, 하였 is usually shortened to 했.

Future Tense
= -(으)ㄹ 거예요

To create a future tense sentence, add either -을 거예요 or -ㄹ 거예요. If the last syllable of the verb stem is a consonant, add -을 거예요, and if the verb stem ends with a vowel, add -ㄹ 거예요. Although -(으)ㄹ 거예요 is basically a future tense sentence ending, you can also use this to express your assumption about something. Depending on the context, -(으)ㄹ 거예요 can be translated as either “it will/I will/they are going to” or “I think/I assume”.

Examples
일어나다 = to get up, to wake up
일어나 + -ㄹ 거예요 = 일어날 거예요. = I will get up. / I think he (she) will get up.

입다 = to wear, to put on
입 + -을 거예요 = 입을 거예요. = I will wear. / I think she (he) will wear.

Modifier (1)
= -(으)ㄴ

Used after a verb stem, this suffix changes a verb into a modifying adjective (in the past tense) to be used in front of a noun. This is similar to the role of a clause such as "that I found" or "that I bought yesterday" that is typically used after a noun in English.

Examples
찾다 = to find
찾은 = that I found, that they found
어제 찾은 책 = the book that she found yesterday

Modifier (2)
= -는

Used after a verb stem, this suffix changes a verb into a modifying adjective (in the present tense) to be used in front of a noun. This is similar to the role of a clause such as "that I like" or "that I use everyday" that is typically used after a noun in English.

Examples
가다 = to go
가는 = that I go to
매일 가는 곳 = a place that I go to every day

Modifier (3) = -(으)ㄹ

Used after a verb stem, this suffix changes a verb into a modifying adjective (in the future tense) to be used in front of a noun. This is similar to the role of a clause such as "that will start tomorrow" or "that you will see there" that is typically used after a noun in English.

Examples
연습하다 = to practice
연습할 = that I will practice
연습할 계획 = a plan that I will practice, a plan to practice

Passive Voice = -이/히/리/기- & -되다

Although there is no set-in-stone rule when it comes to passive voice, the general rules are as follows:

(1) 이

When the dictionary form of the verb ends in -ㅎ다, 이 is added to the verb stem ending and changes to -ㅎ이다.

Examples
놓다 (to put down) → 놓이다 (to be put down)
쌓다 (to pile up) → 쌓이다 (to be piled up)

(2) 히

When the dictionary form of the verb ends in -ㄱ다, -ㄷ다 or ㅂ다, 히 is added to the verb stem ending and changes to -ㄱ히다, ㄷ히다 or ㅂ히다.

Examples
막다 (to block) → 막히다 (to be blocked)
닫다 (to close) → 닫히다 (to be closed)

(3) 리

When the dictionary form of the verb ends in -ㄹ다, -리 is added to the verb stem ending and changes to -ㄹ리다.

Examples

열다 (to open) → 열리다 (to be opened)
팔다 (to sell) → 팔리다 (to be sold)

(4) 기

When the dictionary form of the verb ends in -ㄴ다, ㅁ다, ㅅ다 or ㅊ다, -기 is added to the verb stem ending and changes to -ㄴ기다, -ㅁ기다, -ㅅ기다 or -ㅊ기다.

Examples

안다 (to hug) → 안기다 (to be hugged)
담다 (to put something in a basket/bag) → 담기다 (to be put into a basket/bag)

Passive Voice of 하다 Verbs

하다 verbs are combinations of nouns + 하다. For example:

시작 (start, begin) + 하다 = to start, to begin
걱정(worry) + (하다) = to worry

To change these 하다 verbs into passive voice, change 하다 to 되다.

Examples

시작하다 → 시작되다 (to be started)
걱정하다 → 걱정되다 (to be worried)

Conjugation of Adjectives

In English, adjectives such as “pretty”, “big”, and “tall” are already in the correct format to be used in a sentence. In Korean, however, adjectives must be conjugated because they are in the infinitive form. For example:

예쁘다 = to be pretty

크다 = to be big

높다 = to be tall

To use these to modify a noun (pretty girl, big dog, tall mountain), you must conjugate the word into the modifier format: drop the -다 to get the adjective stem by itself, and if the stem ends with a vowel, add -ㄴ as the final consonant. If the stem ends with a consonant, add -은.

Examples

크다 = to be big (adjective in the infinitive form)

큰 = big (base adjective form)

높다 = to be high (adjective in the infinitive form)

높은 = high (base adjective form)

When adjectives are used as predicate adjectives rather than as modifiers, such as in "OOO is pretty", "OOO is big", and "OOO is important", you can conjugate the adjectives just as you would verbs depending on the tense.

Examples

바쁘다

Present Tense: 바쁘 + -아요 → 바쁘아요 → 바빠요. (OOO is busy.)

- When ㅡ meets another vowel, ㅡ is omitted to become 바빠요, not 바쁘아요.

Past Tense: 바쁘 + -았어요 → 바쁘았어요 → 바빴어요. (OOO was busy.)

- When ㅡ meets another vowel, ㅡ is omitted to become 바빴어요, not 바쁘았어요.

Future Tense: 바쁘 + -(으)ㄹ 거예요 → 바쁠 거예요. (OOO will be busy.)

Adverbs = -게

If you add -게 to an adjective stem, it become an adverb.

Examples

조용하다 = to be quiet
조용하게 = quietly

싸다 = to be cheap
싸게 = cheaply

Conjugation of Irregular Verbs/Adjectives

Irregulars: ㅂ

When the following verbs or adjectives are followed by a suffix which starts with a vowel, the ㅂ is eliminated and becomes 우.

더럽다 = to be dirty
무섭다 = to be scary
차갑다 = to be cold
덥다 = to be hot (weather)
눕다 = to lie down
뜨겁다 = to be hot
시끄럽다 = to be noisy

어둡다 = to be dark
귀엽다 = to be cute
무겁다 = to be heavy
춥다 = to be cold (weather)
어렵다 = to be difficult
가깝다 = to be close
쉽다 = to be easy
가볍다 = to be light

Example

더럽다

Present Tense: 더럽 + -어요 → 더러우 + -어요 → 더러우어요 → 더러워요
Past Tense: 더럽 + -었어요 → 더러우 + -었어요 → 더러우었어요 → 더러웠어요
Future Tense: 더럽 + -(으)ㄹ 거예요 → 더러우 + -(으)ㄹ 거예요 → 더러울 거예요

Irregulars: 르

When the following verbs or adjectives are followed by -아/어/여요 (present tense) or -았/었/였어요 (past tense), 르 is changed to ㄹ and placed at the end of the previous syllable, while one more ㄹ is added to the verb/adjective ending.

배부르다 = to be full
바르다 = to apply
부르다 = to call
모르다 = to not know
다르다 = to be different
고르다 = to pick, to choose

Example

배부르다

Present Tense: 배부르 + -어요 → 배불ㄹ + -어요 → 배불러요

Past Tense: 배부르 + -었어요 → 배불ㄹ + -었어요 → 배불렀어요

Irregulars: ㄷ

When the following verbs are followed by a suffix which starts with a vowel, ㄷ is changed to ㄹ.

듣다 = to hear
걷다 = to walk
알아듣다 = to understand

Example
듣다
Present Tense: 듣 + -어요 → 들 + -어요 → 들어요
Past Tense: 듣 + -었어요 → 들 + -었어요 → 들었어요
Future Tense: 듣 + -(으)ㄹ 거예요 → 들 + -(으)ㄹ 거예요 → 들을 거예요

To be + Noun

Present Tense = NOUN + -이에요/예요

Add -이에요/예요 after the noun. If the noun has a final consonant in the last letter, add -이에요, and if it does not have a final consonant and ends in a vowel, add -예요.

Examples
주말 = weekend
주말 + -이에요 = 주말이에요. (It is the weekend.)

의자 = chair
의자 + -예요 = 의자예요. (It is a chair.)

Past Tense = NOUN + -이었어요/였어요

Add -이었어요/였어요 after the noun. If the noun has a final consonant in the last letter, add -이었어요, and if it does not have a final consonant and ends in a vowel, add -였어요.

Examples
주말 = weekend
주말 + -이었어요 = 주말이었어요. (It was the weekend.)

의자 = chair
의자 + -였어요 = 의자였어요. (It was a chair.)

Future Tense = NOUN + -일 거예요

Add -일 거예요 after the noun.

Examples
주말 = weekend
주말 + -일 거예요 = 주말일 거예요. (It will be the weekend.)

의자 = chair
의자 + -일 거예요 = 의자일 거예요. (It will be a chair.)

Conjunctions

Conjunctions connect two sentences together and are used at the beginning of the second sentence in Korean. Listed below are the conjunctions used in this book.

그래서	so, therefore
그리고	and
하지만	but, however (used when the second sentence is in direct contradiction to the first sentence)
그런데	but, however, by the way (used when the second sentence is in contradiction to the first sentence, or when the second sentence is slightly changing the direction of the topic)
그래도	but, still

Numbers

In Korean, there are two number systems: sino-Korean numbers (based on the Chinese number system) and native Korean numbers.

	sino-Korean	native Korean
0	영/공	-
1	일	하나
2	이	둘
3	삼	셋
4	사	넷
5	오	다섯
6	육/륙	여섯
7	칠	일곱

8	팔	여덟
9	구	아홉
10	십	열

Telling Time

Both sino-Korean numbers and native Korean numbers are used when telling time. When you say the hour (시), native Korean numbers (하나, 둘, 셋, 넷, etc.) are used, but when you say the minute (분), sino-Korean numbers (일, 이, 삼, 사, etc.) are used.

1 o'clock	1시	한 시
2 o'clock	2시	두 시
3 o'clock	3시	세 시
4 o'clock	4시	네 시
5 o'clock	5시	다섯 시
6 o'clock	6시	여섯 시
7 o'clock	7시	일곱 시
8 o'clock	8시	여덟 시
9 o'clock	9시	아홉 시
10 o'clock	10시	열 시
11 o'clock	11시	열한 시
12 o'clock	12시	열두 시

1 minute	1분	일 분	**31 minutes**	31분	삼십일 분
2 minutes	2분	이 분	**32 minutes**	32분	삼십이 분
3 minutes	3분	삼 분	**33 minutes**	33분	삼십삼 분
4 minutes	4분	사 분	**34 minutes**	34분	삼십사 분
5 minutes	5분	오 분	**35 minutes**	35분	삼십오 분
6 minutes	6분	육 분	**36 minutes**	36분	삼십육 분
7 minutes	7분	칠 분	**37 minutes**	37분	삼십칠 분
8 minutes	8분	팔 분	**38 minutes**	38분	삼십팔 분
9 minutes	9분	구 분	**39 minutes**	39분	삼십구 분
10 minutes	10분	십 분	**40 minutes**	40분	사십 분
11 minutes	11분	십일 분	**41 minutes**	41분	사십일 분
12 minutes	12분	십이 분	**42 minutes**	42분	사십이 분
13 minutes	13분	십삼 분	**43 minutes**	43분	사십삼 분
14 minutes	14분	십사 분	**44 minutes**	44분	사십사 분
15 minutes	15분	십오 분	**45 minutes**	45분	사십오 분
16 minutes	16분	십육 분	**46 minutes**	46분	사십육 분
17 minutes	17분	십칠 분	**47 minutes**	47분	사십칠 분
18 minutes	18분	십팔 분	**48 minutes**	48분	사십팔 분
19 minutes	19분	십구 분	**49 minutes**	49분	사십구 분
20 minutes	20분	이십 분	**50 minutes**	50분	오십 분
21 minutes	21분	이십일 분	**51 minutes**	51분	오십일 분
22 minutes	22분	이십이 분	**52 minutes**	52분	오십이 분
23 minutes	23분	이십삼 분	**53 minutes**	53분	오십삼 분
24 minutes	24분	이십사 분	**54 minutes**	54분	오십사 분
25 minutes	25분	이십오 분	**55 minutes**	55분	오십오 분
26 minutes	26분	이십육 분	**56 minutes**	56분	오십육 분
27 minutes	27분	이십칠 분	**57 minutes**	57분	오십칠 분
28 minutes	28분	이십팔 분	**58 minutes**	58분	오십팔 분
29 minutes	29분	이십구 분	**59 minutes**	59분	오십구 분
30 minutes	30분	삼십 분	**60 minutes**	60분	육십 분

Counters

When counting things or people in Korean, you often need to use what is called a "counter" or a "counter unit". In English, if you want to talk about books, and there happen to be three of them, you can simply say "three books"; however in Korean, you need to use the format of "book + three + counter". Listed below are the counters used in this book.

Counter	Used with
개	things in general
명	people
마리	animals

Grammar Points Introduced in This Book

All of the examples in this section appear in this book.

NOUN + -은/는 (Day 1)

(topic marking particles)
Ex) 저희 집에는 = at our house

NOUN + -에 (Day 1)

at
Ex) 회사에 있다 = to be at work

on
Ex) 의자에 앉다 = to sit on a chair

in
Ex) 쓰레기통에 버리다 = to throw away in a trash bin

	into Ex) 서점에 들어가다 = to go into a bookstore **to** Ex) 시장에 가다 = to go to the market
NOUN + -을/를 **(Day 1)**	**(object marking particles)** Ex) 종이를 찢어요. = I tear some paper.
NOUN + -도 **(Day 2)**	**also, too** Ex) 지하철도 = the subway, too
NOUN + -이/가 **(Day 3)**	**(subject marking particles)** Ex) 해가 떠요. = The sun rises.
NOUN + -에서 **(Day 3)**	**at** Ex) 시장에서 사다 = at the market **from** Ex) 필통에서 = from a pencil case **in** Ex) 사전에서 = in a dictionary **out of** Ex) 세 개 중에서 = out of three
NOUN + -와/과 **(Day 3)**	**with** Ex) 저희와 = with us **and** Ex) 때와 장소 = time and place

NOUN + -(으)로 **(Day 3)**	**to, into** Ex) 방으로 = into a room **with** Ex) 칼로 = with a knife **through/via** Ex) 인터넷으로 = via the Internet **for** Ex) 아침으로 = for breakfast **as** Ex) 생일 선물로 = as a birthday present
NOUN + -부터 **(Day 4)**	**since, from** Ex) 언제부터 = since when
NOUN + -까지 **(Day 4)**	**until, up to** Ex) 지금까지 = until now 여기까지 = up to here
NOUN + -(이)랑 **(Day 4)**	**NOUN and NOUN** Ex) 빵이랑 음료수 = bread and a drink/beverage **with** Ex) 가족이랑 = with my family
NOUN + -한테 **(Day 4)**	**to** Ex) 엄마한테 = to (my) mom **by** Ex) 선생님한테 = by (my) teacher

	from Ex) 친구한테 돈을 빌렸어요. = I borrowed money from a friend.
NOUN + -보다 **(Day 5)**	**than** Ex) 가수들보다 = than singers
NOUN + -들 **(Day 5)**	**(a plural suffix)** Ex) 남자들 = men
NOUN + -만 **(Day 7)**	**only** Ex) 바지만 = only pants
NOUN + -의 **(Day 17)**	**of** Ex) 옆집 부부의 딸 = the daughter of the next door couple
NOUN + -에게 **(Day 23)**	**to** Ex) 나에게 = to me
NOUN + -을/를 위해(서) **(Day 29)**	**in order for, for** Ex) 엄마를 위해서 = for (my) mom
NOUN + -이나 **(Day 46)**	**or** Ex) 신문이나 종이 = newspapers or paper
VERB + -(으)면 **(Day 1)**	**if** Ex) 졸면 = if I doze off
VERB/ADJECTIVE + -아/어/여서 **(Day 1)**	**(connecting reason and result)** Ex) 공항이 너무 넓어서 길을 잃어버렸어요. = The airport is so spacious that I lost my way.

	(connecting an action and another action which takes place after the first action) Ex) 카페에 가서 커피를 마셔요. = I go to a café and drink coffee. **(connecting an action and the purpose or the plan after the action)** Ex) 지구를 떠나서 우주로 갔어요. = He left Earth and went to outer space.
VERB + -거나 **(Day 1)**	**or** Ex) 영화를 보거나 = watch a movie or
VERB + -고 **(Day 2)**	**VERB and VERB** Ex) 물을 마시고 세수를 해요. = I drink water and wash my face.
ADJECTIVE + -아/어/여지다 **(Day 3)**	**to become ADJECTIVE** Ex) 건강해지다 = to become healthy 건강해져요. = I become healthy.
VERB + -고 싶다 **(Day 6)**	**to want to VERB** Ex) 놀고 싶다 = to want to hang out 놀고 싶어요 = I want to hang out.
VERB/ADJECTIVE + -지 않다 **(Day 9)**	**not** Ex) 먹지 않다 = to not eat 먹지 않아요. = I don't eat. / One doesn't eat.
VERB + -(으)ㄹ 수 있다 **(Day 10)**	**can, be able to** Ex) 구별할 수 있다 = to be able to distinguish 구별할 수 있어요. = You can distinguish them.

VERB + -아/어/여 주다 (Day 10)	**to VERB for someone** Ex) 가르쳐 주다 = to teach 가르쳐 줘요. = I teach.
VERB (passive voice) + -어 있다 (Day 10)	**to be put into a certain state (by someone) and stay that way** Ex) 열려 있다 = to be open (and remain open) 열려 있어요. = It is open.
VERB + -아/어/여하다 (Day 11)	**(making intransitive verbs into transitive verbs)** Ex) 궁금해하다 = to feel curious 궁금해해요. = One feels curious.
VERB + -(으)ㄹ까요? (Day 11)	**I wonder** Ex) 기뻐할까요? = I wonder if she will be happy.
VERB + -는 것 (Day 14)	**VERB-ing** Ex) 집에 있는 것 = staying at home **something that one VERB** Ex) 못하는 것 = something that one is not good at
VERB + -기 전에 (Day 20)	**before VERB-ing** Ex) 해가 지기 전에 = before the sun sets
VERB + -고 있다 (Day 26)	**to be VERB-ing** Ex) 배우고 있다 = to be learning 배우고 있어요. = I am learning.

VERB + -(으)ㄴ/는/(으)ㄹ 것 같다 (Day 32)	**to think (SUBJECT) VERB** Ex) 다친 것 같다 = to think (someone) hurt 다친 것 같아요. = I think I am hurt.
VERB + -는데 (Day 32)	**but** Ex) 약속이 있는데 늦었어요. = I had plans, but I was late. **(explaining the situation first before explaining what happened)** Ex) 집에 가는데 비가 왔어요. = On my way home, it rained.
VERB + -기 위해서 (Day 33)	**in order to VERB** Ex) 듣기 위해서 = in order to listen
VERB + -아/어/여 보다 (Day 33)	**to try VERB-ing** Ex) 입어 보다 = to try putting on, to try on (clothes) 입어 봐요. = I try it on.
VERB + -다가 (Day 36)	**while VERB-ing** Ex) 운동을 하다가 = while working out
VERB + -기 힘들다 (Day 36)	**to be hard to VERB** Ex) 먹기 힘들다 = to be hard to eat 먹기 힘들어요. = It's hard to eat.
VERB + -자마자 (Day 37)	**as soon as** Ex) 집에 오자마자 = as soon as I come home
SUBJECT + VERB + -다고 (Day 38)	**(to say/believe/hear) that SUBJECT VERB** Ex) 벌레가 있다고 했어요. = He said that there was a bug.

VERB + -아/어/여야 하다 (Day 39)	**must** Ex) 먹어야 하다 = must eat 먹어야 해요. = I must eat.
VERB + -(으)ㄴ/는지 (Day 41)	**(marking the end of a question inside a compound sentence)** Ex) 언제부터 좋아했는지 몰라요. = I don't know since when I have liked it.
VERB + -(으)ㄴ 다음에 (Day 45)	**after VERB-ing** Ex) 결혼한 다음에 = after getting married
VERB + -기로 정하다 (Day 45)	**to decide to VERB** Ex) 하기로 정하다 = to decide to do 하기로 정해요. = I decide to do.
VERB + -기도 하다 (Day 46)	**also VERB** Ex) 유리창을 닦기도 하다 = to also wipe the glass window 유리창을 닦기도 해요. = I also wipe the glass window.
SUBJECT + VERB/ ADJECTIVE + -(으)ㄹ 때 (Day 46)	**when SUBJECT VERB/ADJECTIVE** Ex) 손님이 없을 때 = when there are no customers
VERB + -(으)ㄹ 수도 있다 (Day 47)	**might, maybe** Ex) 실수할 수도 있다 = to maybe make a mistake 실수할 수도 있어요. = You might make a mistake.

LET'S BEGIN!

Day 01

Check off the words
you already know.

- 나
- 회사원
- 너무
- 바쁘다
- 우리
- 보통
- 주말
- 만나다
- 영화
- 카페

After you study these words,
come back and check off the ones
you have memorized.

Day 01 LET'S WARM UP!

Imagine the situation in the story below to help you remember the ten Korean words in context.

01

나 회사원
My friend is a company employee.

너무 바쁘다
She is too busy.

우리 보통 만나다 주말
So, we usually meet on the weekends.

영화
When we meet, we either watch a movie

카페
or go to a café and drink coffee.

LET'S KEEP THE BALL ROLLING!

Word	Meaning	Related Words	Meaning
나 *na*	I, me	저 *jeo*	I (polite)
		제 *je*	I, my (polite)
		내 *nae*	I, my (casual)
		너 *neo*	you (casual)
회사원 *hoe-sa-won*	company employee	회사 *hoe-sa*	company
		일하다 *il-ha-da*	to work
너무 *neo-mu*	too, very	너무 바쁘다 *neo-mu ba-ppeu-da*	to be too busy
		너무 예쁘다 *neo-mu ye-ppeu-da*	to be very pretty
바쁘다 *ba-ppeu-da*	to be busy	요즘 바쁘다 *yo-jeum ba-ppeu-da*	to be busy these days
		바쁜 사람 *ba-ppeun sa-ram*	busy person
		바쁘게 *ba-ppeu-ge*	busily
		한가하다 *han-ga-ha-da*	to be free, to not be busy

우리 *u-ri*	we, our	우리 나라 *u-ri na-ra*	our country, my country
		우리 집 *u-ri jip*	our house, my house
		우리 학교 *u-ri hak-kkyo*	our school, my school
		저희 *jeo-hui*	we, our (polite, excluding the listener)
보통 *bo-tong*	usually, usual, regular	보통 때 *bo-tong ttae*	usually, normally
		보통 사람 *bo-tong sa-ram*	regular person
주말 *ju-mal*	weekend	이번 주말 *i-beon ju-mal*	this weekend
		주말에 *ju-ma-re*	on the weekend
		주말마다 *ju-mal-ma-da*	every weekend
		쉬다 *swi-da*	to rest
		평일 *pyeong-il*	weekday

만나다 *man-na-da*	to meet	우연히 만나다 *u-yeo-ni man-na-da*	to bump into
		못 만나다 *mot man-na-da*	to not be able to meet
		안 만나다 *an man-na-da*	to not meet
		헤어지다 *he-eo-ji-da*	to say good-bye, to part

영화 *yeong-hwa*	movie	영화를 보다 *yeong-hwa-reul bo-da*	to watch a movie
		영화관 *yeong-hwa-gwan*	movie theater
		주인공 *ju-in-gong*	main character
		영화배우 *yeong-hwa-bae-u*	movie actor/actress

카페 *ka-pe*	café	카페에 가다 *ka-pe-e ga-da*	to go to a café
		커피 *keo-pi*	coffee
		차 *cha*	tea

LET'S REVIEW!

Read the story again, but this time in Korean!

제 친구는 **회사원**이에요.

그 친구는 **너무 바빠요.**

그래서 **저희**는 **보통 주말**에 **만나요.**

만나면 **영화**를 보거나

카페에 가서 커피를 마셔요.

Translation

My friend is a company employee. She is too busy. So, we usually meet on the weekends. When we meet, we either watch a movie or go to a café and drink coffee.

Match each Korean word to its English translation.

주말 ·	· I, me
만나다 ·	· to meet
보통 ·	· movie
카페 ·	· to be busy
너무 ·	· café
바쁘다 ·	· we, our
나 ·	· usually, usual, regular
회사원 ·	· weekend
영화 ·	· company employee
우리 ·	· too, very

Crossword Puzzle

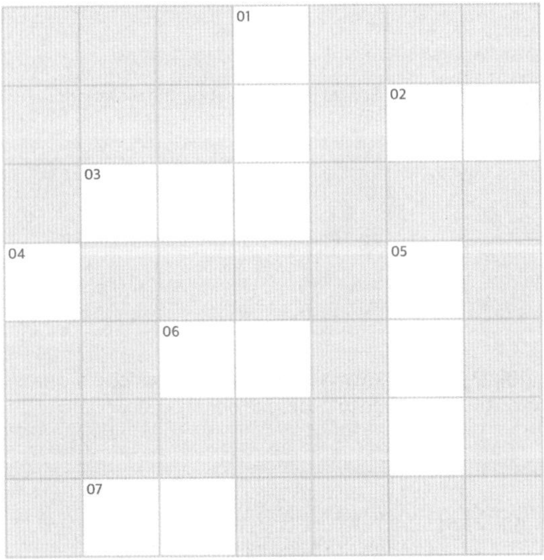

01 to meet
02 weekend
03 to be busy
04 I, me
05 company employee
06 we, our
07 usually, usual, regular

Fill in the blanks using one of the words that you learned in Day 01.
(Please refer to page 017 to review how to conjugate verbs/adjectives.)

01 (   ) 친구는 회사원이에요. My friend is a company employee.

02 제 친구는 (   )이에요. My friend is a company employee.

03 그 친구는 (   ) 바빠요. She is too busy.

04 그 친구는 너무 (   ). She is too busy.

05 그래서 (   )는 보통 주말에 만나요. So, we usually meet on the weekends.

06 그래서 저희는 (   ) 주말에 만나요. So, we usually meet on the weekends.

07 그래서 저희는 보통 (   )에 만나요. So, we usually meet on the weekends.

08 그래서 저희는 보통 주말에 (   ). So, we usually meet on the weekends.

09 만나면 (   )를 보거나 카페에 가서 커피를 마셔요. When we meet, we either watch a movie or go to a café and drink coffee.

10 만나면 영화를 보거나 (   )에 가서 커피를 마셔요. When we meet, we either watch a movie or go to a café and drink coffee.

Day 02

- 매일
- 일찍
- 일어나다
- 물
- 마시다
- 세수
- 옷
- 입다
- 화장
- 회사

Day 02 LET'S WARM UP!

Imagine the situation in the story below to help you remember the ten Korean words in context.

02

일어나다 일찍 매일
I wake up early every morning.

마시다 물 세수
I drink water and wash my face.

입다 옷 화장
I put on clothes and put on make-up.

회사
Then I go to work.

I can do it again today!

LET'S KEEP THE BALL ROLLING!

Word	Meaning	Related Words	Meaning
매일 *mae-il*	every day	매일 만나다 *mae-il man-na-da*	to meet every day
		매일 한 시간 *mae-il han si-gan*	one hour every day
		매일매일 *mae-il-mae-il*	every day, every single day
일찍 *il-jjik*	early	아침 일찍 *a-chim il-jjik*	early in the morning
		일찍 자다 *il-jjik ja-da*	to go to bed early
		일찍 일어나다 *il-jjik i-reo-na-da*	to wake up early
		일찍 도착하다 *il-jjik do-cha-ka-da*	to arrive early
일어나다 *i-reo-na-da*	to get up, to wake up	늦게 일어나다 *neut-kke i-reo-na-da*	to wake up late
		먼저 일어나다 *meon-jeo i-reo-na-da*	to wake up first
		눕다 *nup-tta*	to lie down
		앉다 *an-tta*	to sit down

물 *mul*	water	물을 마시다 *mu-reul ma-si-da*	to drink water
		차가운 물 *cha-ga-un mul*	cold water
		물을 끓이다 *mu-reul kkeu-ri-da*	to boil water
마시다 *ma-si-da*	to drink	차를 마시다 *cha-reul ma-si-da*	to drink tea
		천천히 마시다 *cheon-cheo-ni ma-si-da*	to drink slowly
		다 마시다 *da ma-si-da*	to drink up, to drink all
세수 *se-su*	washing one's face	세수하다 *se-su-ha-da*	to wash one's face
		세수를 하다 *se-su-reul ha-da*	to wash one's face
옷 *ot*	clothes	옷을 사다 *o-seul sa-da*	to buy clothes
		옷 가게 *ot ga-ge*	clothing store
		새 옷 *sae ot*	new clothes

입다 *ip-tta*	to wear, to put on	옷을 입다 *o-seul ip-tta*	to put on clothes
		벗다 *beot-tta*	to take off clothes
		갈아입다 *ga-ra-ip-tta*	to change clothes
		입어 보다 *i-beo bo-da*	to try on clothes

화장 *hwa-jang*	make-up	화장을 하다 *hwa-jang-eul ha-da*	to put on make-up
		화장하다 *hwa-jang-ha-da*	to put on make-up
		화장한 얼굴 *hwa-jang-han eol-gul*	a face with make-up on, a made-up face
		화장품 *hwa-jang-pum*	make-up product, cosmetic product

회사 *hoe-sa*	company	회사에 들어가다 *hoe-sa-e deu-reo-ga-da*	to join a company
		회사원 *hoe-sa-won*	company employee
		회사에 다니다 *hoe-sa-e da-ni-da*	to work at a company

LET'S REVIEW!

Read the story again, but this time in Korean!

저는 **매일** 아침 **일찍 일어나요.**

물을 **마시고 세수**를 해요.

옷을 **입고 화장**을 해요.

그리고 **회사**에 가요.

오늘도 화이팅!

Translation

I wake up early every morning. I drink water and wash my face.
I put on clothes and put on make-up. Then I go to work. I can do it again today!

Match each Korean word to its English translation.

회사 ·	· make-up
물 ·	· to wear, to put on
일찍 ·	· clothes
세수 ·	· to drink
일어나다 ·	· water
마시다 ·	· every day
매일 ·	· company
옷 ·	· early
입다 ·	· to get up, to wake up
화장 ·	· washing one's face

Crossword Puzzle

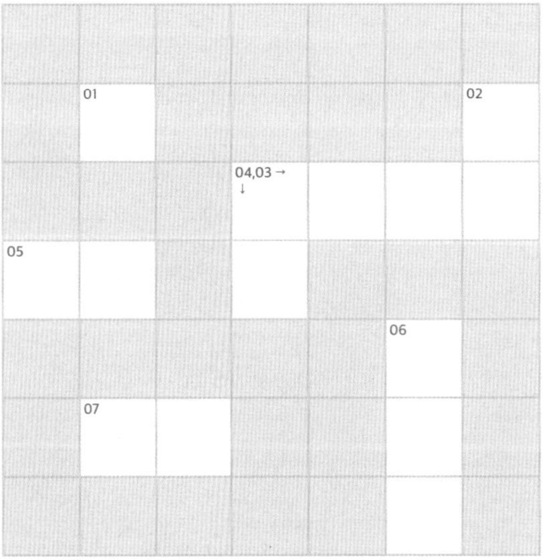

01 water
02 to wear, to put on
03 to get up, to wake up
04 early
05 make-up
06 to drink
07 company

Fill in the blanks using one of the words that you learned in Day 02.
(Please refer to page 017 to review how to conjugate verbs/adjectives.)

01 저는 (   ) 아침 일찍 일어나요. I wake up early every morning.

02 저는 매일 아침 (   ) 일어나요. I wake up early every morning.

03 저는 매일 아침 일찍 (   ). I wake up early every morning.

04 (   )을 마시고 세수를 해요. I drink water and wash my face.

05 물을 (   ) 세수를 해요. I drink water and wash my face.

06 물을 마시고 (   )를 해요. I drink water and wash my face.

07 (   )을 입고 화장을 해요. I put on clothes and put on make-up.

08 옷을 (   ) 화장을 해요. I put on clothes and put on make-up.

09 옷을 입고 (   )을 해요. I put on clothes and put on make-up.

10 그리고 (   )에 가요. Then I go to work.

Day 03

- 시험
- 의자
- 책상
- 더럽다
- 위
- 청소
- 깨끗하다
- 공책
- 필통
- 시작하다

Day 03 LET'S WARM UP!

Imagine the situation in the story below to help you remember the ten Korean words in context.

03

시험
I have an exam tomorrow.

의자
I sat down on the chair.

책상 더럽다
The desk is too dirty.

청소하다 위
I clean the top of my desk.

깨끗하다
Now it's clean.

공책 필통
I take out my notebook and my pencil case from my bag.

시작하다
I start studying.

LET'S KEEP THE BALL ROLLING!

Word	Meaning	Related Words	Meaning
시험 *si-heom*	test, exam	시험을 보다 *si-heo-meul bo-da*	to take an exam
		시험 문제 *si-heom mun-je*	exam question
		시험 공부 *si-heom gong-bu*	study for an exam
		시험 기간 *si-heom gi-gan*	exam period
		성적 *seong-jeok*	exam score
의자 *ui-ja*	chair	의자에 앉다 *ui-ja-e an-tta*	to sit on a chair
		나무 의자 *na-mu ui-ja*	wooden chair
		편안한 의자 *pyeo-na-nan ui-ja*	comfortable chair
책상 *chaek-ssang*	desk	책상 위 *chaek-ssang wi*	on the desk
		내 책상 *nae chaek-ssang*	my desk
		책상을 정리하다 *chaek-ssang-eul jeong-li-ha-da*	to organize one's desk

더럽다 *deo-reop-tta*	to be dirty	옷이 더럽다 *o-si deo-reop-tta*	the clothes are dirty
		더러운 손 *deo-reo-un son*	dirty hand
		더럽히다 *deo-reo-pi-da*	to make dirty, to dirty up
위 *wi*	up, top	위를 보다 *wi-reul bo-da*	to look up
		위로 *wi-ro*	up, upward
		위에서 *wi-e-seo*	from up
		아래 *a-rae*	down, below
청소 *cheong-so*	cleaning	화장실 청소 *hwa-jang-sil cheong-so*	cleaning the bathroom
		청소하다 *cheong-so-ha-da*	to clean
		교실을 청소하다 *gyo-si-reul cheong-so-ha-da*	to clean the classroom
		청소기 *cheong-so-gi*	cleaner

깨끗하다 *kkae-kkeu-ta-da*	to be clean	물이 깨끗하다 *mu-ri kkae-kkeu-ta-da*	the water is clean
		깨끗한 손 *kkae-kkeu-tan son*	clean hand
		깨끗하게 *kkae-kkeu-ta-ge*	cleanly
		깨끗해지다 *kkae-kkeu-tae-ji-da*	to become clean

공책 *gong-chaek*	notebook	공책 열 권 *gong-chaek yeol gwon*	ten notebooks
		공책에 쓰다 *gong-chae-ge sseu-da*	to write in a notebook
		노트 *no-teu*	note

필통 *pil-tong*	pencil case	필통에 담다 *pil-tong-e dam-tta*	to put into a pencil case
		필통 속 *pil-tong sok*	inside a pencil case
		필통을 꺼내다 *pil-tong-eul kkeo-nae-da*	to take out one's pencil case
		필통에서 꺼내다 *pil-tong-e-seo kkeo-nae-da*	to take out from one's pencil case

시작하다 *si-ja-ka-da*	to begin, to start	청소를 시작하다 *cheong-so-reul si-ja-ka-da*	to start cleaning
		시작되다 *si-jak-ttoe-da*	to be started
		시작 *si-jak*	start

LET'S REVIEW!

Read the story again, but this time in Korean!

내일 **시험**이 있어요. **의자**에 앉았어요.

책상 위가 너무 **더러워요.**

책상 **위**를 **청소**해요.

이제 **깨끗해요.**

가방에서 **공책**과 **필통**을 꺼내요.

공부를 **시작해요.**

Translation

I have an exam tomorrow. I sat down on the chair. The desk is too dirty. I clean the top of my desk. Now it's clean. I take out my notebook and my pencil case from my bag. I start studying.

Match each Korean word to its English translation.

공책 ·	· pencil case
더럽다 ·	· up, top
청소 ·	· notebook
깨끗하다 ·	· desk
시험 ·	· to begin, to start
시작하다 ·	· to be clean
필통 ·	· test, exam
의자 ·	· chair
책상 ·	· to be dirty
위 ·	· cleaning

Crossword Puzzle

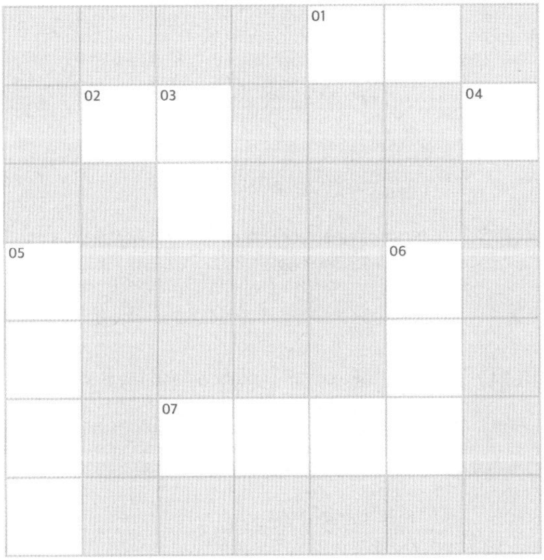

01 pencil case
02 notebook
03 desk
04 up, top
05 to be clean
06 to be dirty
07 to begin, to start

Fill in the blanks using one of the words that you learned in Day 03.
(Please refer to page 017 to review how to conjugate verbs/adjectives.)

01 내일 ( )이 있어요. — I have an exam tomorrow.

02 ( )에 앉았어요. — I sat down on the chair.

03 ( ) 위가 너무 더러워요. — The desk is too dirty.

04 책상 위가 너무 ( ). — The desk is too dirty.

05 책상 ( )를 청소해요. — I clean the top of my desk.

06 책상 위를 ( )해요. — I clean the top of my desk.

07 이제 ( ). — Now it's clean.

08 가방에서 ( )과 필통을 꺼내요. — I take out my notebook and my pencil case from my bag.

09 가방에서 공책과 ( )을 꺼내요. — I take out my notebook and my pencil case from my bag.

10 공부를 ( ). — I start studying.

Day 04

- 배고프다
- 아까
- 빵
- 음료수
- 주다
- 지금
- 배부르다
- 졸다
- 선생님
- 무섭다

Day 04 *LET'S WARM UP!*

Imagine the situation in the story below to help you remember the ten Korean words in context.

04

배고프다

I am so hungry.

아까 주다 빵 음료수

Earlier, my friend gave me some bread and a beverage.

지금

Now I am eating the bread and beverage.

배부르다

Now I'm full.

But I'm so sleepy.

졸다 선생님

If I doze off in my class, I get scolded by my teacher.

무섭다

My teacher is so scary.

LET'S KEEP THE BALL ROLLING!

Word	Meaning	Related Words	Meaning
배고프다 *bae-go-peu-da*	to be hungry	배가 고프다 *bae-ga go-peu-da*	to be hungry
		배고픈 사람 *bae-go-peun sa-ram*	hungry person
아까 *a-kka*	earlier	아까부터 *a-kka-bu-teo*	from earlier, since earlier
		방금 *bang-geum*	just now
		나중에 *na-jung-e*	later
		이따가 *i-tta-ga*	a short time later
빵 *ppang*	bread	빵을 먹다 *ppang-eul meok-tta*	to eat bread
		빵을 굽다 *ppang-eul gup-tta*	to bake bread
		빵집 *ppang-jjip*	bakery
음료수 *eum-nyo-su*	beverage	음료수를 마시다 *eum-nyo-su-reul ma-si-da*	to drink a beverage
		음료수 한 병 *eum-nyo-su han byeong*	one bottle of a beverage

주다 *ju-da*	to give	선물을 주다 *seon-mu-reul ju-da*	to give a present
		받다 *bat-tta*	to receive
		주고받다 *ju-go-bat-tta*	to give and receive

지금 *ji-geum*	now	지금 당장 *ji-geum dang-jang*	right now
		지금부터 *ji-geum-bu-teo*	from now
		지금까지 *ji-geum-kka-ji*	until now
		지금 시작하다 *ji-geum si-ja-ka-da*	to start now

배부르다 *bae-bu-reu-da*	to be full (opposite of hungry)	배가 부르다 *bae-ga bu-reu-da*	to be full
		배부르게 먹다 *bae-bu-reu-ge meok-tta*	to eat until one is full

졸다 *jol-da*	to doze	잠깐 졸다 *jam-kkan jol-da*	to doze for a short while
		깜빡 졸다 *kkam-ppak jol-da*	to doze for a short while
		조는 사람 *jo-neun sa-ram*	person who is dozing
		졸리다 *jol-li-da*	to feel sleepy

선생님 *seon-saeng-nim*	teacher	수학 선생님 *su-hak seon-saeng-nim*	math teacher
		의사 선생님 *ui-sa seon-saeng-nim*	doctor
		학생 *hak-ssaeng*	student
무섭다 *mu-seop-tta*	to be scary, to be scared	무서워하다 *mu-seo-wo-ha-da*	to dread
		무서운 영화 *mu-seo-un yeong-hwa*	scary movie
		무서운 선생님 *mu-seo-un seon-saeng-nim*	scary teacher

LET'S REVIEW!

Read the story again, but this time in Korean!

너무 **배고파요.**

아까 친구가 **빵**이랑 **음료수**를 **줬어요.**

지금 빵이랑 음료수를 먹어요.

이제 **배불러요.** 그런데 너무 졸려요.

수업 시간에 **졸면 선생님**한테 혼나요.

저희 선생님은 정말 **무서워요.**

Translation

I am so hungry. Earlier, my friend gave me some bread and a beverage. Now I am eating the bread and beverage. Now I'm full. But I'm so sleepy. If I doze off in my class, I get scolded by my teacher. My teacher is so scary.

Match each Korean word to its English translation.

졸다 ·	· to be full (opposite of hungry)
무섭다 ·	· to doze
배고프다 ·	· teacher
아까 ·	· to be scary, to be scared
빵 ·	· to give
선생님 ·	· now
음료수 ·	· earlier
주다 ·	· bread
지금 ·	· beverage
배부르다 ·	· to be hungry

Crossword Puzzle

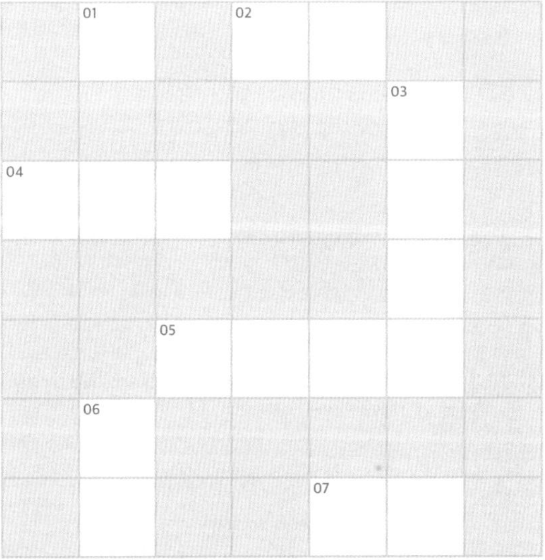

01 bread
02 to give
03 to be full (opposite of hungry)
04 beverage
05 to be hungry
06 earlier
07 now

Fill in the blanks using one of the words that you learned in Day 04.
(Please refer to page 017 to review how to conjugate verbs/adjectives.)

01 너무 ( ). — I am so hungry.

02 ( ) 친구가 빵이랑 음료수를 줬어요. — Earlier, my friend gave me some bread and a beverage.

03 아까 친구가 ( )이랑 음료수를 줬어요. — Earlier, my friend gave me some bread and a beverage.

04 아까 친구가 빵이랑 ( )를 줬어요. — Earlier, my friend gave me some bread and a beverage.

05 아까 친구가 빵이랑 음료수를 ( ). — Earlier, my friend gave me some bread and a beverage.

06 ( ) 빵이랑 음료수를 먹어요. — Now I am eating the bread and beverage.

07 이제 ( ). — Now I'm full.

08 수업 시간에 ( ) 선생님한테 혼나요. — If I doze off in my class, I get scolded by my teacher.

09 수업 시간에 졸면 ( )한테 혼나요. — If I doze off in my class, I get scolded by my teacher.

10 저희 선생님은 정말 ( ). — My teacher is so scary.

Day 05

어린이

학교

가족

공원

많다

어른

아기

적다

신기하다

어떻게

Day 05 LET'S WARM UP!

Imagine the situation in the story below to help you remember the ten Korean words in context.

05

어린이
Today is Children's Day.

학교
On Children's Day, you don't go to school.

공원 가족
I went to the park with my family.

많다
There were so many people.

어른 아기
There were many adults and also many babies.

적다 신기하다
There were not many children. It was interesting.

어떻게
How can there be more adults than children at a park?

LET'S KEEP THE BALL ROLLING!

Word	Meaning	Related Words	Meaning
어린이 *eo-ri-ni*	child	어린이날 *eo-ri-ni-nal*	Children's Day
		착한 어린이 *cha-kan eo-ri-ni*	good child
		어른 *eo-reun*	adult
		청소년 *cheong-so-nyeon*	youth, adolescent
학교 *hak-kkyo*	school	학교에 가다 *hak-kkyo-e ga-da*	to go to school
		초등학교 *cho-deung-hak-kkyo*	elementary school
		중학교 *jung-hak-kkyo*	middle school
		고등학교 *go-deung-hak-kkyo*	high school
가족 *ga-jok*	family	가족끼리 *ga-jok-kki-ri*	among family members, with family
		가족사진 *ga-jok-ssa-jin*	family photo
		가족 모임 *ga-jok mo-im*	family gathering
		친척 *chin-cheok*	relative

공원 *gong-won*	park	**공원을 산책하다** *gong-wo-neul san-chae-ka-da*	to take a walk in the park
		놀이공원 *no-ri-gong-won*	amusement park
		공원에서 놀다 *gong-wo-ne-seo nol-da*	to hang out in the park
많다 *man-ta*	to be a lot, to be numerous	**사람이 많다** *sa-ra-mi man-ta*	to be many people
		돈이 많다 *do-ni man-ta*	to have a lot of money
		시간이 많다 *si-ga-ni man-ta*	to have a lot of time
어른 *eo-reun*	adult, grown-up	**어른이 되다** *eo-reu-ni doe-da*	to become an adult
		어른 같다 *eo-reun gat-tta*	to be like an adult
		어른들 *eo-reun-deul*	adults
		아이 *a-i*	child
아기 *a-gi*	baby	**아기를 낳다** *a-gi-reul na-ta*	to give birth to a baby
		아기가 태어나다 *a-gi-ga tae-eo-na-da*	a baby is born
		우리 아기 *u-ri a-gi*	my baby, our baby

적다 *jeok-tta*	to be few, to be little	사람이 적다 *sa-ra-mi jeok-tta*	to not be many people
		양이 적다 *yang-i jeok-tta*	to not be much
		적은 월급 *jeo-geun wol-geup*	small salary
신기하다 *sin-gi-ha-da*	to be interesting, to be fascinating	신기한 물건 *sin-gi-han mul-geon*	interesting object
		신기하게 *sin-gi-ha-ge*	interestingly
어떻게 *eo-tteo-ke*	how	왜 *wae*	why
		언제 *eon-je*	when
		어디에서 *eo-di-e-seo*	where

LET'S REVIEW!

Read the story again, but this time in Korean!

오늘은 **어린이**날이에요. 어린이날은 **학교**에 안 가요.

저는 **가족**이랑 **공원**에 갔어요.

사람이 정말 **많았어요.**

어른도 많고 **아기**도 많았어요.

어린이는 **적었어요. 신기했어요.**

어떻게 공원에 어린이보다 어른이 더 많아요?

Translation

Today is Children's Day. On Children's Day, you don't go to school. I went to the park with my family. There were so many people. There were many adults and also many babies. There were not many children. It was interesting. How can there be more adults than children at a park?

Match each Korean word to its English translation.

어른 ·	· to be a lot, to be numerous
공원 ·	· adult, grown-up
아기 ·	· child
신기하다 ·	· to be few, to be little
어떻게 ·	· park
학교 ·	· family
적다 ·	· baby
어린이 ·	· school
가족 ·	· to be interesting, to be fascinating
많다 ·	· how

Crossword Puzzle

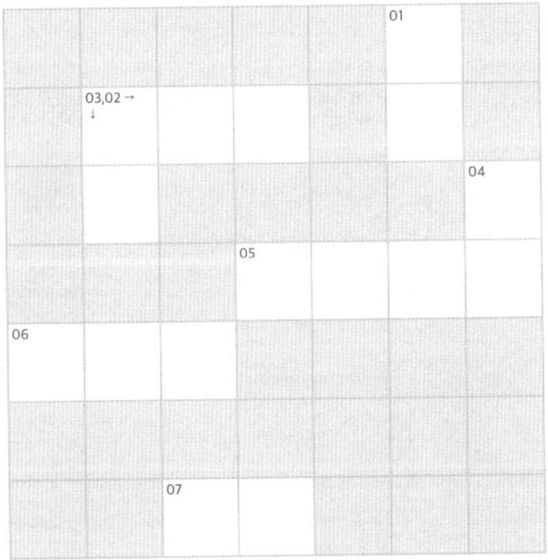

01 school
02 child
03 adult, grown-up
04 to be few, to be little
05 to be interesting, to be fascinating
06 how
07 family

Fill in the blanks using one of the words that you learned in Day 05.
(Please refer to page 017 to review how to conjugate verbs/adjectives.)

01 오늘은 ( )날이에요. Today is Children's Day.

02 어린이날은 ( )에 안 가요. On Children's Day, you don't go to school.

03 저는 ( )이랑 공원에 갔어요. I went to the park with my family.

04 저는 가족이랑 ( )에 갔어요. I went to the park with my family.

05 사람이 정말 ( ). There were so many people.

06 ( )도 많고 아기도 많았어요. There were many adults and also many babies.

07 어른도 많고 ( )도 많았어요. There were many adults and also many babies.

08 어린이는 ( ). There were not many children.

09 ( ). It was interesting.

10 ( ) 공원에 어린이보다 어른이 더 많아요? How can there be more adults than children at a park?

Day 06

- 겨울
- 방학
- 할머니
- 가다
- 버스
- 지하철
- 타다
- 고양이
- 동물
- 놀다

Day 06 LET'S WARM UP!

Imagine the situation in the story below to help you remember the ten Korean words in context.

06

겨울 방학
It is winter vacation time.

가다 할머니
I go to my grandmother's house.

버스 타다 지하철
I take the bus and I take the subway, too.

고양이
My grandmother has a cat.

동물
I really like animals.

놀다
I want to play with her cat soon.

LET'S KEEP THE BALL ROLLING!

Word	Meaning	Related Words	Meaning
겨울 *gyeo-ul*	winter	겨울옷 *gyeo-u-rot*	winter clothes
		겨울 날씨 *gyeo-ul nal-ssi*	winter weather
		춥다 *chup-tta*	to be cold
		눈 *nun*	snow
방학 *bang-hak*	school vacation	여름 방학 *yeo-reum bang-hak*	summer vacation
		겨울 방학 *gyeo-ul bang-hak*	winter vacation
		방학 숙제 *bang-hak suk-jje*	vacation homework
		개학 *gae-hak*	beginning of a semester
할머니 *hal-meo-ni*	grandmother	외할머니 *oe-hal-meo-ni*	maternal grandmother
		친할머니 *chi-nal-meo-ni*	paternal grandmother
		할아버지 *ha-ra-beo-ji*	grandfather
		할머니 집 *hal-meo-ni jip*	grandmother's house

가다 *ga-da*	to go	**만나러 가다** *man-na-reo ga-da*	to go meet (someone)
		집에 가다 *ji-be ga-da*	to go home
		오다 *o-da*	to come
버스 *beo-sseu*	bus	**버스를 타다** *beo-sseu-reul ta-da*	to take the bus
		버스 기사 *beo-sseu gi-sa*	bus driver
		버스 정류장 *beo-sseu jeong-nyu-jang*	bus stop
지하철 *ji-ha-cheol*	subway	**지하철을 타다** *ji-ha-cheo-reul ta-da*	to take the subway
		지하철역 *ji-ha-cheol-lyeok*	subway station
		지하철에서 내리다 *ji-ha-cheo-re-seo nae-ri-da*	to get off the subway
타다 *ta-da*	to ride	**차를 타다** *cha-reul ta-da*	to ride in a car
		자전거를 타다 *ja-jeon-geo-reul ta-da*	to ride a bicycle
		배를 타다 *bae-reul ta-da*	to ride a boat
		말을 타다 *ma-reul ta-da*	to ride a horse

고양이 *go-yang-i*	cat	**새끼 고양이** *sae-kki go-yang-i*	kitten
		길 고양이 *gil go-yang-i*	stray cat
		고양이를 키우다 *go-yang-i-reul ki-u-da*	to raise a cat
동물 *dong-mul*	animal	**동물원** *dong-mu-rwon*	zoo
		동물 병원 *dong-mul byeong-won*	veterinary clinic
		식물 *sing-mul*	plant
놀다 *nol-da*	to hang out, to play	**친구랑 놀다** *chin-gu-rang nol-da*	to hang out with a friend
		놀러 가다 *nol-leo ga-da*	to go out
		놀고 싶다 *nol-go sip-tta*	to want to play

LET'S REVIEW!

Read the story again, but this time in Korean!

겨울 방학이에요.

할머니 집에 가요.

버스도 타고 지하철도 타요.

할머니는 고양이를 키워요.

저는 동물이 정말 좋아요.

고양이랑 빨리 놀고 싶어요.

Translation

It is winter vacation time. I go to my grandmother's house. I take the bus and I take the subway, too. My grandmother has a cat. I really like animals. I want to play with her cat soon.

Match each Korean word to its English translation.

동물 ·	· bus
가다 ·	· subway
겨울 ·	· to ride
타다 ·	· school vacation
놀다 ·	· winter
할머니 ·	· cat
방학 ·	· animal
지하철 ·	· to hang out, to play
고양이 ·	· grandmother
버스 ·	· to go

Crossword Puzzle

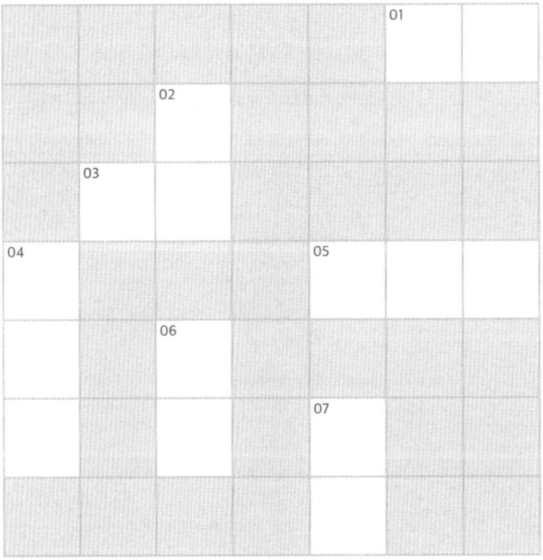

01 animal
02 to hang out, to play
03 to go
04 subway
05 grandmother
06 school vacation
07 winter

Fill in the blanks using one of the words that you learned in Day 06.
(Please refer to page 017 to review how to conjugate verbs/adjectives.)

01 (   ) 방학이에요. It is winter vacation time.

02 겨울 (   )이에요. It is winter vacation time.

03 (   ) 집에 가요. I go to my grandmother's house.

04 할머니 집에 (   ). I go to my grandmother's house.

05 (   )도 타고 지하철도 타요. I take the bus and I take the subway, too.

06 버스도 타고 (   )도 타요. I take the bus and I take the subway, too.

07 버스도 타고 지하철도 (   ). I take the bus and I take the subway, too.

08 할머니는 (   )를 키워요. My grandmother has a cat.

09 저는 (   )이 정말 좋아요. I really like animals.

10 고양이랑 빨리 (   ) 싶어요. I want to play with her cat soon.

Day 07

- 휴가
- 남자
- 여자
- 샴푸
- 린스
- 속옷
- 양말
- 드라이기
- 바지
- 티셔츠

Day 07 LET'S WARM UP!

Imagine the situation in the story below to help you remember the ten Korean words in context.

07

휴가
I went on vacation with my family.

남자
The men brought one bag each.

여자
The women brought two bags each.

샴푸 린스
In the women's bags, there were shampoo, hair conditioner,

속옷 양말
underwear, and socks.

드라이기
There was also a hairdryer.

바지 티셔츠
In the men's bags, there were only pants and t-shirts.

LET'S KEEP THE BALL ROLLING!

Word	Meaning	Related Words	Meaning
휴가 *hyu-ga*	vacation, leave	휴가를 가다 *hyu-ga-reul ga-da*	to go on a vacation
		휴가를 받다 *hyu-ga-reul bat-tta*	to get a vacation, to get time off
		여름 휴가 *yeo-reum hyu-ga*	summer vacation
남자 *nam-ja*	man	남자 화장실 *nam-ja hwa-jang-sil*	men's room
		남자 아이 *nam-ja a-i*	boy
		남학생 *na-mak-ssaeng*	male student
여자 *yeo-ja*	woman	여자 화장실 *yeo-ja hwa-jang-sil*	women's room
		여자 아이 *yeo-ja a-i*	girl
		여학생 *yeo-hak-ssaeng*	female student
샴푸 *syam-pu*	shampoo	샴푸 냄새 *syam-pu naem-sae*	shampoo smell
		머리를 감다 *meo-ri-reul gam-tta*	to wash one's hair
		비누 *bi-nu*	soap

린스 *rin-sseu*	hair conditioner	린스를 바르다 *rin-sseu-reul ba-reu-da*	to apply hair conditioner
		머리를 헹구다 *meo-ri-reul heng-gu-da*	to rinse one's hair
속옷 *so-got*	underwear	속옷 몇 벌 *so-got myeot beol*	a few pieces of underwear
		속치마 *sok-chi-ma*	slip, underskirt
		팬티 *paen-ti*	underpants
		브래지어 *beu-rae-ji-eo*	brassiere, bra
양말 *yang-mal*	socks	양말을 신다 *yang-ma-reul sin-tta*	to put on socks
		양말을 빨다 *yang-ma-reul ppal-da*	to wash socks
		양말 한 짝 *yang-mal han jjak*	a sock
드라이기 *deu-ra-i-gi*	hairdryer	헤어 드라이기 *he-eo deu-ra-i-gi*	hairdryer
		머리를 말리다 *meo-ri-reul mal-li-da*	to dry one's hair

바지 *ba-ji*	pants	**바지가 맞다** *ba-ji-ga mat-tta*	to be the right pants, the pants fit well
		바지를 줄이다 *ba-ji-reul ju-ri-da*	to shorten one's pants
		청바지 *cheong-ba-ji*	jeans
		반바지 *ban-ba-ji*	shorts
티셔츠 *ti-syeo-cheu*	t-shirt	**하얀 티셔츠** *ha-yan ti-syeo-cheu*	white t-shirt
		티셔츠 두 장 *ti-syeo-cheu du jang*	two t-shirts
		티 *ti*	t-shirt

LET'S REVIEW!

Read the story again, but this time in Korean!

가족과 함께 **휴가**를 갔어요.

남자들은 가방을 한 개 가져왔어요.

여자들은 가방을 두 개 가져왔어요.

여자들 가방에는 **샴푸, 린스, 속옷,**

양말이 있었어요. **드라이기**도 있었어요.

남자들 가방에는 **바지**와 **티셔츠**만 있었어요.

Translation

I went on vacation with my family. The men brought one bag each. The women brought two bags each. In the women's bags, there were shampoo, hair conditioner, underwear, and socks. There was also a hairdryer. In the men's bags, there were only pants and t-shirts.

Match each Korean word to its English translation.

샴푀 ·	· underwear
티셔츠 ·	· socks
속옷 ·	· hairdryer
휴가 ·	· t-shirt
남자 ·	· vacation, leave
양말 ·	· pants
드라이기 ·	· man
바지 ·	· shampoo
린스 ·	· woman
여자 ·	· hair conditioner

Crossword Puzzle

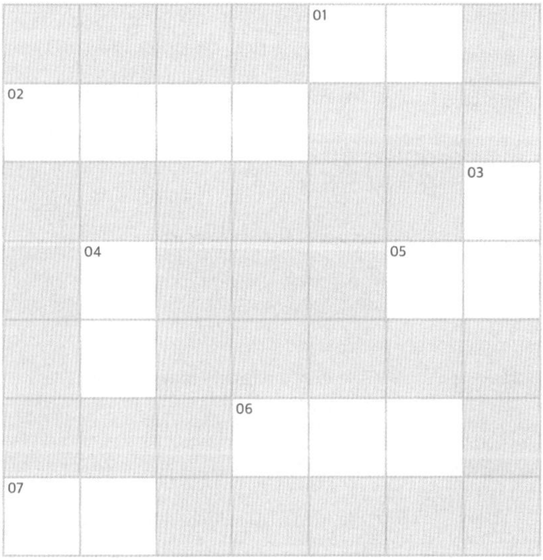

01 socks
02 hairdryer
03 woman
04 hair conditioner
05 man
06 t-shirt
07 shampoo

Fill in the blanks using one of the words that you learned in Day 07.
(Please refer to page 017 to review how to conjugate verbs/adjectives.)

01 가족과 함께 ( )를 갔어요. I went on vacation with my family.

02 ( )들은 가방을 한 개 가져왔어요. The men brought one bag each.

03 ( )들은 가방을 두 개 가져왔어요. The women brought two bags each.

04 여자들 가방에는 ( ), 린스, 속옷, 양말이 있었어요. In the women's bags, there were shampoo, hair conditioner, underwear, and socks.

05 여자들 가방에는 샴푸, ( ), 속옷, 양말이 있었어요. In the women's bags, there were shampoo, hair conditioner, underwear, and socks.

06 여자들 가방에는 샴푸, 린스, ( ), 양말이 있었어요. In the women's bags, there were shampoo, hair conditioner, underwear, and socks.

07 여자들 가방에는 샴푸, 린스, 속옷, ( )이 있었어요. In the women's bags, there were shampoo, hair conditioner, underwear, and socks.

08 ( )도 있었어요. There was also a hairdryer.

09 남자들 가방에는 ( )와 티셔츠만 있었어요. In the men's bags, there were only pants and t-shirts.

10 남자들 가방에는 바지와 ( )만 있었어요. In the men's bags, there were only pants and t-shirts.

Day 08

- 누나
- 텔레비전
- 드라마
- 뉴스
- 싸우다
- 지다
- 방
- 닫다
- 음악
- 듣다

Day 08 LET'S WARM UP!

Imagine the situation in the story below to help you remember the ten Korean words in context.

08

텔레비전 누나
I watched TV in the living room with my older sister.

드라마
She likes TV dramas.

뉴스
I like the news.

싸우다
So, I argued with my sister.

지다
When I fight with my sister, I always lose.

방
I went into my room.

닫다 듣다 음악
I closed the door and listened to music.

LET'S KEEP THE BALL ROLLING!

Word	Meaning	Related Words	Meaning
누나 *nu-na*	older sister (for a boy)	친누나 *chin-nu-na*	real older sister, biological older sister
		사촌 누나 *sa-chon nu-na*	older female cousin (for a boy)
		아는 누나 *a-neun nu-na*	older woman a guy knows
텔레비전 *tel-le-bi-jeon*	television	텔레비전을 보다 *tel-le-bi-jeo-neul bo-da*	to watch television
		텔레비전을 켜다 *tel-le-bi-jeo-neul kyeo-da*	to turn on the television
		텔레비전을 끄다 *tel-le-bi-jeo-neul kkeu-da*	to turn off the television
드라마 *deu-ra-ma*	TV drama	드라마를 보다 *deu-ra-ma-reul bo-da*	to watch a TV drama
		인기 있는 드라마 *in-kki in-neun deu-ra-ma*	popular drama
		주인공 *ju-in-gong*	main character
뉴스 *nyu-sseu*	news	텔레비전 뉴스 *tel-le-bi-jeon nyu-sseu*	television news
		뉴스 기사 *nyu-sseu gi-sa*	news article
		소식 *so-sik*	news about a person

싸우다 *ssa-u-da*	to fight, to argue	크게 싸우다 *keu-ge ssa-u-da*	to have a big fight, to have a big argument
		싸움 *ssa-um*	fight
		말싸움 *mal-ssa-um*	argument, quarrel
		화해하다 *hwa-hae-ha-da*	to make up (with), to reconcile (with)
지다 *ji-da*	to lose	경기에서 지다 *gyeong-gi-e-seo ji-da*	to lose a game/match
		진 사람 *jin sa-ram*	someone who lost, loser
		이기다 *i-gi-da*	to win
방 *bang*	room	방이 넓다 *bang-i neol-tta*	to be a spacious room
		방으로 들어가다 *bang-eu-ro deu-reo-ga-da*	to go into a room
		방에 있다 *bang-e it-tta*	to be in a room
닫다 *dat-tta*	to close	문을 닫다 *mu-neul dat-tta*	to close a door
		닫히다 *da-chi-da*	to be closed
		열다 *yeol-da*	to open

음악 *eu-mak*	music	신나는 음악 *sin-na-neun eu-mak*	exciting music, uplifting music
		음악을 틀다 *eu-ma-geul teul-da*	to turn on music
		음악 소리 *eu-mak so-ri*	music sound
듣다 *deut-tta*	to listen, to hear	음악을 듣다 *eu-ma-geul deut-tta*	to listen to music
		소리를 듣다 *so-ri-reul deut-tta*	to listen to a sound
		들리다 *deul-li-da*	to be heard, can hear
		들어 보다 *deu-reo bo-da*	to have a listen

LET'S REVIEW!

Read the story again, but this time in Korean!

누나랑 거실에서 텔레비전을 봤어요.

누나는 드라마를 좋아해요. 저는 뉴스를 좋아해요.

그래서 누나랑 싸웠어요.

누나랑 싸우면 항상 제가 져요.

저는 방으로 들어갔어요.

문을 닫고 음악을 들었어요.

Translation

I watched TV in the living room with my older sister. She likes TV dramas. I like the news. So, I argued with my sister. When I fight with my sister, I always lose. I went into my room. I closed the door and listened to music.

Match each Korean word to its English translation.

닫다 ·	· TV drama
싸우다 ·	· news
음악 ·	· to lose
듣다 ·	· music
뉴스 ·	· to listen, to hear
방 ·	· older sister (for a boy)
누나 ·	· room
텔레비전 ·	· to fight, to argue
드라마 ·	· television
지다 ·	· to close

Crossword Puzzle

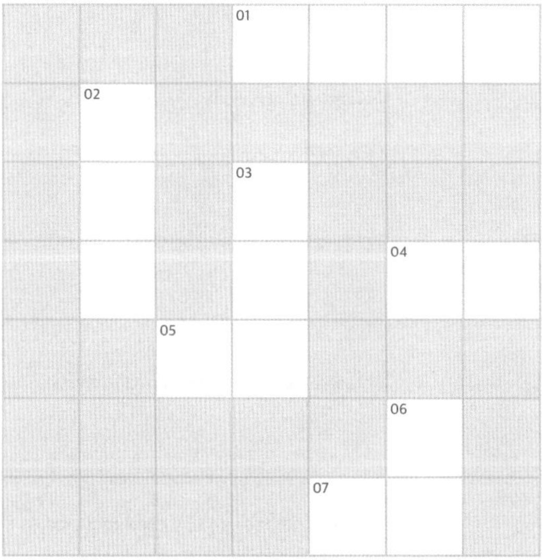

01 television
02 TV drama
03 to fight, to argue
04 older sister (for a boy)
05 to close
06 to listen, to hear
07 to lose

Fill in the blanks using one of the words that you learned in Day 08.
(Please refer to page 017 to review how to conjugate verbs/adjectives.)

01 (   )랑 거실에서 텔레비전을 봤어요. I watched TV in the living room with my older sister.

02 누나랑 거실에서 (   )을 봤어요. I watched TV in the living room with my older sister.

03 누나는 (   )를 좋아해요. She likes TV dramas.

04 저는 (   )를 좋아해요. I like the news.

05 그래서 누나랑 (   ). So, I argued with my sister.

06 누나랑 싸우면 항상 제가 (   ). When I fight with my sister, I always lose.

07 저는 (   )으로 들어갔어요. I went into my room.

08 문을 (   ) 음악을 들었어요. I closed the door and listened to music.

09 문을 닫고 (   )을 들었어요. I closed the door and listened to music.

10 문을 닫고 음악을 (   ). I closed the door and listened to music.

Day 09

- 개
- 있다
- 이름
- 시간
- 살다
- 죽다
- 슬프다
- 동생
- 울다
- 눈물

Day 09 LET'S WARM UP!

Imagine the situation in the story below to help you remember the ten Korean words in context.

09

있다 개
We had one dog at our house.

이름
Her name was Iseul.

살다 시간
She lived with us for a long time.

죽다
But yesterday, Iseul died.

슬프다
I am so sad.

동생 울다
My younger brother and I cried all day long.

눈물
I can't stop shedding tears.

LET'S KEEP THE BALL ROLLING!

Word	Meaning	Related Words	Meaning
개 *gae*	dog	개를 키우다 *gae-reul ki-u-da*	to raise a dog
		개 한 마리 *gae han ma-ri*	one dog
		강아지 *gang-a-ji*	puppy
있다 *it-tta*	to exist, to have, to be (at a place)	돈이 있다 *do-ni it-tta*	to have money
		약속이 있다 *yak-sso-gi it-tta*	to have plans, to have an appointment
		회사에 있다 *hoe-sa-e it-tta*	to be at work
		없다 *eop-tta*	to not have, to not exist, to not be
이름 *i-reum*	name	이름을 짓다 *i-reu-meul jit-tta*	to make up a name
		이름을 물어보다 *i-reu-meul mu-reo-bo-da*	to ask someone their name
		이름을 적다 *i-reu-meul jeok-tta*	to write down someone's name
		이름을 말하다 *i-reu-meul mal-ha-da*	to say someone's name

시간 *si-gan*	time	시간이 있다 *si-ga-ni it-tta*	to have time
		시간이 없다 *si-ga-ni eop-tta*	to not have time
		시 *si*	hour
		분 *bun*	minute

살다 *sal-da*	to live	혼자 살다 *hon-ja sal-da*	to live alone
		오래 살다 *o-rae sal-da*	to live for a long period of time
		살려 주다 *sal-lyeo ju-da*	to spare someone's life
		삶 *sam*	life

죽다 *juk-tta*	to die	일찍 죽다 *il-jjik juk-tta*	to die young
		죽이다 *ju-gi-da*	to kill
		죽음 *ju-geum*	death
		돌아가시다 *do-ra-ga-si-da*	to pass away

슬프다 *seul-peu-da*	to be sad	슬픈 *seul-peun*	sad
		슬프게 울다 *seul-peu-ge ul-da*	to cry sadly
		기쁘다 *gi-ppeu-da*	to be happy
동생 *dong-saeng*	younger sibling, younger brother, younger sister	동생이 있다 *dong-saeng-i it-tta*	to have a younger sibling
		여동생 *yeo-dong-saeng*	younger sister
		남동생 *nam-dong-saeng*	younger brother
울다 *ul-da*	to cry	펑펑 울다 *peong-peong ul-da*	to cry one's eyes out
		우는 *u-neun*	crying
		울음 *u-reum*	cry, weeping
		울음을 그치다 *u-reu-meul geu-chi-da*	to stop crying
눈물 *nun-mul*	tear	눈물이 나다 *nun-mu-ri na-da*	to shed tears, tears come out
		눈물을 닦다 *nun-mu-reul dak-tta*	to wipe one's tears
		눈물을 흘리다 *nun-mu-reul heul-li-da*	to shed tears

LET'S REVIEW!

Read the story again, but this time in Korean!

저희 집에는 **개**가 한 마리 **있었어요.**

이름은 이슬이었어요.

오랜 **시간** 동안 저희와 함께 **살았어요.**

그런데 어제 이슬이가 **죽었어요.** 너무 **슬퍼요.**

저와 제 **동생**은 하루 종일 **울었어요.**

눈물이 멈추지 않아요.

Translation

We had one dog at our house. Her name was Iseul. She lived with us for a long time. But yesterday, Iseul died. I am so sad. My younger brother and I cried all day long. I can't stop shedding tears.

Match each Korean word to its English translation.

죽다 ·	· name
슬프다 ·	· time
동생 ·	· to live
개 ·	· tear
시간 ·	· younger sibling
있다 ·	· dog
살다 ·	· to cry
이름 ·	· to exist, to have, to be (at a place)
눈물 ·	· to be sad
울다 ·	· to die

Crossword Puzzle

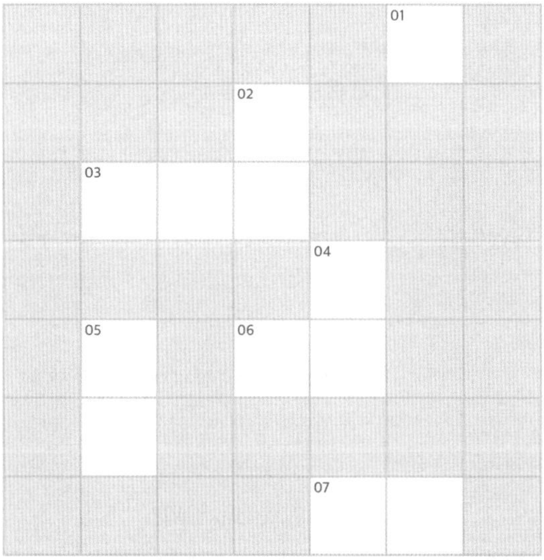

01 dog
02 to cry
03 to be sad
04 to exist, to have, to be (at a place)
05 name
06 to live
07 time

Fill in the blanks using one of the words that you learned in Day 09.
(Please refer to page 017 to review how to conjugate verbs/adjectives.)

01 저희 집에는 ( )가 한 마리 있었어요. We had one dog at our house.

02 저희 집에는 개가 한 마리 ( ). We had one dog at our house.

03 ( )은 이슬이었어요. Her name was Iseul.

04 오랜 ( ) 동안 저희와 함께 살았어요. She lived with us for a long time.

05 오랜 시간 동안 저희와 함께 ( ). She lived with us for a long time.

06 그런데 어제 이슬이가 ( ). But yesterday, Iseul died.

07 너무 ( ). I am so sad.

08 저와 제 ( )은 하루 종일 울었어요. My younger brother and I cried all day long.

09 저와 제 동생은 하루 종일 ( ). My younger brother and I cried all day long.

10 ( )이 멈추지 않아요. I can't stop shedding tears.

Day 10

- 수영
- 수건
- 가게
- 돈
- 빌리다
- 비누
- 차갑다
- 어깨
- 힘
- 가르치다

Day 10 LET'S WARM UP!

Imagine the situation in the story below to help you remember the ten Korean words in context.

10

수영
I wanted to **swim**. I went to the swimming pool.

수건 가게
But, I didn't have a **towel**. I went to a **store** nearby.

돈 빌리다
But, I didn't have **money**. I **borrowed** money from a friend.

비누
I bought a towel. I bought **soap**.

차갑다
The water in the swimming pool was **cold**.

어깨 힘 가르치다
My **shoulders** **tightened**. My swimming teacher **taught** me.

So, I was able to relax my shoulders.

LET'S KEEP THE BALL ROLLING!

Word	Meaning	Related Words	Meaning
수영 *su-yeong*	swimming	수영을 배우다 *su-yeong-eul bae-u-da*	to learn to swim
		수영하다 *su-yeong-ha-da*	to swim
		수영장 *su-yeong-jang*	swimming pool
		수영복 *su-yeong-bok*	swimwear
수건 *su-geon*	towel	수건으로 닦다 *su-geo-neu-ro dak-tta*	to wipe with a towel
		마른 수건 *ma-reun su-geon*	dry towel
		흰 수건 *huin su-geon*	white towel
		손수건 *son-su-geon*	handkerchief
가게 *ga-ge*	store	가게에 가다 *ga-ge-e ga-da*	to go to a store
		가게에서 사다 *ga-ge-e-seo sa-da*	to buy at a store
		가게가 열려 있다 *ga-ge-ga yeol-lyeo it-tta*	the store is open
		가게 주인 *ga-ge ju-in*	store owner

돈 *don*	money	돈을 벌다 *do-neul beol-da*	to earn money
		돈을 쓰다 *do-neul sseu-da*	to spend money
		돈이 없다 *do-ni eop-tta*	to have no money
		돈을 모으다 *do-neul mo-eu-da*	to save money
빌리다 *bil-li-da*	to borrow, to rent	돈을 빌리다 *do-neul bil-li-da*	to borrow money
		책을 빌리다 *chae-geul bil-li-da*	to borrow a book
		빌린 차 *bil-lin cha*	rented car
비누 *bi-nu*	soap	비누로 씻다 *bi-nu-ro ssit-tta*	to wash with soap
		비누 거품 *bi-nu geo-pum*	soap foam
		비누칠 *bi-nu-chil*	lathering
차갑다 *cha-gap-tta*	to be cold	물이 차갑다 *mu-ri cha-gap-tta*	the water is cold
		차가운 바람 *cha-ga-un ba-ram*	cold wind
		뜨겁다 *tteu-geop-tta*	to be hot

어깨 *eo-kkae*	shoulder	어깨가 넓다 *eo-kkae-ga neol-tta*	one's shoulders are broad
		어깨를 펴다 *eo-kkae-reul pyeo-da*	to straighten one's shoulders
		어깨에 메다 *eo-kkae-e me-da*	to carry over one's shoulders
힘 *him*	strength, power	힘이 세다 *hi-mi se-da*	to be strong
		힘이 들어가다 *hi-mi deu-reo-ga-da*	to clench, to tighten
		힘주다 *him-ju-da*	to tense your muscles, to emphasize
		힘을 빼다 *hi-meul ppae-da*	to relax one's body, to relax a certain body part
가르치다 *ga-reu-chi-da*	to teach	운전을 가르치다 *un-jeo-neul ga-reu-chi-da*	to teach driving
		잘 가르치다 *jal ga-reu-chi-da*	to teach well
		가르쳐 주다 *ga-reu-chyeo ju-da*	to teach
		선생님 *seon-saeng-nim*	teacher

LET'S REVIEW!

Read the story again, but this time in Korean!

수영을 하고 싶었어요. 수영장에 갔어요.

그런데 **수건**이 없었어요. 근처 **가게**에 갔어요.

그런데 **돈**이 없었어요. 친구한테 돈을 **빌렸어요.**

수건을 샀어요. **비누**도 샀어요. 수영장 물이 **차가웠어요.**

어깨에 **힘**이 들어갔어요. 수영 선생님이 **가르쳐** 줬어요.

그래서 어깨에 힘을 뺄 수 있었어요.

Translation

I wanted to swim. I went to the swimming pool. But, I didn't have a towel. I went to a store nearby. But, I didn't have money.
I borrowed money from a friend. I bought a towel. I bought soap. The water in the swimming pool was cold. My shoulders tightened. My swimming teacher taught me. So, I was able to relax my shoulders.

Match each Korean word to its English translation.

수영 ·	· store
수건 ·	· soap
차갑다 ·	· to teach
돈 ·	· strength, power
어깨 ·	· swimming
빌리다 ·	· to be cold
비누 ·	· towel
가게 ·	· money
가르치다 ·	· shoulder
힘 ·	· to borrow, to rent

Crossword Puzzle

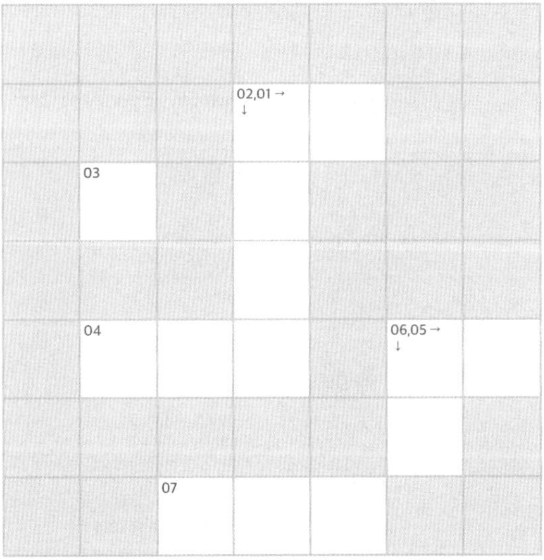

01 store
02 to teach
03 strength, power
04 to borrow, to rent
05 towel
06 swimming
07 to be cold

Fill in the blanks using one of the words that you learned in Day 10.
(Please refer to page 017 to review how to conjugate verbs/adjectives.)

01 (　　　　　　)을 하고 싶었어요. I wanted to swim.

02 그런데 (　　　　　　)이 없었어요. But, I didn't have a towel.

03 근처 (　　　　　　)에 갔어요. I went to a store nearby.

04 그런데 (　　　　　　)이 없었어요. But, I didn't have money.

05 친구한테 돈을 (　　　　　　). I borrowed money from a friend.

06 (　　　　　　)도 샀어요. I bought soap, too.

07 수영장 물이 (　　　　　　). The water in the swimming pool was cold.

08 (　　　　　　)에 힘이 들어갔어요. My shoulders tightened.

09 어깨에 (　　　　　　)이 들어갔어요. My shoulders tightened.

10 수영 선생님이 (　　　　　　) 줬어요. My swimming teacher taught me.

QUIZ

DAY 01-10

01 In Korean, 나 means "I, me". How do you say **"we, us"**?

a. 우리 b. 여자 c. 아기 d. 어른

02 Choose the term that is an edible item.

a. 린스 b. 싸우다 c. 음료수 d. 어떻게

03 Which one syllable word means **"bread"**?

a. 뻥 b. 빵 c. 뽕 d. 팡

04 How do you say **"name"** in Korean?

a. 의자 b. 뉴스 c. 이름 d. 휴가

05 In Korean, what is the name of the animal pictured?

a. 고임이
b. 고은이
c. 고엉이
d. 고양이

06 Which of the following is **NOT** a place?

a. 학교 b. 주말 c. 카페 d. 공원

07 Choose the item that is **NOT** a toiletry.

a. 동물 b. 수건 c. 비누 d. 샴푸

08 Which of the following words is **NOT** related to school?

a. 시험 b. 회사원 c. 선생님 d. 방학

09 Which of the following words is **NOT** related to time?

a. 일찍 b. 아까 c. 가게 d. 지금

10 Choose the term that is **NOT** a loanword from English.

a. 매일 b. 텔레비전 c. 드라마 d. 버스

11 What does 책상 위 mean?

a. beside the desk b. in front of the desk

c. on the desk d. under the desk

12 Which season is 겨울?

a. spring b. summer c. fall/autumn d. winter

13 Which word is not related to the others?

a. 바지 b. 티셔츠 c. 양말 d. 눈물

14 What is the Korean word for the item in the picture?

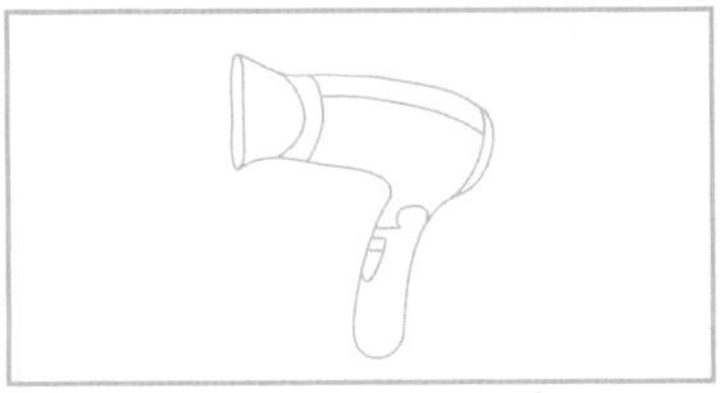

a. 드라이
b. 드라이기
c. 드로이기
d. 드러이기

15 Choose the pair of antonyms that are matched incorrectly.

a. 울다 - 슬프다 b. 살다 - 죽다
c. 배고프다 - 배부르다 d. 깨끗하다 - 더럽다

16 Choose which term also includes the others.

a. 할머니 b. 누나 c. 동생 d. 가족

17 Puppy is 강아지 in Korean. What is **"dog"** in Korean?

a. 힘 b. 개 c. 방 d. 물

18 Which of the following does **NOT** make sense if it comes after 너무?

a. 바쁘다 b. 시작하다 c. 무섭다 d. 차갑다

19 Choose the noun-verb pair that is matched incorrectly.

a. 지하철 - 타다 b. 옷 - 입다

c. 음악 - 듣다 d. 세수 - 만나다

20 Which of the following does **NOT** become a verb if you attach -하다?

a. 수영 b. 청소 c. 어깨 d. 화장

QUIZ

DAY 01-10

Answers : a c b c d / b a b c a / c d d b a / d b b d c

Day 11

- 내일
- 친하다
- 쓰다[01]
- 받다
- 기쁘다
- 선물
- 무엇
- 좋다
- 귀고리
- 목걸이

Day 11

LET'S WARM UP!

Imagine the situation in the story below to help you remember the ten Korean words in context.

11

내일 친하다
Tomorrow is my close friend's birthday.

쓰다 01
Therefore, I am going to write a congratulatory letter.

기쁘다 받다
Will they be happy when they receive the letter?

무엇 좋다 선물
What will be a good present?

귀고리
Will earrings be good?

목걸이
Will a necklace be good?

LET'S KEEP THE BALL ROLLING!

Word	Meaning	Related Words	Meaning
내일 *nae-il*	tomorrow	내일 날씨 *nae-il nal-ssi*	tomorrow's weather
		다음날 *da-eum-nal*	the next day
		모레 *mo-re*	the day after tomorrow
친하다 *chin-ha-da*	to be close (with someone)	동생이랑 친하다 *dong-saeng-i-rang chin-ha-da*	to be close to one's younger sibling
		친한 형 *chin-han hyeong*	a close older male friend (for a boy)
		친하게 지내다 *chin-ha-ge ji-nae-da*	to be close to someone
쓰다 01 *sseu-da*	to write	이름을 쓰다 *i-reu-meul sseu-da*	to write a name
		글씨를 쓰다 *geul-ssi-reul sseu-da*	to write (by hand)
		일기를 쓰다 *il-gi-reul sseu-da*	to write in one's journal
		쓰이다 *sseu-i-da*	to be written

받다 *bat-tta*	to receive	선물을 받다 *seon-mu-reul bat-tta*	to receive a present
		공을 받다 *gong-eul bat-tta*	to receive a ball, to catch a ball
		전화를 받다 *jeo-nwa-reul bat-tta*	to receive a phone call, to answer a phone call
기쁘다 *gi-ppeu-da*	to be glad, to be happy	정말 기쁘다 *jeong-mal gi-ppeu-da*	to be really glad, to be really happy
		기쁜 마음 *gi-ppeun ma-eum*	joyful heart, glad heart
		기뻐하다 *gi-ppeo-ha-da*	to be glad, to be joyful
		슬프다 *seul-peu-da*	to be sad
선물 *seon-mul*	present, gift	선물하다 *seon-mul-ha-da*	to give as a present
		축하 선물 *chu-ka seon-mul*	congratulatory present
		선물을 주다 *seon-mu-reul ju-da*	to give a present
무엇 *mu-eot*	what	뭐 *mwo*	what, something
		무슨 *mu-seun*	what kind of

좋다 *jo-ta*	to be good	성격이 좋다 *seong-kkyeo-gi jo-ta*	to have a good personality
		좋은 사람 *jo-eun sa-ram*	good person, nice person
		좋아하다 *jo-a-ha-da*	to like

귀고리 *gwi-go-ri*	earrings	귀고리를 끼다 *gwi-go-ri-reul kki-da*	to put on earrings
		귀고리를 하다 *gwi-go-ri-reul ha-da*	to wear earrings
		은 귀고리 *eun gwi-go-ri*	silver earrings
		귀걸이 *gwi-geo-ri*	earrings (different spelling, same meaning)

목걸이 *mok-kkeo-ri*	necklace	진주 목걸이 *jin-ju mok-kkeo-ri*	pearl necklace
		금 목걸이 *geum mok-kkeo-ri*	gold necklace
		목걸이를 하다 *mok-kkeo-ri-reul ha-da*	to wear a necklace

LET'S REVIEW!

Read the story again, but this time in Korean!

내일은 친한 친구 생일이에요.

그래서 축하 편지를 쓸 거예요.

편지를 받으면 기뻐할까요?

선물은 뭐가 좋을까요?

귀고리가 좋을까요?

목걸이가 좋을까요?

Translation

Tomorrow is my close friend's birthday. Therefore, I am going to write a congratulatory letter. Will they be happy when they receive the letter? What will be a good present? Will earrings be good? Will a necklace be good?

Match each Korean word to its English translation.

쓰다 01 ·	· to receive
기쁘다 ·	· to be good
받다 ·	· earrings
무엇 ·	· necklace
목걸이 ·	· to write
좋다 ·	· tomorrow
선물 ·	· to be close (with someone)
친하다 ·	· present, gift
귀고리 ·	· to be glad, to be happy
내일 ·	· what

Crossword Puzzle

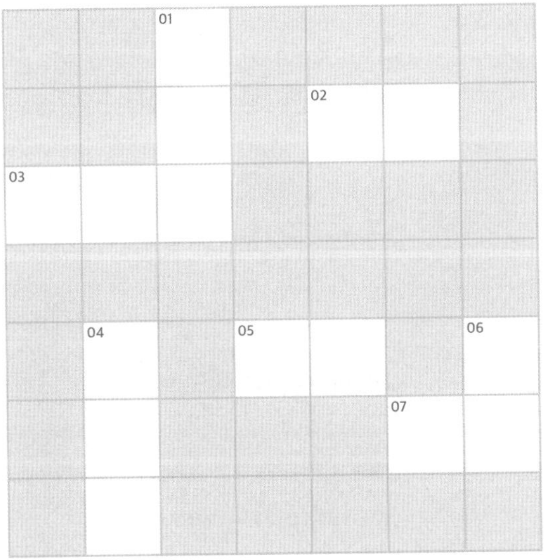

01 to be glad, to be happy
02 tomorrow
03 to be close (with someone)
04 earrings
05 present, gift
06 to be good
07 to receive

Fill in the blanks using one of the words that you learned in Day 11.
(Please refer to page 017 to review how to conjugate verbs/adjectives.)

01 (   )은 친한 친구 생일이에요. Tomorrow is my close friend's birthday.

02 내일은 (   ) 친구 생일이에요. Tomorrow is my close friend's birthday.

03 그래서 축하 편지를 (   ) 거예요. Therefore, I am going to write a congratulatory letter.

04 편지를 (   ) 기뻐할까요? Will they be happy when they receive the letter?

05 편지를 받으면 (   )? Will they be happy when they receive the letter?

06 (   )은 뭐가 좋을까요? What will be a good present?

07 선물은 (   )가 좋을까요? What will be a good present?

08 선물은 뭐가 (   )? What will be a good present?

09 (   )가 좋을까요? Will earrings be good?

10 (   )가 좋을까요? Will a necklace be good?

Day 12

- 오늘
- 생일
- 교실
- 먹다
- 친구
- 노래
- 춤
- 축하하다
- 재미있다
- 하루

Day 12

LET'S WARM UP!

Imagine the situation in the story below to help you remember the ten Korean words in context.

12

오늘 생일

Today is my birthday.

교실

We had a birthday party in the classroom.

먹다

We ate cake and also ate snacks.

친구 노래

My friends sang a song for me.

춤

We also sang and danced.

축하하다

I was happy because my friends celebrated my birthday.

재미있다 하루

It was a really fun day.

LET'S KEEP THE BALL ROLLING!

Word	Meaning	Related Words	Meaning
오늘 *o-neul*	today	어제 *eo-je*	yesterday
		내일 *nae-il*	tomorrow
생일 *saeng-il*	birthday	친구 생일 *chin-gu saeng-il*	friend's birthday
		생일 파티 *saeng-il pa-ti*	birthday party
		생일 선물 *saeng-il seon-mul*	birthday present
		생신 *saeng-sin*	birthday (honorific)
교실 *gyo-sil*	classroom	학교 *hak-kkyo*	school
		칠판 *chil-pan*	blackboard
		책상 *chaek-ssang*	desk
		의자 *ui-ja*	chair

먹다 *meok-tta*	to eat	밥을 먹다 *ba-beul meok-tta*	to have a meal
		많이 먹다 *ma-ni meok-tta*	to eat a lot
		마시다 *ma-si-da*	to drink
친구 *chin-gu*	friend	친구를 사귀다 *chin-gu-reul sa-gwi-da*	to make a friend
		친한 친구 *chi-nan chin-gu*	close friend
		친구들 *chin-gu-deul*	friends
노래 *no-rae*	song	노래하다 *no-rae-ha-da*	to sing
		노래를 듣다 *no-rae-reul deut-tta*	to listen to a song
		노래를 부르다 *no-rae-reul bu-reu-da*	to sing a song
춤 *chum*	dance	춤추다 *chum-chu-da*	to dance
		춤을 추다 *chu-meul chu-da*	to dance
		춤을 잘 추다 *chu-meul jal chu-da*	to dance well
		음악 *eu-mak*	music

축하하다 *chu-ka-ha-da*	to congratulate, to celebrate	생일을 축하하다 *saeng-i-reul chu-ka-ha-da*	to celebrate someone's birthday
		졸업을 축하하다 *jo-reo-beul chu-ka-ha-da*	to celebrate someone's graduation
		축하해 주다 *chu-ka-hae ju-da*	to congratulate, to celebrate
		축하 파티 *chu-ka pa-ti*	celebration, congratulatory party
재미있다 *jae-mi-it-tta*	to be fun	재미있는 *jae-mi-in-neun*	fun
		정말 재미있다 *jeong-mal jae-mi-it-tta*	to be a lot of fun
		재미없다 *jae-mi-eop-tta*	to be boring, to not be fun
하루 *ha-ru*	day, one day	하루 종일 *ha-ru jong-il*	all day long
		하루를 시작하다 *ha-ru-reul si-ja-ka-da*	to start one's day
		하루 동안 *ha-ru dong-an*	for a day

LET'S REVIEW!

Read the story again, but this time in Korean!

오늘은 제 **생일**이에요. **교실**에서 생일 파티를 했어요.

케이크도 먹고 과자도 **먹었어요**.

친구들이 **노래**를 불러 줬어요.

노래도 부르고 **춤**도 췄어요.

친구들이 **축하해** 줘서 기분이 좋았어요.

정말 **재미있는 하루**였어요.

Translation

Today is my birthday. We had a birthday party in the classroom. We ate cake and also ate snacks. My friends sang a song for me. We also sang and danced. I was happy because my friends celebrated my birthday. It was a really fun day.

Match each Korean word to its English translation.

친구 ·	· to congratulate, to celebrate
축하하다 ·	· birthday
춤 ·	· friend
오늘 ·	· day, one day
먹다 ·	· song
생일 ·	· today
하루 ·	· classroom
재미있다 ·	· to eat
교실 ·	· dance
노래 ·	· to be fun

Crossword Puzzle

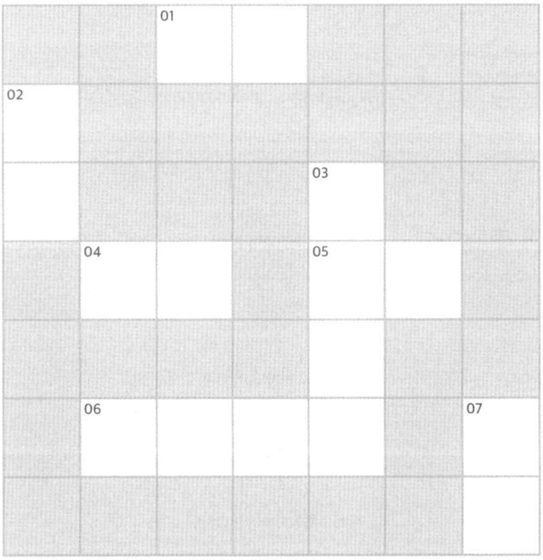

01 today
02 to eat
03 to congratulate, to celebrate
04 song
05 day, one day
06 to be fun
07 friend

Fill in the blanks using one of the words that you learned in Day 12.
(Please refer to page 017 to review how to conjugate verbs/adjectives.)

01 (   )은 제 생일이에요. Today is my birthday.

02 오늘은 제 (   )이에요. Today is my birthday.

03 (   )에서 생일 파티를 했어요. We had a birthday party in the classroom.

04 케이크도 먹고 과자도 (   ). We ate cake and also ate snacks.

05 (   )들이 노래를 불러 줬어요. My friends sang a song for me.

06 친구들이 (   )를 불러 줬어요. My friends sang a song for me.

07 노래도 부르고 (   )도 췄어요. We also sang and danced.

08 친구들이 (   ) 줘서 기분이 좋았어요. I was happy because my friends celebrated my birthday.

09 정말 (   ) 하루였어요. It was a really fun day.

10 정말 재미있는 (   )였어요. It was a really fun day.

Day 13

- 아빠
- 바다
- 걷다
- 식당
- 맛있다
- 음식
- 커피
- 별
- 보다
- 행복하다

Day 13

LET'S WARM UP!

Imagine the situation in the story below to help you remember the ten Korean words in context.

13

바다 아빠

I went to the ocean with my dad.

걷다

We walked along the beach.

식당 맛있다 음식

We went to a restaurant and had delicious food.

커피

We went to a café and drank coffee.

보다 별

Night fell. We also saw the stars.

행복하다

I was very happy.

LET'S KEEP THE BALL ROLLING!

Word	Meaning	Related Words	Meaning
아빠 *a-ppa*	dad	우리 아빠 *u-ri a-ppa*	my dad
		새아빠 *sae-a-ppa*	stepfather
		아빠가 되다 *a-ppa-ga doe-da*	to become a dad
		엄마 *eom-ma*	mom
바다 *ba-da*	sea, ocean	바다에 가다 *ba-da-e ga-da*	to go to the ocean
		바다낚시 *ba-da-nak-ssi*	sea fishing
		바닷가 *ba-dat-kka*	beach
		바닷물 *ba-dan-mul*	sea water
걷다 *geot-tta*	to walk	길을 걷다 *gi-reul geot-tta*	to walk in the street
		빨리 걷다 *ppal-li geot-tta*	to walk quickly
		천천히 걷다 *cheon-cheo-ni geot-tta*	to walk slowly
		걸어가다 *geo-reo-ga-da*	to walk (somewhere)

식당 *sik-ttang*	restaurant	식당에 가다 *sik-ttang-e ga-da*	to go to a restaurant
		맛있는 식당 *ma-sin-neun sik-ttang*	delicious place, restaurant with delicious food
		유명한 식당 *yu-myeong-han sik-ttang*	famous restaurant
		새로운 식당 *sae-ro-un sik-ttang*	new restaurant
맛있다 *ma-sit-tta*	to be delicious	밥이 맛있다 *ba-bi ma-sit-tta*	the food is delicious, the meal is delicious
		맛있는 음식 *ma-sin-neun eum-sik*	delicious food
		맛없다 *ma-deop-tta*	to not be tasty, to be a bad taste
음식 *eum-sik*	food	음식을 먹다 *eum-si-geul meok-tta*	to eat food
		음식을 만들다 *eum-si-geul man-deul-da*	to make food
		밀가루 음식 *mil-kka-ru eum-sik*	flour-based food
커피 *keo-pi*	coffee	커피 한 잔 *keo-pi han jan*	a cup of coffee
		따뜻한 커피 *tta-tteu-tan keo-pi*	hot coffee
		커피를 마시다 *keo-pi-reul ma-si-da*	to drink coffee

별 *byeol*	star	반짝반짝 *ban-jjak-ban-jjak*	twinkling
		빛나다 *bin-na-da*	to shine
		달 *dal*	moon
		해 *hae*	sun
		하늘 *ha-neul*	sky

보다 *bo-da*	to see, to watch, to meet, to read	영화를 보다 *yeong-haw-reul bo-da*	to watch a movie
		신문을 보다 *sin-mu-neul bo-da*	to read the newspaper
		보이다 *bo-i-da*	to be visible, to be seen, can see
		보여 주다 *bo-yeo ju-da*	to show

행복하다 *haeng-bo-ka-da*	to be happy	너무 행복하다 *neo-mu haeng-bo-ka-da*	to be very happy
		행복하게 살다 *haeng-bo-ka-ge sal-da*	to live happily
		행복한 사람 *haeng-bo-kan sa-ram*	happy person
		행복 *haeng-bok*	happiness

LET'S REVIEW!

Read the story again, but this time in Korean!

아빠랑 같이 **바다**에 갔어요.

바닷가를 **걸었어요.**

식당에 가서 **맛있는 음식**을 먹었어요.

카페에 가서 **커피**를 마셨어요.

밤이 됐어요. **별**도 **봤어요.**

너무 **행복했어요.**

Translation

I went to the ocean with my dad. We walked along the beach. We went to a restaurant and had delicious food. We went to a café and drank coffee. Night fell. We also saw the stars. I was very happy.

Match each Korean word to its English translation.

보다 ·	· restaurant
커피 ·	· to walk
음식 ·	· to see, to watch, to meet, to read
식당 ·	· dad
아빠 ·	· to be happy
행복하다 ·	· sea, ocean
바다 ·	· coffee
별 ·	· to be delicious
맛있다 ·	· star
걷다 ·	· food

Crossword Puzzle

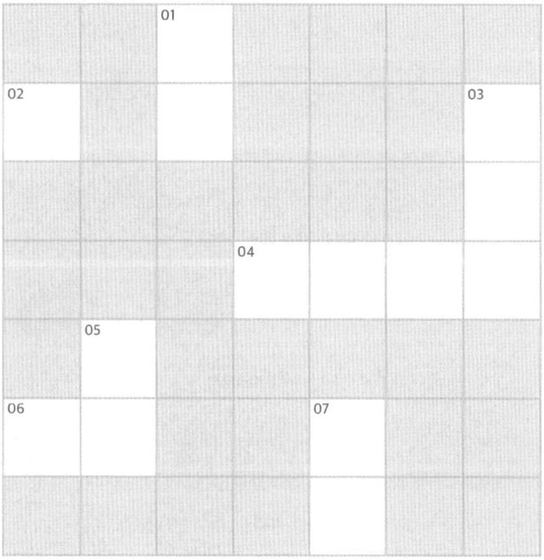

01 coffee
02 star
03 to be delicious
04 to be happy
05 to see, to watch
06 sea, ocean
07 food

Fill in the blanks using one of the words that you learned in Day 13.
(Please refer to page 017 to review how to conjugate verbs/adjectives.)

01 (   )랑 같이 바다에 갔어요. I went to the ocean with my dad.

02 아빠랑 같이 (   )에 갔어요. I went to the ocean with my dad.

03 바닷가를 (   ). We walked along the beach.

04 (   )에 가서 맛있는 음식을 먹었어요. We went to a restaurant and had delicious food.

05 식당에 가서 (   ) 음식을 먹었어요. We went to a restaurant and had delicious food.

06 식당에 가서 맛있는 (   )을 먹었어요. We went to a restaurant and had delicious food.

07 카페에 가서 (   )를 마셨어요. We went to a café and drank coffee.

08 (   )도 봤어요. We also saw the stars.

09 별도 (   ). We also saw the stars.

10 너무 (   ). I was very happy.

Day 14

- 여름
- 싫어하다
- 덥다
- 밖
- 나가다
- 집
- 에어컨
- 켜다
- 시원하다
- 얼음

Day 14

LET'S WARM UP!

Imagine the situation in the story below to help you remember the ten Korean words in context.

14

싫어하다 여름

I hate summer.

덥다

In the summer it is too hot. So, I hate summer.

나가다 밖

During the summer, I don't go outside that often.

켜다 에어컨 집

I turn on the air conditioner at home.

시원하다 얼음

I drink cold ice water.

In the summer, I like staying at home the most.

LET'S KEEP THE BALL ROLLING!

Word	Meaning	Related Words	Meaning
여름 *yeo-reum*	summer	여름 방학 *yeo-reum bang-hak*	summer vacation
		여름옷 *yeo-reu-mot*	summer clothes
		덥다 *deop-tta*	to be hot
싫어하다 *si-reo-ha-da*	to dislike, to hate	싫어하는 *si-reo-ha-neun*	that one hates
		싫어하는 사람 *si-reo-ha-neun sa-ram*	a person who one dislikes
		하기 싫어하다 *ha-gi si-reo-ha-da*	to hate doing something
덥다 *deop-tta*	to be hot	더운 *deo-un*	hot
		더운 날씨 *deo-un nal-ssi*	hot weather
		여름 *yeo-reum*	summer
밖 *bak*	outside	밖에 나가다 *ba-kke na-ga-da*	to go outside
		밖으로 *ba-kkeu-ro*	to the outside
		안 *an*	inside

나가다 *na-ga-da*	to go out	방에서 나가다 *bang-e-seo na-ga-da*	to leave the room
		들어오다 *deu-reo-o-da*	to come in
		들어가다 *deu-reo-ga-da*	to go in
		나오다 *na-o-da*	to come out

집 *jip*	house, home	집에 오다 *ji-be o-da*	to come home
		집에 가다 *ji-be ga-da*	to go home
		집에 있다 *ji-be it-tta*	to stay at home
		가족 *ga-jok*	family

에어컨 *e-eo-keon*	air conditioner	에어컨을 켜다 *e-eo-keo-neul kyeo-da*	to turn on the air conditioner
		에어컨을 끄다 *e-eo-keo-neul kkeu-da*	to turn off the air conditioner
		에어컨 바람 *e-eo-keon ba-ram*	wind from the air conditioner

켜다 *kyeo-da*	to turn on	불을 켜다 *bu-reul kyeo-da*	to turn on the light
		텔레비전을 켜다 *tel-le-bi-jeo-neul kyeo-da*	to turn on the television
		끄다 *kkeu-da*	to turn off

시원하다 *si-wo-na-da*	to be cool (temperature)	**시원한** *si-wo-nan*	cool, cold
		시원한 물 *si-wo-nan mul*	cold water
		바람이 시원하다 *ba-ra-mi si-wo-na-da*	the wind is cool

얼음 *eo-reum*	ice	**얼음이 얼다** *eo-reu-mi eol-da*	ice forms
		얼음이 녹다 *eo-reu-mi nok-tta*	ice melts
		얼음물 *eo-reum-mul*	ice water

LET'S REVIEW!

Read the story again, but this time in Korean!

저는 **여름**을 **싫어해요.**

여름에는 너무 **더워요.** 그래서 여름을 싫어해요.

여름에는 **밖**에 잘 안 **나가요.**

집에서 **에어컨**을 **켜요.**

시원한 얼음물을 마셔요.

여름에는 집에 있는 것이 제일 좋아요.

Translation

I hate summer. In the summer it is too hot. So, I hate summer. During the summer, I don't go outside that often. I turn on the air conditioner at home. I drink cold ice water. In the summer, I like staying at home the most.

Match each Korean word to its English translation.

집 ·	· to be hot
나가다 ·	· summer
얼음 ·	· to be cool (temperature)
에어컨 ·	· to turn on
여름 ·	· to dislike, to hate
시원하다 ·	· outside
덥다 ·	· to go out
싫어하다 ·	· ice
켜다 ·	· house, home
밖 ·	· air conditioner

Crossword Puzzle

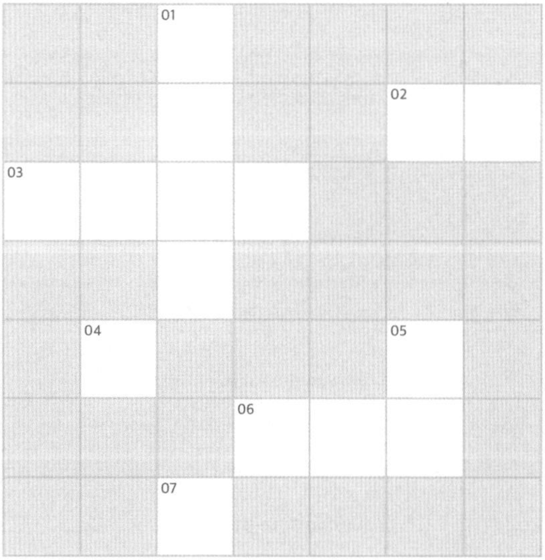

01 to dislike, to hate
02 summer
03 to be cool (temperature)
04 outside
05 to turn on
06 to go out
07 house, home

Fill in the blanks using one of the words that you learned in Day 14.
(Please refer to page 017 to review how to conjugate verbs/adjectives.)

01 저는 ( )을 싫어해요. I hate summer.

02 저는 여름을 ( ). I hate summer.

03 여름에는 너무 ( ). In the summer it is too hot.

04 여름에는 ( )에 잘 안 나가요. During the summer, I don't go outside that often.

05 여름에는 밖에 잘 안 ( ). During the summer, I don't go outside that often.

06 ( )에서 에어컨을 켜요. I turn on the air conditioner at home.

07 집에서 ( )을 켜요. I turn on the air conditioner at home.

08 집에서 에어컨을 ( ). I turn on the air conditioner at home.

09 ( ) 얼음물을 마셔요. I drink cold ice water.

10 시원한 ( )물을 마셔요. I drink cold ice water.

Day 15

- 벌써
- 밤
- 침대
- 눕다
- 잠
- 화장실
- 책
- 읽다
- 냉장고
- 우유

Day 15 LET'S WARM UP!

Imagine the situation in the story below to help you remember the ten Korean words in context.

15

벌써 밤

It is already 12 o'clock at night.

눕다 침대 잠

I lie down in my bed. But I can't sleep.

화장실

I go to the bathroom and come back.

읽다 책

I read a book. But I still can't sleep.

냉장고

I take out some milk from the refrigerator.

우유

I drink milk. Now I can sleep. I sleep well.

LET'S KEEP THE BALL ROLLING!

Word	Meaning	Related Words	Meaning
벌써 *beol-sseo*	already	벌써 10년 *beol-sseo sim-nyeon*	already 10 years
		벌써 끝나다 *beol-sseo kkeun-na-da*	to already be over
		이미 *i-mi*	already
밤 *bam*	night	오늘 밤 *o-neul bam*	tonight
		밤 10시 *bam yeol-ssi*	10 o'clock at night
		낮 *nat*	day, daytime
		캄캄하다 *kam-ka-ma-da*	to be dark
침대 *chim-dae*	bed	침대에 눕다 *chim-dae-e nup-tta*	to lie in the bed
		싱글 침대 *ssing-geul chim-dae*	single bed
		더블 침대 *deo-beul chim-dae*	double bed
		이층 침대 *i-cheung chim-dae*	bunk bed

눕다 *nup-tta*	to lie down	**침대에 눕다** *chim-dae-e nup-tta*	to lie in the bed
		똑바로 눕다 *ttok-ppa-ro nup-tta*	to lie flat on one's back
		누워 있다 *nu-wo it-tta*	to be lying (down)
		일어나다 *i-reo-na-da*	to get up
잠 *jam*	sleep	**늦잠** *neut-jjam*	oversleep, sleeping in
		자다 *ja-da*	to sleep
		잠을 자다 *ja-meul ja-da*	to sleep
		낮잠 *nat-jjam*	nap
화장실 *hwa-jang-sil*	bathroom	**화장실에 가다** *hwa-jang-si-re ga-da*	to go to the bathroom
		화장지 *hwa-jang-ji*	toilet paper
책 *chaek*	book	**책을 읽다** *chae-geul ik-tta*	to read a book
		책을 펴다 *chae-geul pyeo-da*	to open a book
		책을 덮다 *chae-geul deop-tta*	to close a book

읽다 *ik-tta*	to read	잡지를 읽다 *jap-jji-reul ik-tta*	to read a magazine
		읽기 *il-kki*	reading
		빨리 읽다 *ppal-li ik-tta*	to read quickly
		다 읽다 *da ik-tta*	to finish reading, to read all
냉장고 *naeng-jang-go*	refrigerator	냉장고 문 *naeng-jang-go mun*	refrigerator door
		큰 냉장고 *keun naeng-jang-go*	big refrigerator
		냉장고에 넣다 *naeng-jang-go-e neo-ta*	to put in the refrigerator
		냉장고를 열다 *naeng-jang-go-reul yeol-da*	to open the refrigerator
우유 *u-yu*	milk	우유 한 잔 *u-yu han jan*	a glass of milk
		우유를 마시다 *u-yu-reul ma-si-da*	to drink milk

LET'S REVIEW!

Read the story again, but this time in Korean!

벌써 밤 12시예요.

침대에 **누워요.** 그런데 **잠**이 안 와요.

화장실에 갔다 와요.

책을 **읽어요.** 그래도 잠이 안 와요.

냉장고에서 우유를 꺼내요.

우유를 마셔요. 이제 잠이 와요. 잘 자요.

Translation

It is already 12 o'clock at night. I lie down in my bed. But I can't sleep. I go to the bathroom and come back. I read a book. But I still can't sleep. I take out some milk from the refrigerator. I drink milk. Now I can sleep. I sleep well.

Match each Korean word to its English translation.

눕다 ·	· bed
벌써 ·	· book
읽다 ·	· milk
냉장고 ·	· already
침대 ·	· bathroom
잠 ·	· to read
화장실 ·	· night
우유 ·	· to lie down
밤 ·	· sleep
책 ·	· refrigerator

Crossword Puzzle

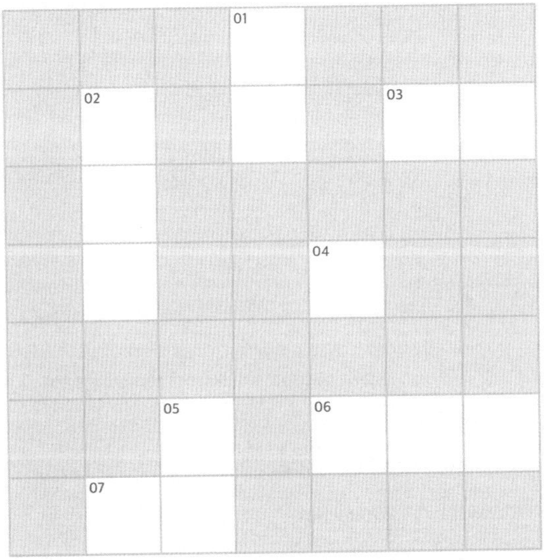

01 bed
02 refrigerator
03 milk
04 night
05 to lie down
06 bathroom
07 to read

Fill in the blanks using one of the words that you learned in Day 15.
(Please refer to page 017 to review how to conjugate verbs/adjectives.)

01 (   ) 밤 12시예요. It is already 12 o'clock at night.

02 벌써 (   ) 12시예요. It is already 12 o'clock at night.

03 (   )에 누워요. I lie down in my bed.

04 침대에 (   ). I lie down in my bed.

05 그런데 (   )이 안 와요. But I can't sleep.

06 (   )에 갔다 와요. I go to the bathroom and come back.

07 (   )을 읽어요. I read a book.

08 책을 (   ). I read a book.

09 (   )에서 우유를 꺼내요. I take out some milk from the refrigerator.

10 (   )를 마셔요. I drink milk.

Day 16

- 컵
- 뜨겁다
- 컴퓨터
- 이메일
- 노트북
- 충전하다
- 중요하다
- 거울
- 화장품
- 바르다

Day 16 LET'S WARM UP!

Imagine the situation in the story below to help you remember the ten Korean words in context.

16

뜨겁다 컵

I pour hot coffee into a cup.

컴퓨터

I turn on my computer.

이메일

I read my e-mails.

충전하다 노트북

I charge my phone with my laptop computer.

중요하다

I have an important appointment in the afternoon.

거울

I look in the mirror.

바르다 화장품

I put on make-up.

LET'S KEEP THE BALL ROLLING!

Word	Meaning	Related Words	Meaning
컵 *keop*	cup	컵에 따르다 *keo-be tta-reu-da*	to pour into a cup
		컵을 씻다 *keo-beul ssit-tta*	to wash a cup
		빈 컵 *bin keop*	empty cup
		한 컵 *han keop*	one cup
뜨겁다 *tteu-geop-tta*	to be hot	냄비가 뜨겁다 *naem-bi-ga tteu-geop-tta*	the pot is hot
		온몸이 뜨겁다 *on-mo-mi tteu-geop-tta*	one's whole body is hot
		뜨거운 커피 *tteu-geo-un keo-pi*	hot coffee
		차갑다 *cha-gap-tta*	to be cold
컴퓨터 *keom-pyu-teo*	computer	컴퓨터를 켜다 *keom-pyu-teo-reul kyeo-da*	to turn on a computer
		컴퓨터가 오래되다 *keom-pyu-teo-ga o-rae-doe-da*	the computer is old
		컴퓨터 한 대 *keom-pyu-teo han dae*	one computer
		컴퓨터하다 *keom-pyu-teo-ha-da*	to use a computer, to work on a computer

이메일 *i-me-il*	e-mail	이메일이 오다 *i-me-i-ri o-da*	an e-mail comes, to receive an e-mail
		이메일을 읽다 *i-me-i-reul ik-tta*	to read an e-mail
		이메일을 쓰다 *i-me-i-reul sseu-da*	to write an e-mail
		이메일을 보내다 *i-me-i-reul bo-nae-da*	to send an e-mail
노트북 *no-teu-buk*	laptop computer	노트북 컴퓨터 *no-teu-buk keom-pyu-teo*	laptop computer
		노트북으로 일하다 *no-teu-bu-geu-ro il-ha-da*	to work on a laptop computer
충전하다 *chung-jeon-ha-da*	to charge	노트북을 충전하다 *no-teu-bu-geul chung-jeon-ha-da*	to charge a laptop computer
		휴대폰을 충전하다 *hyu-dae-po-neul chung-jeon-ha-da*	to charge a cell phone
		충전기 *chung-jeon-gi*	charger
		배터리가 없다 *bae-teo-ri-ga eop-tta*	to have no battery
중요하다 *jung-yo-ha-da*	to be important	중요한 약속 *jung-yo-han yak-ssok*	important appointment
		중요한 시험 *jung-yo-han si-heom*	important test

거울 *geo-ul*	mirror	거울을 보다 *geo-u-reul bo-da*	to look in the mirror
		거울이 깨지다 *geo-u-ri kkae-ji-da*	the mirror breaks
		큰 거울 *keun geo-ul*	big mirror
		손거울 *son-kkeo-ul*	hand mirror

화장품 *hwa-jang-pum*	make-up product	화장품을 바르다 *hwa-jang-pu-meul ba-reu-da*	to apply make-up
		화장품을 다 쓰다 *hwa-jang-pu-meul da sseu-da*	to run out of a make-up product
		새 화장품 *sae hwa-jang-pum*	a new make-up product
		화장품 정리 *hwa-jang-pum jeong-li*	organizing make-up products

바르다 *ba-reu-da*	to apply, to put on	로션을 바르다 *lo-syeo-neul ba-reu-da*	to apply lotion
		연고를 바르다 *yeon-go-reul ba-reu-da*	to apply ointment
		잼을 바르다 *jae-meul ba-reu-da*	to spread jam (on bread, cracker, etc.)

LET'S REVIEW!

Read the story again, but this time in Korean!

컵에 **뜨거운** 커피를 따라요.

컴퓨터를 켜요. **이메일**을 읽어요.

노트북으로 휴대폰을 **충전해요.**

오후에 **중요한** 약속이 있어요.

거울을 봐요.

화장품을 **발라요.**

Translation

I pour hot coffee into a cup. I turn on my computer. I read my e-mails. I charge my phone with my laptop computer. I have an important appointment in the afternoon. I look in the mirror. I put on make-up.

Match each Korean word to its English translation.

뜨겁다 ·	· computer
이메일 ·	· to charge
중요하다 ·	· to be hot
컵 ·	· e-mail
바르다 ·	· make-up product
컴퓨터 ·	· cup
충전하다 ·	· to be important
화장품 ·	· to apply, to put on
거울 ·	· laptop computer
노트북 ·	· mirror

Crossword Puzzle

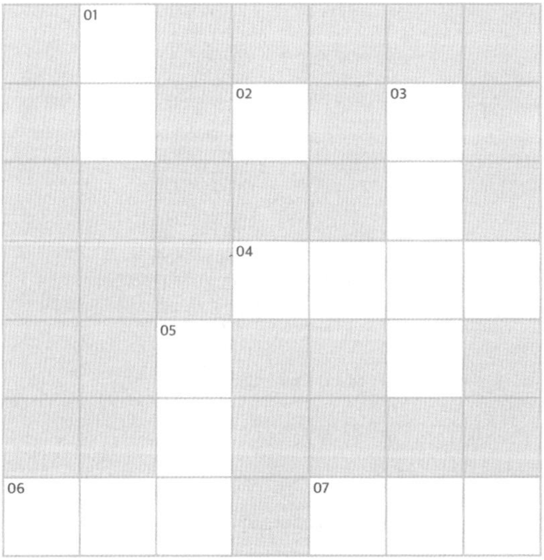

01 mirror
02 cup
03 to charge
04 to be important
05 to apply, to put on
06 to be hot
07 laptop computer

Fill in the blanks using one of the words that you learned in Day 16.
(Please refer to page 017 to review how to conjugate verbs/adjectives.)

01 (   )에 뜨거운 커피를 따라요. I pour hot coffee into a cup.

02 컵에 (   ) 커피를 따라요. I pour hot coffee into a cup.

03 (   )를 켜요. I turn on my computer.

04 (   )을 읽어요. I read my e-mails.

05 (   )으로 휴대폰을 충전해요. I charge my phone with my laptop computer.

06 노트북으로 휴대폰을 (   ). I charge my phone with my laptop computer.

07 오후에 (   ) 약속이 있어요. I have an important appointment in the afternoon.

08 (   )을 봐요. I look in the mirror.

09 (   )을 발라요. I put on make-up.

10 화장품을 (   ). I put on make-up.

Day 17

- 옆
- 부부
- 초대
- 오후
- 도착
- 딸
- 나이
- 같다
- 유치원
- 사이

Day 17

LET'S WARM UP!

Imagine the situation in the story below to help you remember the ten Korean words in context.

17

초대하다 옆 부부

Today I **invited** the **next** door **couple** over.

도착 오후

They will **arrive** at my house at 6 **p.m.**

딸

The **daughter** of the next door couple

같다 나이

and my daughter are the **same** **age**.

유치원

They both go to the same **kindergarten**.

사이

So they have a good **relationship**.

LET'S KEEP THE BALL ROLLING!

Word	Meaning	Related Words	Meaning
옆 *yeop*	side, next to	옆집 *yeop-jjip*	next door, next house
		옆자리 *yeop-jja-ri*	next seat
		옆 사람 *yeop sa-ram*	next person
		옆에 *yeo-pe*	next to
부부 *bu-bu*	married couple	부부 사이 *bu-bu sa-i*	between a married couple, married couple
		부부 싸움 *bu-bu ssa-um*	married couple's fight, fight between husband and wife
		남편 *nam-pyeon*	husband
		아내 *a-nae*	wife
초대 *cho-dae*	invitation	초대하다 *cho-dae-ha-da*	to invite
		초대를 받다 *cho-dae-reul bat-tta*	to be invited, to receive an invitation
		저녁 초대 *jeo-nyeok cho-dae*	invitation to dinner
		초대장 *cho-dae-jjang*	invitation, invitation card

오후 *o-hu*	afternoon	오늘 오후 *o-neul o-hu*	this afternoon
		오전 *o-jeon*	morning
		오후에 *o-hu-e*	in the afternoon
도착 *do-chak*	arrival	도착하다 *do-cha-ka-da*	to arrive
		도착 시간 *do-chak si-gan*	arrival time
		늦게 도착하다 *neut-kke do-cha-ka-da*	to arrive late
		일찍 도착하다 *il-jjik do-cha-ka-da*	to arrive early
딸 *ttal*	daughter	첫째 딸 *cheot-jjae ttal*	first daughter
		막내 딸 *mang-nae ttal*	youngest daughter, last daughter
		딸을 낳다 *tta-reul na-ta*	to give birth to a daughter
		아들 *a-deul*	son

나이 *na-i*	age	나이가 어리다 *na-i-ga eo-ri-da*	to be young
		나이가 많다 *na-i-ga man-ta*	to be old
		나이가 들다 *na-i-ga deul-da*	to get older
		나이를 먹다 *na-i-reul meok-tta*	to get older
		살 *sal*	counting unit for age

같다 *gat-tta*	to be the same, to be like	나이가 같다 *na-i-ga gat-tta*	to be the same age
		같은 *ga-teun*	the same
		같은 유치원 *ga-teun yu-chi-won*	the same kindergarten
		똑같다 *ttok-kkat-tta*	to be exactly the same

유치원 *yu-chi-won*	kindergarten	유치원에 다니다 *yu-chi-wo-ne da-ni-da*	to attend kindergarten
		유치원 놀이터 *yu-chi-won no-ri-teo*	playground at the kindergarten

사이 *sa-i*	relationship, relation	사이가 좋다 *sa-i-ga jo-ta*	to be on good terms
		친구 사이 *chin-gu sa-i*	(to be) friends, friendly relationship
		친한 사이 *chi-nan sa-i*	(to be) close friends, close relationship

LET'S REVIEW!

Read the story again, but this time in Korean!

오늘 **옆집 부부**를 **초대**했어요.

오후 6시에 집에 **도착**할 거예요.

옆집 부부의 **딸**과 제 딸은 **나이**가 **같아요.**

둘 다 같은 **유치원**에 다녀요.

그래서 **사이**가 좋아요.

Translation

Today I invited the next door couple over. They will arrive at my house at 6 p.m. The daughter of the next door couple and my daughter are the same age. They both go to the same kindergarten. So they have a good relationship.

Match each Korean word to its English translation.

부부 ·	· invitation
오후 ·	· arrival
딸 ·	· side, next to
같다 ·	· age
사이 ·	· kindergarten
옆 ·	· married couple
유치원 ·	· relationship, relation
초대 ·	· afternoon
나이 ·	· daughter
도착 ·	· to be the same, to be like

Crossword Puzzle

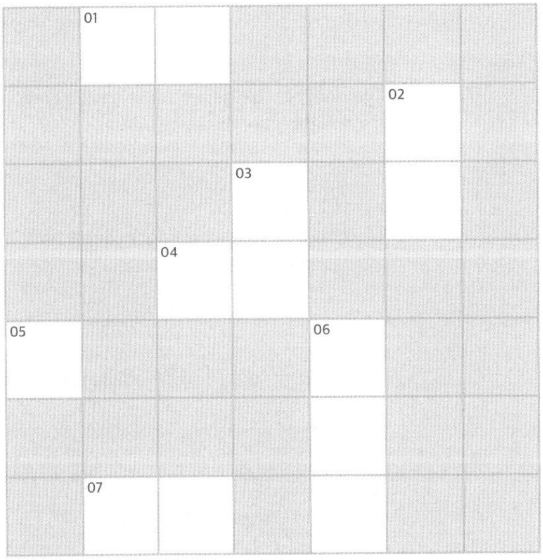

01 afternoon
02 married couple
03 age
04 relationship, relation
05 daughter
06 kindergarten
07 invitation

Fill in the blanks using one of the words that you learned in Day 17.
(Please refer to page 017 to review how to conjugate verbs/adjectives.)

01 오늘 ( )집 부부를 초대했어요. Today I invited the next door couple over.

02 오늘 옆집 ( )를 초대했어요. Today I invited the next door couple over.

03 오늘 옆집 부부를 ( )했어요. Today I invited the next door couple over.

04 ( ) 6시에 집에 도착할 거예요. They will arrive at my house at 6 p.m.

05 오후 6시에 집에 ( )할 거예요. They will arrive at my house at 6 p.m.

06 옆집 부부의 ( )과 제 딸은 나이가 같아요. The daughter of the next door couple and my daughter are the same age.

07 옆집 부부의 딸과 제 딸은 ( )가 같아요. The daughter of the next door couple and my daughter are the same age.

08 옆집 부부의 딸과 제 딸은 나이가 ( ). The daughter of the next door couple and my daughter are the same age.

09 둘 다 같은 ( )에 다녀요. They both go to the same kindergarten.

10 그래서 ( )가 좋아요. So they have a good relationship.

Day 18

아들

게임

요일

아침

점심

밥

화나다

걱정

왜

공부

Day 18 LET'S WARM UP!

Imagine the situation in the story below to help you remember the ten Korean words in context.

18

아들 게임
My son plays video games all day long.

토요일
Today is a Saturday.

아침 점심
My son played video games in the morning and also at lunch.

밥
He even skipped meals and played games.

화나다 걱정
I was really angry. And I was worried.

왜
Why does my son only play video games?

공부
Why doesn't he study?

LET'S KEEP THE BALL ROLLING!

Word	Meaning	Related Words	Meaning
아들 *a-deul*	son	첫째 아들 *cheot-jjae a-deul*	first son
		막내 아들 *mang-nae a-deul*	last son, youngest son
		아들을 낳다 *a-deu-reul na-ta*	to give birth to a son
		딸 *ttal*	daughter
게임 *kke-im*	game	게임을 하다 *kke-i-meul ha-da*	to play a game
		컴퓨터 게임 *keom-pyu-teo kke-im*	computer game
		보드게임 *bo-deu-kke-im*	board game
요일 *yo-il*	day of the week	월요일 *wo-ryo-il*	Monday
		화요일 *hwa-yo-il*	Tuesday
		수요일 *su-yo-il*	Wednesday
		목요일 *mo-gyo-il*	Thursday
		금요일 *geu-myo-il*	Friday
		토요일 *to-yo-il*	Saturday
		일요일 *i-ryo-il*	Sunday

아침 *a-chim*	morning	**아침에** *a-chi-me*	in the morning
		아침 인사 *a-chim in-sa*	morning greeting
		아침 일찍 *a-chim il-jjik*	early in the morning
		아침밥 *a-chim-ppap*	breakfast
점심 *jeom-sim*	lunch	**점심시간** *jeom-sim-ssi-gan*	lunch time
		늦은 점심 *neu-jeun jeom-sim*	late lunch
		점심을 먹다 *jeom-si-meul meok-tta*	to have lunch
밥 *bap*	rice, food, meal	**밥을 먹다** *ba-beul meok-tta*	to eat (a meal)
		밥을 차리다 *ba-beul cha-ri-da*	to prepare a meal
		저녁밥 *jeo-nyeok-ppap*	dinner, supper
		비빔밥 *bi-bim-ppap*	mixed rice, rice mixed with various ingredients
화나다 *hwa-na-da*	to feel angry, to get angry	**화난** *hwa-nan*	angry
		화가 나다 *hwa-ga na-da*	to feel angry
		화내다 *hwa-nae-da*	to get angry at someone, to show one's anger

걱정 *geok-jjeong*	worry, concern	걱정하다 *geok-jjeong-ha-da*	to worry
		걱정되다 *geok-jjeong-doe-da*	to be worried
		걱정이 없다 *geok-jjeong-i eop-tta*	to have no worries
왜 *wae*	why	왜 그렇게 *wae geu-reo-ke*	why so
		때문에 *ttae-mu-ne*	because, because of
공부 *gong-bu*	study	공부하다 *gong-bu-ha-da*	to study
		공부를 안 하다 *gong-bu-reul an ha-da*	to not study
		열심히 공부하다 *yeol-ssi-mi gong-bu-ha-da*	to study hard

LET'S REVIEW!

Read the story again, but this time in Korean!

제 **아들**은 하루 종일 **게임**을 해요.

오늘은 **토요일**이에요.

아들은 **아침**에도 **점심**에도 게임을 했어요.

밥도 안 먹고 게임을 했어요.

저는 정말 **화났어요.** 그리고 **걱정**되었어요.

제 아들은 **왜** 게임만 할까요? 왜 **공부**를 안 할까요?

Translation

My son plays video games all day long. Today is a Saturday. My son played video games in the morning and also at lunch. He even skipped meals and played games. I was really angry. And I was worried. Why does my son only play video games? Why doesn't he study?

Match each Korean word to its English translation.

아침 ·	· game
점심 ·	· rice, food, meal
아들 ·	· to feel angry, to get angry
화나다 ·	· morning
걱정 ·	· son
공부 ·	· why
밥 ·	· lunch
게임 ·	· study
왜 ·	· day of the week
요일 ·	· worry, concern

Crossword Puzzle

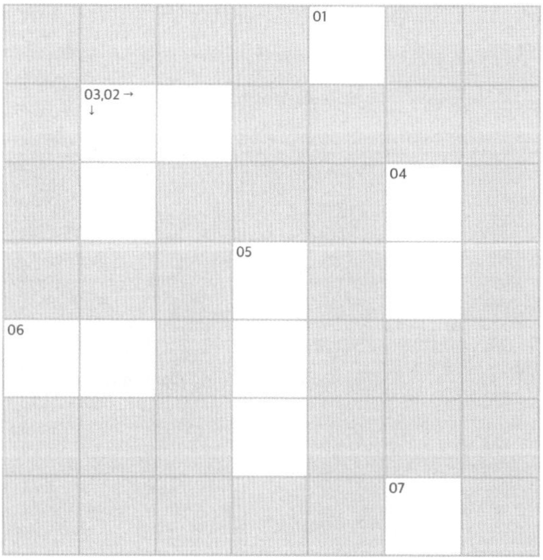

01 rice, food, meal
02 morning
03 son
04 day of the week
05 to feel angry, to get angry
06 worry, concern
07 why

Fill in the blanks using one of the words that you learned in Day 18.
(Please refer to page 017 to review how to conjugate verbs/adjectives.)

01 제 (   )은 하루 종일 게임을 해요. — My son plays video games all day long.

02 제 아들은 하루 종일 (   )을 해요. — My son plays video games all day long.

03 오늘은 (   )이에요. — Today is a Saturday.

04 아들은 (   )에도 점심에도 게임을 했어요. — My son played video games in the morning and also at lunch.

05 아들은 아침에도 (   )에도 게임을 했어요. — My son played video games in the morning and also at lunch.

06 (   )도 안 먹고 게임을 했어요. — He even skipped meals and played games.

07 저는 정말 (   ). — I was really angry.

08 그리고 (   )되었어요. — And I was worried.

09 제 아들은 (   ) 게임만 할까요? — Why does my son only play video games?

10 왜 (   )를 안 할까요? — Why doesn't he study?

Day 19

- 느낌
- 달력
- 날짜
- 모양
- 아래
- 전화번호
- 잊어버리다
- 빨리
- 예약
- 출발하다

Day 19 LET'S WARM UP!

Imagine the situation in the story below to help you remember the ten Korean words in context.

19

I worked until late again today.

느낌 달력
I had a weird **feeling**, so I checked the **calendar**.

날짜 모양
On today's **date**, there is a circle **shape**.

아래 전화번호
Below the date, there is also a **phone number**.

잊어버리다
Oh, it's my dad's birthday today! I **forgot**.

빨리 예약
I **quickly** **reserved** a restaurant.

출발하다
I am **leaving** for the restaurant now.

LET'S KEEP THE BALL ROLLING!

Word	Meaning	Related Words	Meaning
느낌 *neu-kkim*	feeling	느낌이 들다 *neu-kki-mi deul-da*	to feel, to have a certain feeling
		느낌이 이상하다 *neu-kki-mi i-sang-ha-da*	to have a weird feeling
		좋은 느낌 *jo-eun neu-kkim*	good feeling
		그런 느낌 *geu-reon neu-kkim*	such a feeling, feeling like that
달력 *dal-lyeok*	calendar	달력을 보다 *dal-lyeo-geul bo-da*	to check the calendar
		달력에 표시하다 *dal-lyeo-ge pyo-si-ha-da*	to mark the calendar
		년 *nyeon*	year
		월 *wol*	month
		일 *il*	day
날짜 *nal-jja*	date	오늘 날짜 *o-neul nal-jja*	today's date
		약속 날짜 *yak-ssok nal-jja*	date of appointment
		결혼 날짜 *gyeo-ron nal-jja*	wedding date
		날짜를 잡다 *nal-jja-reul jap-tta*	to set a date

모양 *mo-yang*	shape	같은 모양 *ga-teun mo-yang*	same shape
		다른 모양 *da-reun mo-yang*	different shape
		비슷한 모양 *bi-seu-tan mo-yang*	similar shape
		동그라미 *dong-geu-ra-mi*	circle
		세모 *se-mo*	triangle
		네모 *ne-mo*	rectangle

아래 *a-rae*	down, below	책상 아래 *chaek-ssang a-rae*	below the desk
		나무 아래에서 *na-mu a-rae-e-seo*	below a tree
		위 *wi*	up, top
		옆 *yeop*	side

전화번호 *jeo-nwa-beo-no*	phone number	집 전화번호 *jip jeo-nwa-beo-no*	home phone number
		전화번호를 외우다 *jeo-nwa-beo-no-reul oe-u-da*	to memorize a number
		전화번호를 물어보다 *jeo-nwa-beo-no-reul mu-reo-bo-da*	to ask someone's number
		전화번호를 알려 주다 *jeo-nwa-beo-no-reul al-lyeo ju-da*	to give one's number

잊어버리다 *i-jeo-beo-ri-da*	to forget	깜빡 잊어버리다 *kkam-ppak i-jeo-beo-ri-da*	to forget, something slips one's mind
		약속을 잊어버리다 *yak-sso-geul i-jeo-beo-ri-da*	to forget about a plan/ appointment
		기억하다 *gi-eo-ka-da*	to remember

빨리 *ppal-li*	fast, quickly	빨리 가다 *ppal-li ga-da*	to go quickly
		빠르다 *ppa-reu-da*	to be quick
		빠르게 *ppa-reu-ge*	quickly

예약 *ye-yak*	reservation	예약하다 *ye-ya-ka-da*	to reserve
		전화로 예약하다 *jeo-nwa-ro ye-ya-ka-da*	to reserve on the phone
		예약 취소 *ye-yak chwi-so*	reservation cancellation

출발하다 *chul-bal-ha-da*	to depart	일찍 출발하다 *il-jjik chul-bal-ha-da*	to depart early
		서울로 출발하다 *seo-ul-lo chul-bal-ha-da*	to depart for Seoul
		출발 *chul-bal*	departure
		도착하다 *do-cha-ka-da*	to arrive

LET'S REVIEW!

Read the story again, but this time in Korean!

오늘도 늦게까지 일을 했어요.

느낌이 이상해서 **달력**을 봤어요.

오늘 **날짜**에 동그라미 **모양**이 있어요.

날짜 **아래 전화번호**도 있어요.

아, 오늘 아빠 생신이에요! 깜빡 **잊어버렸어요.**

빨리 식당을 **예약**했어요. 지금 식당으로 **출발해요.**

Translation

I worked until late again today. I had a weird feeling, so I checked the calendar. On today's date, there is a circle shape. Below the date, there is also a phone number. Oh, it's my dad's birthday today! I forgot. I quickly reserved a restaurant. I am leaving for the restaurant now.

Match each Korean word to its English translation.

날짜 ·	· feeling
전화번호 ·	· calendar
빨리 ·	· to forget
느낌 ·	· shape
아래 ·	· date
출발하다 ·	· phone number
잊어버리다 ·	· reservation
달력 ·	· to depart
예약 ·	· fast, quickly
모양 ·	· down, below

Crossword Puzzle

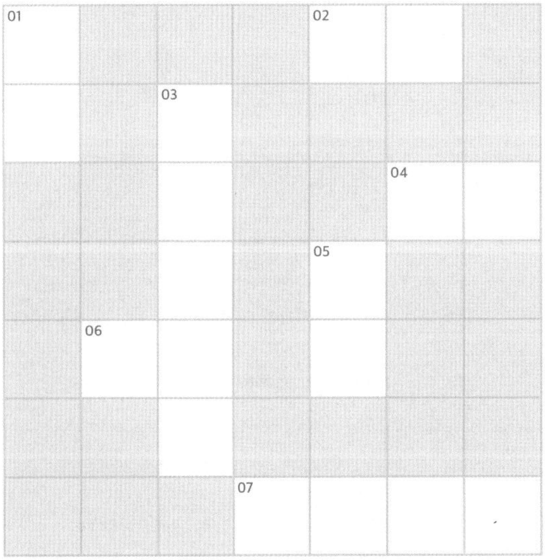

01 down, below
02 shape
03 to forget
04 calendar
05 feeling
06 fast, quickly
07 phone number

Fill in the blanks using one of the words that you learned in Day 19.
(Please refer to page 017 to review how to conjugate verbs/adjectives.)

01 (   )이 이상해서 달력을 봤어요.
I had a weird feeling, so I checked the calendar.

02 느낌이 이상해서 (   )을 봤어요.
I had a weird feeling, so I checked the calendar.

03 오늘 (   )에 동그라미 모양이 있어요.
On today's date, there is a circle shape.

04 오늘 날짜에 동그라미 (   )이 있어요.
On today's date, there is a circle shape.

05 날짜 (   ) 전화번호도 있어요.
Below the date, there is also a phone number.

06 날짜 아래 (   )도 있어요.
Below the date, there is also a phone number.

07 깜빡 (   ).
I forgot.

08 (   ) 식당을 예약했어요.
I quickly reserved a restaurant.

09 빨리 식당을 (   )했어요.
I quickly reserved a restaurant.

10 지금 식당으로 (   ).
I am leaving for the restaurant now.

Day 20

- 시골
- 도시
- 시끄럽다
- 조용하다
- 등산
- 높다
- 낮다
- 해
- 어둡다
- 내려가다

Day 20 LET'S WARM UP!

Imagine the situation in the story below to help you remember the ten Korean words in context.

20

시골

I was born in the countryside.

도시 시끄럽다

Now I live in the city. The city is too noisy.

조용하다

But if I go to the mountain, it's really quiet.

등산

So, I like hiking up the mountain.

높다 낮다

I like both high mountains and low mountains.

I usually go to the mountain in the morning.

어둡다 해 내려가다

It is dark when the sun sets. So, I go down before the sun sets.

LET'S KEEP THE BALL ROLLING!

Word	Meaning	Related Words	Meaning
시골 *si-gol*	countryside	시골 사람 *si-gol sa-ram*	country person
		시골 풍경 *si-gol pung-gyeong*	rural scene
		시골에서 태어나다 *si-go-re-seo tae-eo-na-da*	to be born in the countryside
도시 *do-si*	city	도시 생활 *do-si saeng-hwal*	city life
		대도시 *dae-do-si*	big city
		도시에 살다 *do-si-e sal-da*	to live in a city
시끄럽다 *si-kkeu-reop-tta*	to be noisy	교실이 시끄럽다 *gyo-si-ri si-kkeu-reop-tta*	to be noisy in the classroom
		시끄러운 소리 *si-kkeu-reo-un so-ri*	noisy sound, loud sound
		시끄럽게 *si-kkeu-reop-kke*	noisily, loudly
		시끄럽게 하다 *si-kkeu-reop-kke ha-da*	to make a loud noise

조용하다 *jo-yong-ha-da*	to be quiet	**집이 조용하다** *ji-bi jo-yong-ha-da*	the house is quiet
		조용한 동네 *jo-yong-han dong-ne*	quiet neighborhood
		조용하게 *jo-yong-ha-ge*	quietly
		조용하게 말하다 *jo-yong-ha-ge mal-ha-da*	to talk quietly

등산 *deung-san*	hiking	**등산을 가다** *deung-sa-neul ga-da*	to go hiking in the mountain
		등산을 하다 *deung-sa-neul ha-da*	to hike in the mountain
		등산하다 *deung-sa-na-da*	to hike in the mountain

높다 *nop-tta*	to be high	**하늘이 높다** *ha-neu-ri nop-tta*	the sky is high
		천장이 높다 *cheon-jang-i nop-tta*	the ceiling is high
		높은 건물 *no-peun geon-mul*	tall building

낮다 *nat-tta*	to be low	**책상이 낮다** *chaek-ssang-i nat-tta*	the desk is low
		낮은 산 *na-jeun san*	low mountain
		낮은 계단 *na-jeun gye-dan*	low steps

해 *hae*	the sun	해가 뜨다 *hae-ga tteu-da*	the sun rises
		해가 지다 *hae-ga ji-da*	the sun sets
		햇빛 *haet-ppit*	sunlight

어둡다 *eo-dup-tta*	to be dark	색깔이 어둡다 *saek-kka-ri eo-dup-tta*	the color is dark
		어두운 골목 *eo-du-un gol-mok*	dark alley
		어두워지다 *eo-du-wo-ji-da*	to get dark
		밝다 *bak-tta*	to be bright

내려가다 *nae-ryeo-ga-da*	to go down	산을 내려가다 *sa-neul nae-ryeo-ga-da*	to go down the mountain
		지하실로 내려가다 *ji-ha-sil-lo nae-ryeo-ga-da*	to go down to the basement
		내려가는 엘리베이터 *nae-ryeo-ga-neun el-li-be-i-teo*	descending elevator
		올라가다 *ol-la-ga-da*	to go up

LET'S REVIEW!

Read the story again, but this time in Korean!

저는 **시골**에서 태어났어요.

지금은 **도시**에 살아요. 도시는 너무 **시끄러워요.**

그런데 산에 가면 정말 **조용해요.**

그래서 **등산**을 좋아해요. **높은** 산도 **낮은** 산도 다 좋아요.

보통 아침에 산에 가요. **해**가 지면 **어두워요.**

그래서 해가 지기 전에 산을 **내려가요.**

Translation

I was born in the countryside. Now I live in the city. The city is too noisy. But if I go to the mountain, it's really quiet. So, I like hiking up the mountain. I like both high mountains and low mountains. I usually go to the mountain in the morning. It is dark when the sun sets. So, I go down before the sun sets.

Match each Korean word to its English translation.

도시 ·	· to be quiet
등산 ·	· the sun
낮다 ·	· to be noisy
내려가다 ·	· to be high
어둡다 ·	· to go down
시골 ·	· hiking
시끄럽다 ·	· city
해 ·	· to be dark
높다 ·	· to be low
조용하다 ·	· countryside

Crossword Puzzle

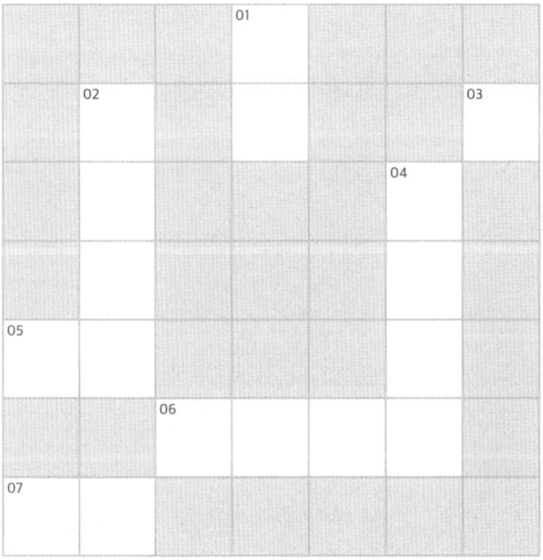

01 city
02 to go down
03 the sun
04 to be noisy
05 to be low
06 to be quiet
07 hiking

Fill in the blanks using one of the words that you learned in Day 20.
(Please refer to page 017 to review how to conjugate verbs/adjectives.)

01	저는 ( )에서 태어났어요.	I was born in the countryside.
02	지금은 ( )에 살아요.	Now I live in the city.
03	도시는 너무 ( ).	The city is too noisy.
04	그런데 산에 가면 정말 ( ).	But if I go to the mountain, it's really quiet.
05	그래서 ( )을 좋아해요.	So, I like hiking up the mountain.
06	( ) 산도 낮은 산도 다 좋아요.	I like both high mountains and low mountains.
07	높은 산도 ( ) 산도 다 좋아요.	I like both high mountains and low mountains.
08	( )가 지면 어두워요.	It is dark when the sun sets.
09	해가 지면 ( ).	It is dark when the sun sets.
10	그래서 해가 지기 전에 ( ).	So, I go down before the sun sets.

QUIZ

DAY 11-20

01 How do you say **"calendar"** in Korean?

a. 사이 b. 달력 c. 예약 d. 아들

02 Which word is related to 여름?

a. 쓰다 b. 노트북 c. 덥다 d. 맛있다

03 Choose the word that is a non-edible item.

a. 우유 b. 커피 c. 시골 d. 밥

04 Choose the term that is **NOT** a loanword from English.

a. 컴퓨터 b. 내일 c. 이메일 d. 게임

05 How do you say **"to be glad"** or **"to be happy"** in Korean?

a. 기뿌다 b. 기쁘다 c. 기뽀다 d. 기뻐다

06 Choose the word pair that is matched incorrectly.

a. 낮다 - to be high
b. 어둡다 - to be dark
c. 재미있다 - to be fun
d. 행복하다 - to be happy

07 Which of the following Korean words means **"one day"**?

a. 하루 b. 아빠 c. 오늘 d. 교실

08 Which word do Korean people commonly refer to as **"air conditioner"**?

a. 에어컨디셔너 b. 에어린스 c. 에어컨디 d. 에어컨

09 Choose the word that best replaces ○○.

월○○ **화**○○ **수**○○ **목**○○ **금**○○ **토**○○ **일**○○

a. 선물 b. 요일 c. 아침 d. 얼음

10 What is the antonym of 시끄럽다?

a. 출발하다 b. 충전하다 c. 중요하다 d. 조용하다

11 Which of the following does **NOT** become a verb if you attach -하다?

a. 거울 b. 등산 c. 걱정 d. 노래

12 Which one syllable word means **"sleep"**?

a. 잠 b. 밤 c. 집 d. 밖

13 How do you say **"married couple"** in Korean?

a. 도도 b. 두두 c. 부부 d. 보보

14 Choose the noun-verb pair that is matched incorrectly.

a. 생일 - 축하하다
b. 전화번호 - 잊어버리다
c. 화장품 - 바르다
d. 귀고리 - 목걸이

15 Choose the word that best replaces ○○.

○○에 눕다 **싱글○○** **더블○○** **이층○○**

a. 초대 b. 점심 c. 침대 d. 친구

16 Which of the following does **NOT** refer to an action?

a. 내려가다 b. 나가다 c. 걷다 d. 높다

17 Which of the following is the equivalent of **"why"** in Korean?

a. 딸 b. 왜 c. 춤 d. 옆

18 What does 나이가 같다 mean?

a. to be old
b. to be young
c. to be the same age
d. to be different ages

19 What kind of 모양 is the item in the picture?

a. 해 모양
b. 컵 모양
c. 책 모양
d. 별 모양

20 What is the Korean word for the place in the picture?

a. 바다
b. 식당
c. 도시
d. 화장실

QUIZ
DAY 11-20

Answers : b c c b b / a a d b d / a a c d c / d b c d a

Day 21

- 연예인
- 누구
- 키
- 크다
- 웃다
- 얼굴
- 귀엽다
- 눈[01]
- 다리
- 길다

Day 21 LET'S WARM UP!

Imagine the situation in the story below to help you remember the ten Korean words in context.

21

누구 연예인

Who do you think is my favorite celebrity?

키가 크다

He is tall.

웃다 얼굴 귀엽다

His smiling face is really cute.

눈[01] 길다 다리

He has big eyes and long legs.

LET'S KEEP THE BALL ROLLING!

Word	Meaning	Related Words	Meaning
연예인 *yeo-nye-in*	entertainer, celebrity	유명한 연예인 *yu-myeong-han yeo-nye-in*	famous celebrity
		연예인이 되다 *yeo-nye-i-ni doe-da*	to become a celebrity
		연예인을 만나다 *yeo-nye-i-neul man-na-da*	to meet a celebrity
누구 *nu-gu*	who	누가 *nu-ga*	who (subject)
		누구든지 *nu-gu-deun-ji*	whoever, anyone
		누구나 *nu-gu-na*	anyone
키 *ki*	one's height	키가 크다 *ki-ga keu-da*	to be tall
		키가 작다 *ki-ga jak-tta*	to be short
		키를 재다 *ki-reul jae-da*	to measure someone's height
크다 *keu-da*	to be big	옷이 크다 *o-si keu-da*	the clothes are big
		큰 눈 *keun nun*	big eyes
		작다 *jak-tta*	to be small

웃다 *ut-tta*	to laugh, to smile	**크게 웃다** *keu-ge ut-tta*	to laugh loudly
		웃음 *u-seum*	laughter
		웃음소리 *u-seum-sso-ri*	laughter sound
		미소 *mi-so*	smile
얼굴 *eol-gul*	face	**웃는 얼굴** *un-neun eol-gul*	laughing face, smiling face
		얼굴이 예쁘다 *eol-gu-ri ye-ppeu-da*	one's face is pretty
		표정 *pyo-jeong*	facial expression, look
귀엽다 *gwi-yeop-tta*	to be cute	**강아지가 귀엽다** *gang-a-ji-ga gwi-yeop-tta*	the puppy is cute
		귀여운 얼굴 *gwi-yeo-un eol-gul*	cute face
		귀엽게 생기다 *gwi-yeop-kke saeng-gi-da*	to look cute, to have a cute face
눈 01 *nun*	eye	**눈을 뜨다** *nu-neul tteu-da*	to open one's eyes
		눈을 감다 *nu-neul gam-tta*	to close one's eyes
		눈동자 *nun-ttong-ja*	pupil

다리 *da-ri*	leg	다리를 다치다 *da-ri-reul da-chi-da*	to hurt one's leg(s)
		다리가 아프다 *da-ri-ga a-peu-da*	one's leg hurts
		팔 *pal*	arm
		팔다리 *pal-da-ri*	arms and legs, limbs

길다 *gil-da*	to be long	줄이 길다 *ju-ri gil-da*	the line is long
		머리가 길다 *meo-ri-ga gil-da*	one's hair is long
		긴 다리 *gin da-ri*	long legs

LET'S REVIEW!

Read the story again, but this time in Korean!

제가 좋아하는 **연예인**은 **누구**일까요?

키가 **커요.**

웃는 얼굴이 정말 **귀여워요.**

눈이 크고 **다리**가 **길어요.**

Translation

Who do you think is my favorite celebrity? He is tall.
His smiling face is really cute. He has big eyes and long legs.

Match each Korean word to its English translation.

키 ·	· eye
얼굴 ·	· to be big
웃다 ·	· entertainer, celebrity
귀엽다 ·	· who
연예인 ·	· one's height
눈 01 ·	· to be long
길다 ·	· face
다리 ·	· to laugh, to smile
크다 ·	· to be cute
누구 ·	· leg

Crossword Puzzle

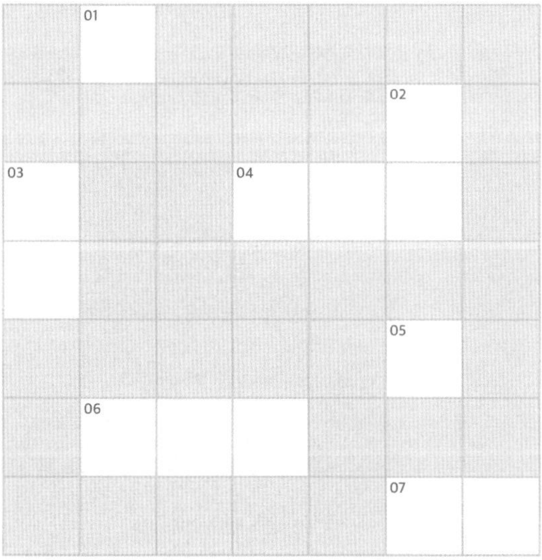

01 one's height
02 to be long
03 who
04 to be cute
05 eye
06 entertainer, celebrity
07 leg

Fill in the blanks using one of the words that you learned in Day 21.
(Please refer to page 017 to review how to conjugate verbs/adjectives.)

01 제가 좋아하는 (   )은 누구일까요? Who do you think is my favorite celebrity?

02 제가 좋아하는 연예인은 (   )일까요? Who do you think is my favorite celebrity?

03 (   )가 커요. He is tall.

04 키가 (   ). He is tall.

05 (   ) 얼굴이 정말 귀여워요. His smiling face is really cute.

06 웃는 (   )이 정말 귀여워요. His smiling face is really cute.

07 웃는 얼굴이 정말 (   ). His smiling face is really cute.

08 (   )이 크고 다리가 길어요. He has big eyes and long legs.

09 눈이 크고 (   )가 길어요. He has big eyes and long legs.

10 눈이 크고 다리가 (   ). He has big eyes and long legs.

Day 22

- 언니
- 같이
- 여행
- 비행기
- 처음
- 창문
- 앉다
- 이따가
- 하늘
- 구름

Day 22 LET'S WARM UP!

Imagine the situation in the story below to help you remember the ten Korean words in context.

22

여행 같이 언니
I am going on a trip together with my older sister.

비행기
We will go there by airplane.

처음
I will ride in an airplane for the first time.

앉다 창문
I sat in the seat next to the window.

하늘 이따가
I will be able to see the sky later.

구름
Will I be able to see the clouds, too?

LET'S KEEP THE BALL ROLLING!

Word	Meaning	Related Words	Meaning
언니 *eon-ni*	older sister (for a girl)	친언니 *chi-neon-ni*	biological older sister (for a girl)
		사촌 언니 *sa-chon eon-ni*	older female cousin (for a girl)
		친한 언니 *chi-nan eon-ni*	close older female friend (for a girl)
같이 *ga-chi*	together	친구랑 같이 *chin-gu-rang ga-chi*	together with a friend
		다 같이 *da ga-chi*	all together
		같이 하다 *ga-chi ha-da*	to do something together
여행 *yeo-haeng*	travel	여행하다 *yeo-haeng-ha-da*	to travel
		여행 가다 *yeo-haeng ga-da*	to go on a trip
		기차 여행 *gi-cha yeo-haeng*	train trip
비행기 *bi-haeng-gi*	airplane	비행기를 타다 *bi-haeng-gi-reul ta-da*	to ride in an airplane
		공항 *gong-hang*	airport
		비행기 표 *bi-haeng-gi pyo*	airplane ticket

처음 *cheo-eum*	beginning, for the first time	처음 보다 *cheo-eum bo-da*	to see for the first time
		맨 처음 *maen cheo-eum*	in the very beginning
		처음에 *cheo-eu-me*	at first
		처음으로 *cheo-eu-meu-ro*	for the first time
창문 *chang-mun*	window	창문을 열다 *chang-mu-neul yeol-da*	to open the window
		창문을 닫다 *chang-mu-neul dat-tta*	to close the window
		유리창 *yu-ri-chang*	glass window
		창가 *chang-kka*	by the window
앉다 *an-tta*	to sit	의자에 앉다 *ui-ja-e an-tta*	to sit on a chair
		바닥에 앉다 *ba-da-ge an-tta*	to sit on the floor
		서다 *seo-da*	to stand
이따가 *i-tta-ga*	later	이따가 전화하다 *i-tta-ga jeon-hwa-ha-da*	to call later
		이따가 만나다 *i-tta-ga man-na-da*	to meet later
		아까 *a-kka*	earlier

하늘 *ha-neul*	sky	**파란 하늘** *pa-ran ha-neul*	blue sky
		하늘이 맑다 *ha-neu-ri mak-tta*	the sky is clear
		땅 *ttang*	ground

구름 *gu-reum*	cloud	**구름이 끼다** *gu-reu-mi kki-da*	to be cloudy
		구름이 많다 *gu-reu-mi man-ta*	to be very cloudy
		흐리다 *heu-ri-da*	to be overcast
		흰 구름 *huin gu-reum*	white cloud

LET'S REVIEW!

Read the story again, but this time in Korean!

언니랑 **같이 여행**을 가요.

비행기를 타고 가요.

저는 비행기를 **처음** 타요.

창문 옆자리에 **앉았어요.**

이따가 하늘을 볼 수 있을 거예요.

구름도 볼 수 있을까요?

Translation

I am going on a trip together with my older sister. We will go there by airplane. I will ride in an airplane for the first time. I sat in the seat next to the window. I will be able to see the sky later.
Will I be able to see the clouds, too?

Match each Korean word to its English translation.

비행기 ·	· beginning, for the first time
창문 ·	· together
이따가 ·	· to sit
구름 ·	· later
앉다 ·	· older sister (for a girl)
여행 ·	· sky
언니 ·	· travel
하늘 ·	· cloud
처음 ·	· window
같이 ·	· airplane

Crossword Puzzle

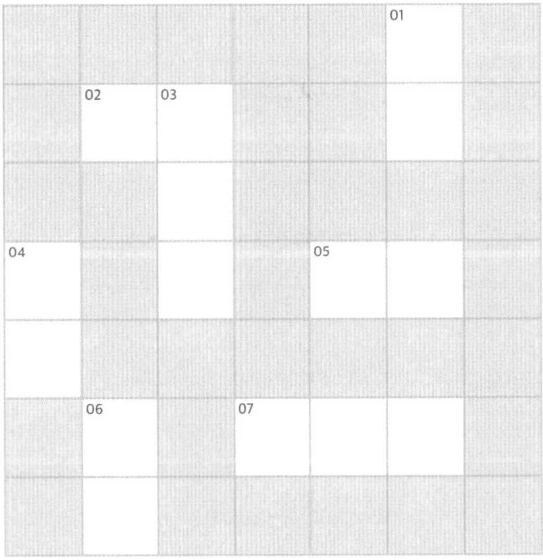

01 older sister (for a girl)
02 together
03 later
04 beginning, for the first time
05 cloud
06 sky
07 airplane

Fill in the blanks using one of the words that you learned in Day 22.
(Please refer to page 017 to review how to conjugate verbs/adjectives.)

01 (   )랑 같이 여행을 가요. — I am going on a trip together with my older sister.

02 언니랑 (   ) 여행을 가요. — I am going on a trip together with my older sister.

03 언니랑 같이 (   )을 가요. — I am going on a trip together with my older sister.

04 (   )를 타고 가요. — We will go there by airplane.

05 저는 비행기를 (   ) 타요. — I will ride in an airplane for the first time.

06 (   ) 옆자리에 앉았어요. — I sat in the seat next to the window.

07 창문 옆자리에 (   ). — I sat in the seat next to the window.

08 (   ) 하늘을 볼 수 있을 거예요. — I will be able to see the sky later.

09 이따가 (   )을 볼 수 있을 거예요. — I will be able to see the sky later.

10 (   )도 볼 수 있을까요? — Will I be able to see the clouds, too?

Day 23

- 연락
- 도와주다
- 층
- 엘리베이터
- 무겁다
- 상자
- 들다
- 넣다
- 좁다
- 빼다

Day 23 LET'S WARM UP!

Imagine the situation in the story below to help you remember the ten Korean words in context.

23

연락
I am moving today. I contacted my friend.

도와주다
My friend will help me move.

층 엘리베이터
My place is on the fifth floor. We don't have an elevator.

들다 무겁다 상자
I go up the stairs carrying a heavy box.

넣다 좁다
I put my bed in the room. But, the room is too small.

빼다
I take the bed out again.

LET'S KEEP THE BALL ROLLING!

Word	Meaning	Related Words	Meaning
연락 *yeol-lak*	contact, contacting	연락이 되다 *yeol-la-gi doe-da*	to be able to reach, to be able to contact, to be within reach
		전화 연락 *jeo-nwa yeol-lak*	contact by phone
		연락하다 *yeol-la-ka-da*	to contact
		연락처 *yeol-lak-cheo*	contact information
도와주다 *do-wa-ju-da*	to help	남을 도와주다 *na-meul do-wa-ju-da*	to help someone else
		일을 도와주다 *i-reul do-wa-ju-da*	to help with work
		도와준 사람 *do-wa-jun sa-ram*	person who helped
		돕다 *dop-tta*	to help
층 *cheung*	floor	5층 *o-cheung*	5th floor
		다른 층 *da-reun cheung*	different floor
		높은 층 *no-peun cheung*	high floor
		몇 층 *myeot cheung*	what floor

엘리베이터 *el-li-be-i-teo*	elevator	엘리베이터를 타다 *el-li-be-i-teo-reul ta-da*	to take an elevator
		엘리베이터에서 내리다 *el-li-be-i-teo-e-seo nae-ri-da*	to get out of an elevator
		엘리베이터가 멈추다 *el-li-be-i-teo-ga meom-chu-da*	the elevator stops

무겁다 *mu-geop-tta*	to be heavy	들기 무겁다 *deul-gi mu-geop-tta*	to be heavy to carry
		무거운 짐 *mu-geo-un jim*	heavy luggage
		무게 *mu-ge*	weight
		가볍다 *ga-byeop-tta*	to be light

상자 *sang-ja*	box	상자를 열다 *sang-ja-reul yeol-da*	to open a box
		상자에 담다 *sang-ja-e dam-tta*	to put in a box
		종이 상자 *jong-i sang-ja*	paper box
		박스 *bak-sseu*	box

들다 *deul-da*	to lift, to carry	상자를 들다 *sang-ja-reul deul-da*	to lift a box, to carry a box
		가방을 들다 *ga-bang-eul deul-da*	to carry a bag
		들고 다니다 *deul-go da-ni-da*	to carry around
		들어 주다 *deu-reo ju-da*	to carry for someone

넣다 *neo-ta*	to put in	봉투에 넣다 *bong-tu-e neo-ta*	to put into an envelope
		바람을 넣다 *ba-ra-meul neo-ta*	to put air in
		설탕을 넣다 *seol-tang-eul neo-ta*	to put sugar in
		넣는 곳 *neon-neun got*	a place to put something

좁다 *jop-tta*	to be narrow	방이 좁다 *bang-i jop-tta*	the room is small
		좁은 길 *jo-beun gil*	narrow road, narrow path
		넓다 *neol-tta*	to be spacious, to be wide

빼다 *ppae-da*	to take out, to pull out	차를 빼다 *cha-reul ppae-da*	to pull out a car
		돈을 빼다 *do-neul ppae-da*	to withdraw money
		3을 빼다 *sa-meul ppae-da*	to subtract three

LET'S REVIEW!

Read the story again, but this time in Korean!

저는 오늘 이사를 가요. 친구에게 **연락**을 했어요.

친구가 이사를 **도와줄** 거예요.

저희 집은 5**층**이에요. **엘리베이터**가 없어요.

무거운 상자를 **들고** 계단을 올라가요.

방에 침대를 **넣어요.** 그런데 방이 너무 **좁아요.**

침대를 다시 **빼요.**

Translation

I am moving today. I contacted my friend. My friend will help me move. My place is on the fifth floor. We don't have an elevator. I go up the stairs carrying a heavy box. I put my bed in the room. But, the room is too small. I take the bed out again.

Match each Korean word to its English translation.

넣다 ·	· to be heavy
엘리베이터 ·	· to lift, to carry
무겁다 ·	· to be narrow
빼다 ·	· floor
들다 ·	· contact, contacting
좁다 ·	· to help
상자 ·	· elevator
도와주다 ·	· to put in
연락 ·	· to take out, to pull out
층 ·	· box

Crossword Puzzle

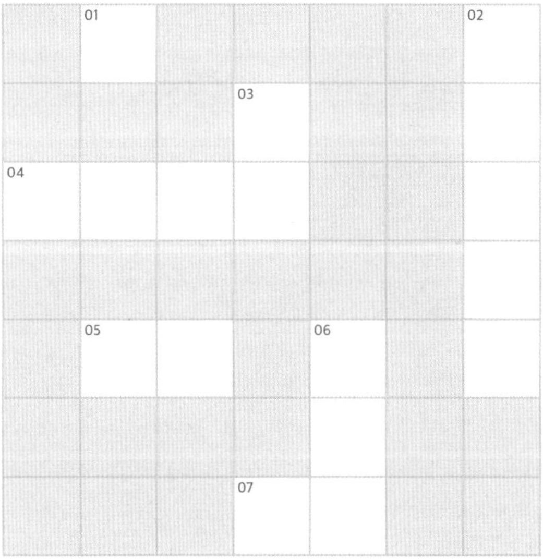

01 floor
02 elevator
03 to lift, to carry
04 to help
05 box
06 to be heavy
07 to put in

Fill in the blanks using one of the words that you learned in Day 23.
(Please refer to page 017 to review how to conjugate verbs/adjectives.)

01 친구에게 ( )을 했어요. I contacted my friend.

02 친구가 이사를 ( ) 거예요. My friend will help me move.

03 저희 집은 5( )이에요. My place is on the fifth floor.

04 ( )가 없어요. We don't have an elevator.

05 ( ) 상자를 들고 계단을 올라가요. I go up the stairs carrying a heavy box.

06 무거운 ( )를 들고 계단을 올라가요. I go up the stairs carrying a heavy box.

07 무거운 상자를 ( ) 계단을 올라가요. I go up the stairs carrying a heavy box.

08 방에 침대를 ( ). I put my bed in the room.

09 그런데 방이 너무 ( ). But, the room is too small.

10 침대를 다시 ( ). I take the bed out again.

Day 24

- 이사
- 혼자
- 멋있다
- 거실
- 벽
- 그림
- 시계
- 부엌
- 만들다
- 쓰다[02]

Day 24 LET'S WARM UP!

Imagine the situation in the story below to help you remember the ten Korean words in context.

24

이사 혼자
I moved yesterday. I am finally living by myself.

멋있다
I want to decorate my house in a cool way.

그림 거실 벽
I want to hang a picture on the living room wall.

시계
I also bought a pretty wall clock.

만들다 부엌
I will also make food by myself in the kitchen.

쓰다 02
I will use new plates.

LET'S KEEP THE BALL ROLLING!

Word	Meaning	Related Words	Meaning
이사 *i-sa*	moving	이사하다 *i-sa-ha-da*	to move (to another place)
		이사 가다 *i-sa ga-da*	to move (to another place)
		이사 오다 *i-sa o-da*	to move in, to move here
		이삿짐 *i-sat-jjim*	things to move
		이삿짐 센터 *i-sat-jjim ssen-teo*	moving company, movers
혼자 *hon-ja*	alone	나 혼자 *na hon-ja*	alone, by myself
		혼자 살다 *hon-ja sal-da*	to live by oneself
		혼잣말 *hon-jan-mal*	talking to oneself
멋있다 *meo-sit-tta*	to be cool, to be awesome	멋있는 사람 *meo-sin-neun sa-ram*	cool person, awesome person
		멋있는 옷 *meo-sin-neun ot*	cool-looking clothes
		멋있게 *meo-sit-kke*	in a cool manner

거실 *geo-sil*	living room	**거실에 앉다** *geo-si-re an-tta*	to sit in the living room
		거실에 모이다 *geo-si-re mo-i-da*	to gather in the living room
		소파 *so-pa*	couch, sofa
벽 *byeok*	wall	**벽이 무너지다** *byeo-gi mu-neo-ji-da*	the wall collapses
		벽에 걸다 *byeo-ge geol-da*	to hang on the wall
		벽을 칠하다 *byeo-geul chil-ha-da*	to paint the wall
그림 *geu-rim*	painting, drawing, picture	**그림을 그리다** *geu-ri-meul geu-ri-da*	to paint a picture
		그림을 걸다 *geu-ri-meul geol-da*	to hang a picture
		액자 *aek-jja*	frame
		사진 *sa-jin*	photo
시계 *si-gye*	clock	**벽시계** *byeok-ssi-gye*	wall clock
		손목시계 *son-mok-ssi-gye*	wrist watch
		시계가 느리다 *si-gye-ga neu-ri-da*	the watch is slow
		시계가 빠르다 *si-gye-ga ppa-reu-da*	the watch is fast

부엌 *bu-eok*	kitchen	부엌에서 요리하다 *bu-eo-ke-seo yo-ri-ha-da*	to cook in the kitchen
		부엌이 좁다 *bu-eo-ki jop-tta*	the kitchen is small
만들다 *man-deul-da*	to make	음식을 만들다 *eum-si-geul man-deul-da*	to make food, to cook food
		직접 만들다 *jik-jjeop man-deul-da*	to make for oneself
		손으로 만들다 *so-neu-ro man-deul-da*	to make with one's hands
쓰다 02 *sseu-da*	to use	집에서 쓰다 *ji-be-seo sseu-da*	to use at home
		쓰는 물건 *sseu-neun mul-geon*	things that are being used
		써 보다 *sseo bo-da*	to try using
		쓰이다 *sseu-i-da*	to be used

LET'S REVIEW!

Read the story again, but this time in Korean!

어제 **이사**했어요. 드디어 **혼자** 살아요.

집을 **멋있게** 꾸미고 싶어요.

거실 벽에 **그림**을 걸고 싶어요.

예쁜 벽**시계**도 샀어요.

부엌에서 음식도 직접 **만들** 거예요.

새 접시를 **쓸** 거예요.

Translation

I moved yesterday. I am finally living by myself. I want to decorate my house in a cool way. I want to hang a picture on the living room wall. I also bought a pretty wall clock. I will also make food by myself in the kitchen. I will use new plates.

Match each Korean word to its English translation.

거실 ·	· clock
그림 ·	· to be cool, to be awesome
혼자 ·	· wall
시계 ·	· alone
부엌 ·	· to make
쓰다 **02** ·	· moving
이사 ·	· living room
벽 ·	· painting, drawing, picture
만들다 ·	· to use
멋있다 ·	· kitchen

Crossword Puzzle

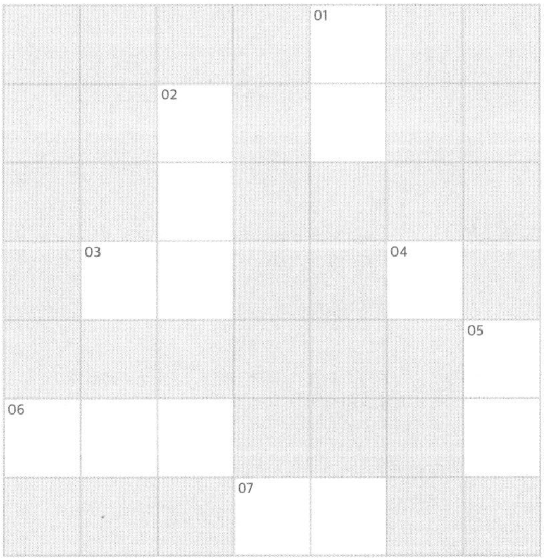

01 alone
02 to make
03 to use
04 wall
05 living room
06 to be cool, to be awesome
07 moving

Fill in the blanks using one of the words that you learned in Day 24.
(Please refer to page 017 to review how to conjugate verbs/adjectives.)

01 어제 (   )했어요. — I moved yesterday.

02 드디어 (   ) 살아요. — I am finally living by myself.

03 집을 (   ) 꾸미고 싶어요. — I want to decorate my house in a cool way.

04 (   ) 벽에 그림을 걸고 싶어요. — I want to hang a picture on the living room wall.

05 거실 (   )에 그림을 걸고 싶어요. — I want to hang a picture on the living room wall.

06 거실 벽에 (   )을 걸고 싶어요. — I want to hang a picture on the living room wall.

07 예쁜 벽(   )도 샀어요. — I also bought a pretty wall clock.

08 (   )에서 음식도 직접 만들 거예요. — I will also make food by myself in the kitchen.

09 부엌에서 음식도 직접 (   ) 거예요. — I will also make food by myself in the kitchen.

10 새 접시를 (   ) 거예요. — I will use new plates.

Day 25

- 지우다
- 씻다
- 버섯
- 당근
- 부르다
- 다
- 산책
- 밝다
- 편하다
- 감사

Day 25 LET'S WARM UP!

Imagine the situation in the story below to help you remember the ten Korean words in context.

25

지우다 씻다
I come home. I wash off my make-up. I wash my hands.

Today's dinner is soybean paste stew.

버섯 당근
I put in mushrooms and carrots.

부르다
I call my kids. We have dinner all together.

산책 다 밝다
We go for a walk all together. The streets are still bright.

편하다
When I walk with my kids, I feel at ease.

감사
I am thankful for another happy day.

LET'S KEEP THE BALL ROLLING!

Word	Meaning	Related Words	Meaning
지우다 *ji-u-da*	to erase, to wash off	화장을 지우다 *hwa-jang-eul ji-u-da*	to wash off make-up
		낙서를 지우다 *nak-sseo-reul ji-u-da*	to erase scribbles
		지우개로 지우다 *ji-u-gae-ro ji-u-da*	to erase with an eraser
씻다 *ssit-tta*	to wash	손을 씻다 *so-neul ssit-tta*	to wash one's hands
		얼굴을 씻다 *eol-gu-reul ssit-tta*	to wash one's face
		깨끗하게 씻다 *kkae-kkeu-ta-ge ssit-tta*	to wash cleanly
버섯 *beo-seot*	mushroom	버섯을 따다 *beo-seo-seul tta-da*	to pick a mushroom
		버섯을 넣다 *beo-seo-seul neo-ta*	to put a mushroom in
		버섯 요리 *beo-seot yo-ri*	mushroom dish
당근 *dang-geun*	carrot	당근을 볶다 *dang-geu-neul bok-tta*	to stir fry a carrot
		당근을 썰다 *dang-geu-neul sseol-da*	to chop a carrot
		생당근 *saeng-dang-geun*	raw carrot

부르다
bu-reu-da

to call

큰 소리로 부르다 *keun so-ri-ro bu-reu-da*	to call out loud
이름을 부르다 *i-reu-meul bu-reu-da*	to call someone's name
아이들을 부르다 *a-i-deu-reul bu-reu-da*	to call the children
부르는 소리 *bu-reu-neun so-ri*	sound of calling someone

다
da

all, every

모두 *mo-du*	all, everyone
전부 *jeon-bu*	all
다 함께 *da ham-kke*	all together

산책
san-chaek

walk

산책을 나가다 *san-chae-geul na-ga-da*	to go out for a walk
공원을 산책하다 *gong-wo-neul san-chae-ka-da*	to take a walk in the park
강아지를 산책시키다 *gang-a-ji-reul san-chaek-si-ki-da*	to walk a dog

밝다 *bak-tta*	to be bright	거리가 밝다 *geo-ri-ga bak-tta*	the street is bright
		표정이 밝다 *pyo-jeong-i bak-tta*	one's facial expression is bright
		밝은 빛 *bal-geun bit*	bright light
		어둡다 *eo-dup-tta*	to be dark
편하다 *pyeon-ha-da*	to be comfortable	마음이 편하다 *ma-eu-mi pyeon-ha-da*	to feel comfortable, to feel at ease
		몸이 편하다 *mo-mi pyeon-ha-da*	one's body is comfortable
		편한 신발 *pyeon-han sin-bal*	comfortable shoes
감사 *gam-sa*	gratitude	감사 편지 *gam-sa pyeon-ji*	thank you letter
		감사 기도 *gam-sa gi-do*	prayer of gratitude
		감사하다 *gam-sa-ha-da*	to thank

LET'S REVIEW!

Read the story again, but this time in Korean!

집에 왔어요. 화장을 **지워요.** 손을 **씻어요.**

오늘 저녁은 된장찌개예요. **버섯**과 **당근**을 넣어요.

아이들을 **불러요.** 저녁을 같이 먹어요.

다 함께 **산책**을 가요. 거리가 아직 **밝아요.**

아이들이랑 산책하면 마음이 **편해요.**

오늘도 행복한 하루에 **감사**해요.

Translation

I come home. I wash off my make-up. I wash my hands. Today's dinner is soybean paste stew. I put in mushrooms and carrots. I call my kids. We have dinner all together. We go for a walk all together. The streets are still bright. When I walk with my kids, I feel at ease. I am thankful for another happy day.

Match each Korean word to its English translation.

부르다 ·	· to wash
편하다 ·	· all, every
버섯 ·	· to call
산책 ·	· mushroom
감사 ·	· gratitude
지우다 ·	· to be comfortable
씻다 ·	· to erase, to wash off
당근 ·	· walk
밝다 ·	· carrot
다 ·	· to be bright

Crossword Puzzle

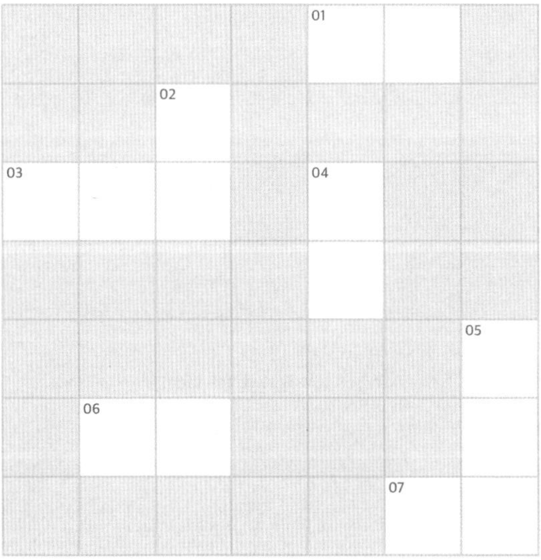

01 mushroom
02 to wash
03 to call
04 gratitude
05 to be comfortable
06 carrot
07 to be bright

Fill in the blanks using one of the words that you learned in Day 25.
(Please refer to page 017 to review how to conjugate verbs/adjectives.)

01 화장을 (   ). — I wash off my make-up.

02 손을 (   ). — I wash my hands.

03 (   )과 당근을 넣어요. — I put in mushrooms and carrots.

04 버섯과 (   )을 넣어요. — I put in mushrooms and carrots.

05 아이들을 (   ). — I call my kids.

06 (   ) 함께 산책을 가요. — We go for a walk all together.

07 다 함께 (   )을 가요. — We go for a walk all together.

08 거리가 아직 (   ). — The streets are still bright.

09 아이들이랑 산책하면 마음이 (   ). — When I walk with my kids, I feel at ease.

10 오늘도 행복한 하루에 (   )해요. — I am thankful for another happy day.

Day 26

- 꿈
- 사진
- 배우다
- 카메라
- 가격
- 비싸다
- 휴대폰
- 찍다
- 연습하다
- 유명하다

Day 26 LET'S WARM UP!

Imagine the situation in the story below to help you remember the ten Korean words in context.

26

꿈
My dream is to be a photographer.

배우다 사진
I am learning photography in school.

카메라
But my camera broke.

가격 비싸다
I want to buy a new camera. But the price is too high.

찍다 휴대폰
So I take photos with my cell phone.

연습하다
I will practice hard.

유명하다
I want to become a famous photographer.

LET'S KEEP THE BALL ROLLING!

Word	Meaning	Related Words	Meaning
꿈 *kkum*	dream	꿈을 꾸다 *kku-meul kku-da*	to dream
		슬픈 꿈 *seul-peun kkum*	sad dream
		꿈을 이루다 *kku-meul i-ru-da*	to realize one's dream
사진 *sa-jin*	photo	사진을 찍다 *sa-ji-neul jjik-tta*	to take a photo
		사진 작가 *sa-jin jak-kka*	photographer
		사진 한 장 *sa-jin han jang*	one photo
		사진이 잘 나오다 *sa-ji-ni jal na-o-da*	the photo turns out well
배우다 *bae-u-da*	to learn	한국어를 배우다 *han-gu-geo-reul bae-u-da*	to learn Korean
		아빠한테 배우다 *a-ppa-han-te bae-u-da*	to learn from one's dad
		가르치다 *ga-reu-chi-da*	to teach

카메라 *ka-me-ra*	camera	비디오카메라 *bi-di-o-ka-me-ra*	video camera
		카메라를 사다 *ka-me-ra-reul sa-da*	to buy a camera
		수동 카메라 *su-dong ka-me-ra*	manual camera
		렌즈 *ren-jeu*	lens
가격 *ga-gyeok*	price	가격이 내리다 *ga-gyeo-gi nae-ri-da*	the price goes down
		가격이 오르다 *ga-gyeo-gi o-reu-da*	the price goes up
		가격을 물어보다 *ga-gyeo-geul mu-reo-bo-da*	to ask the price
비싸다 *bi-ssa-da*	to be expensive	비싼 가방 *bi-ssan ga-bang*	expensive bag
		비싼 가격 *bi-ssan ga-gyeok*	expensive price
		옷이 비싸다 *o-si bi-ssa-da*	the clothes are expensive
		싸다 *ssa-da*	to be cheap

휴대폰 *hyu-dae-pon*	mobile phone, cell phone	휴대폰을 사다 *hyu-dae-po-neul sa-da*	to buy a mobile phone
		휴대폰으로 통화하다 *hyu-dae-po-neu-ro tong-hwa-ha-da*	to talk on the mobile phone
		핸드폰 *haen-deu-pon*	mobile phone, cell phone
		스마트폰 *seu-ma-teu-pon*	smart phone
찍다 *jjik-tta*	to take, to film	사진을 찍다 *sa-ji-neul jjik-tta*	to take a photo
		동영상을 찍다 *dong-yeong-sang-eul jjik-tta*	to take a video
		셀카를 찍다 *ssel-ka-reul jjik-tta*	to take a selfie
연습하다 *yeon-seu-pa-da*	to practice	기타를 연습하다 *gi-ta-reul yeon-seu-pa-da*	to practice the guitar
		열심히 연습하다 *yeol-ssi-mi yeon-seu-pa-da*	to practice hard
		연습 *yeon-seup*	practice
유명하다 *yu-myeong-ha-da*	to be famous	유명한 사람 *yu-myeong-han sa-ram*	famous person
		아주 유명하다 *a-ju yu-myeong-ha-da*	to be very famous
		유명해지다 *yu-myeong-hae-ji-da*	to become famous

LET'S REVIEW!

Read the story again, but this time in Korean!

제 **꿈**은 사진 작가예요.

학교에서 **사진**을 **배우고** 있어요.

그런데 **카메라**가 고장이 났어요.

새 카메라를 사고 싶어요. 그런데 **가격**이 너무 **비싸요.**

그래서 **휴대폰**으로 사진을 **찍어요.**

열심히 **연습할** 거예요. **유명한** 사진 작가가 되고 싶어요.

Translation

My dream is to be a photographer. I am learning photography in school. But my camera broke. I want to buy a new camera. But the price is too high. So I take photos with my cell phone. I will practice hard. I want to become a famous photographer.

Match each Korean word to its English translation.

사진 ·	· camera
비싸다 ·	· price
휴대폰 ·	· to be famous
연습하다 ·	· dream
유명하다 ·	· to learn
찍다 ·	· to be expensive
꿈 ·	· photo
가격 ·	· to practice
카메라 ·	· to take, to film
배우다 ·	· mobile phone, cell phone

Crossword Puzzle

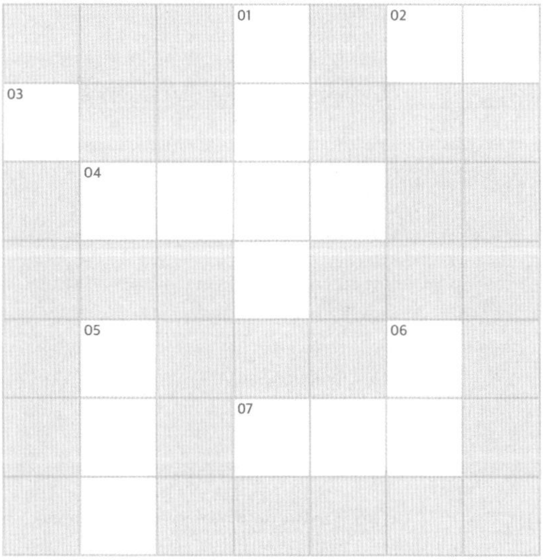

01 to be famous
02 price
03 dream
04 to practice
05 camera
06 to take, to film
07 to learn

Fill in the blanks using one of the words that you learned in Day 26.
(Please refer to page 017 to review how to conjugate verbs/adjectives.)

01 제 (   )은 사진 작가예요. My dream is to be a photographer.

02 학교에서 (   )을 배우고 있어요. I am learning photography in school.

03 학교에서 사진을 (   ) 있어요. I am learning photography in school.

04 그런데 (   )가 고장이 났어요. But my camera broke.

05 그런데 (   )이 너무 비싸요. But the price is too high.

06 그런데 가격이 너무 (   ). But the price is too high.

07 그래서 (   )으로 사진을 찍어요. So I take photos with my cell phone.

08 그래서 휴대폰으로 사진을 (   ). So I take photos with my cell phone.

09 열심히 (   ) 거예요. I will practice hard.

10 (   ) 사진 작가가 되고 싶어요. I want to become a famous photographer.

Day 27

- 봄
- 오다
- 날씨
- 따뜻하다
- 예쁘다
- 꽃
- 딸기
- 빨간색
- 좋아하다
- 과일

Day 27 LET'S WARM UP!

Imagine the situation in the story below to help you remember the ten Korean words in context.

27

봄 오다
Spring has come.

날씨 따뜻하다
The weather is warm.

예쁘다 꽃
Pretty flowers have blossomed.

딸기
In the spring, a lot of strawberries come out.

빨간색
Strawberries are red.

좋아하다 과일
Strawberries are my favorite fruit.

Therefore, I like spring the best.

LET'S KEEP THE BALL ROLLING!

Word	Meaning	Related Words	Meaning
봄 *bom*	spring (season)	3월 *sa-mwol*	March
		따뜻하다 *tta-tteu-ta-da*	to be warm
		계절 *gye-jeol*	season
		가을 *ga-eul*	fall, autumn
오다 *o-da*	to come	빨리 오다 *ppal-li o-da*	to come quickly
		갔다 오다 *gat-tta o-da*	to go and come back
		가다 *ga-da*	to go
날씨 *nal-ssi*	weather	날씨가 좋다 *nal-ssi-ga jo-ta*	the weather is good
		오늘 날씨 *o-neul nal-ssi*	today's weather
		날씨가 흐리다 *nal-ssi-ga heu-ri-da*	the weather is cloudy

따뜻하다 *tta-tteu-ta-da*	to be warm	방이 따뜻하다 *bang-i tta-tteu-ta-da*	the room is warm
		날씨가 따뜻하다 *nal-ssi-ga tta-tteu-ta-da*	the weather is warm
		따뜻한 *tta-tteu-tan*	warm
예쁘다 *ye-ppeu-da*	to be pretty	너무 예쁘다 *neo-mu ye-ppeu-da*	to be very pretty
		예쁜 *ye-ppeun*	pretty
		예쁘게 *ye-ppeu-ge*	prettily, beautifully
꽃 *kkot*	flower	꽃 한 송이 *kkot han song-i*	one flower
		꽃이 피다 *kko-chi pi-da*	a flower blossoms
		꽃이 지다 *kko-chi ji-da*	a flower falls
		꽃다발 *kkot-tta-bal*	a bunch of flowers
딸기 *ttal-gi*	strawberry	맛있는 딸기 *ma-sin-neun ttal-gi*	delicious strawberries
		딸기잼 *ttal-gi-jjaem*	strawberry jam
		딸기를 따다 *ttal-gi-reul tta-da*	to pick strawberries

빨간색 *ppal-gan-saek*	red (color)	빨간 *ppal-gan*	red
		빨간색 옷 *ppal-gan-saek ot*	red clothes
좋아하다 *jo-a-ha-da*	to like	제일 좋아하다 *je-il jo-a-ha-da*	to like the most
		좋아하는 *jo-a-ha-neun*	that one likes
		좋아하는 영화 *jo-a-ha-neun yeong-hwa*	a movie that one likes
과일 *gwa-il*	fruit	과일을 먹다 *gwa-i-reul meok-tta*	to eat fruit
		과일 주스 *gwa-il ju-sseu*	fruit juice
		사과 *sa-gwa*	apple
		채소 *chae-so*	vegetable

LET'S REVIEW!

Read the story again, but this time in Korean!

봄이 **왔어요.**

날씨가 **따뜻해요.**

예쁜 꽃이 피었어요.

봄에는 **딸기**가 많이 나와요. 딸기는 **빨간색**이에요.

딸기는 제가 제일 **좋아하는 과일**이에요.

그래서 저는 봄이 제일 좋아요.

Translation

Spring has come. The weather is warm. Pretty flowers have blossomed. In the spring, a lot of strawberries come out. Strawberries are red. Strawberries are my favorite fruit. Therefore, I like spring the best.

Match each Korean word to its English translation.

오다 ·	· weather
예쁘다 ·	· to be warm
딸기 ·	· flower
빨간색 ·	· to come
과일 ·	· strawberry
봄 ·	· to be pretty
날씨 ·	· red (color)
좋아하다 ·	· fruit
꽃 ·	· spring (season)
따뜻하다 ·	· to like

Crossword Puzzle

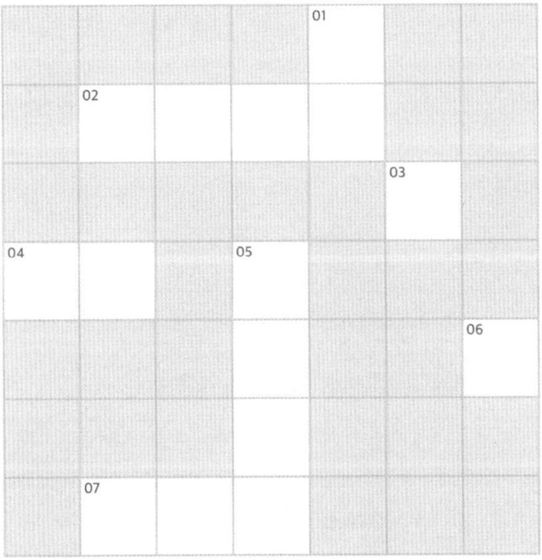

01 to come
02 to be warm
03 flower
04 strawberry
05 to like
06 spring (season)
07 to be pretty

Fill in the blanks using one of the words that you learned in Day 27.
(Please refer to page 017 to review how to conjugate verbs/adjectives.)

01 ( )이 왔어요. Spring has come.

02 봄이 ( ). Spring has come.

03 ( )가 따뜻해요. The weather is warm.

04 날씨가 ( ). The weather is warm.

05 ( ) 꽃이 피었어요. Pretty flowers have blossomed.

06 예쁜 ( )이 피었어요. Pretty flowers have blossomed.

07 봄에는 ( )가 많이 나와요. In the spring, a lot of strawberries come out.

08 딸기는 ( )이에요. Strawberries are red.

09 딸기는 제가 제일 ( ) 과일이에요. Strawberry is my favorite fruit.

10 딸기는 제가 제일 좋아하는 ( ) 이에요. Strawberry is my favorite fruit.

Day 28

- 기다리다
- 눈[02]
- 바람
- 춥다
- 자주
- 안
- 전화하다
- 알다
- 장갑
- 목도리

Day 28 LET'S WARM UP!

Imagine the situation in the story below to help you remember the ten Korean words in context.

28

기다리다 눈[02]

I am **waiting** for a friend. But it suddenly **snows**.

바람 춥다

The **wind** blows, too. It is so **cold**.

자주

I went into a café that I go to **often**.

안 전화하다

I will wait **inside**. I **called** my friend.

알다

My friend also **knows** this café.

I will meet my friend and go shopping.

장갑 목도리

I am going to buy **gloves** and a **scarf**.

LET'S KEEP THE BALL ROLLING!

Word	Meaning	Related Words	Meaning
기다리다 *gi-da-ri-da*	to wait	밖에서 기다리다 *ba-kke-seo gi-da-ri-da*	to wait outside
		방학을 기다리다 *bang-ha-geul gi-da-ri-da*	to wait for school vacation
		잠깐 기다리다 *jam-kkan gi-da-ri-da*	to wait for a little bit
		오래 기다리다 *o-rae gi-da-ri-da*	to wait for a long time
눈 02 *nun*	snow	눈이 오다 *nu-ni o-da*	to snow
		눈이 내리다 *nu-ni nae-ri-da*	to snow
		눈이 쌓이다 *nu-ni ssa-i-da*	the snow piles up
바람 *ba-ram*	wind	바람이 불다 *ba-ra-mi bul-da*	the wind blows
		바람이 세다 *ba-ra-mi se-da*	the wind is strong
		시원한 바람 *si-won-han ba-ram*	cool wind

춥다 *chup-tta*	to be cold	너무 춥다 *neo-mu chup-tta*	to be too cold
		날씨가 춥다 *nal-ssi-ga chup-tta*	the weather is cold
		추운 겨울 *chu-un gyeo-ul*	cold winter
자주 *ja-ju*	often	자주 가다 *ja-ju ga-da*	to go often
		자주 하다 *ja-ju ha-da*	to do often
안 *an*	inside	건물 안 *geon-mul an*	inside a building
		안에서 *a-ne-seo*	inside, indoors
		안으로 *a-neu-ro*	into
		밖 *bak*	outside
전화하다 *jeon-hwa-ha-da*	to call, to telephone	친구한테 전화하다 *chin-gu-han-te jeon-hwa-ha-da*	to call a friend
		집으로 전화하다 *ji-beu-ro jeon-hwa-ha-da*	to call home
		휴대폰으로 전화하다 *hyu-dae-po-neu-ro jeon-hwa-ha-da*	to call on one's cell phone
		전화번호 *jeon-hwa-beon-ho*	phone number

# 알다 *al-da*	to know	잘 알다 *jal al-da*	to know well
		알리다 *al-li-da*	to let someone know, to announce
		알려 주다 *al-lyeo ju-da*	to let someone know
		모르다 *mo-reu-da*	to not know

# 장갑 *jang-gap*	glove	털장갑 *teol-jang-gap*	fur gloves, woolen gloves
		고무장갑 *go-mu-jang-gap*	rubber gloves
		가죽 장갑 *ga-juk jang-gap*	leather gloves

# 목도리 *mok-tto-ri*	scarf	목도리를 하다 *mok-tto-ri-reul ha-da*	to put on a scarf
		목도리를 두르다 *mok-tto-ri-reul du-reu-da*	to wrap a scarf around one's neck
		털목도리 *teol-mok-tto-ri*	woolen scarf

LET'S REVIEW!

Read the story again, but this time in Korean!

친구를 **기다리고** 있어요. 그런데 갑자기 **눈**이 와요.

바람도 불어요. 너무 **추워요**.

자주 가는 카페에 들어갔어요.

안에서 기다릴 거예요. 친구한테 **전화했어요.**

친구도 이 카페를 **알아요**. 친구를 만나서 쇼핑을 할 거예요.

장갑이랑 **목도리**를 살 거예요.

Translation

I am waiting for a friend. But it suddenly snows. The wind blows, too. It is so cold. I went into a café that I go to often. I will wait inside. I called my friend. My friend also knows this café. I will meet my friend and go shopping. I am going to buy gloves and a scarf.

Match each Korean word to its English translation.

눈 02 ·	· to be cold
자주 ·	· inside
전화하다 ·	· wind
목도리 ·	· to wait
장갑 ·	· scarf
기다리다 ·	· snow
알다 ·	· glove
바람 ·	· often
안 ·	· to know
춥다 ·	· to call, to telephone

Crossword Puzzle

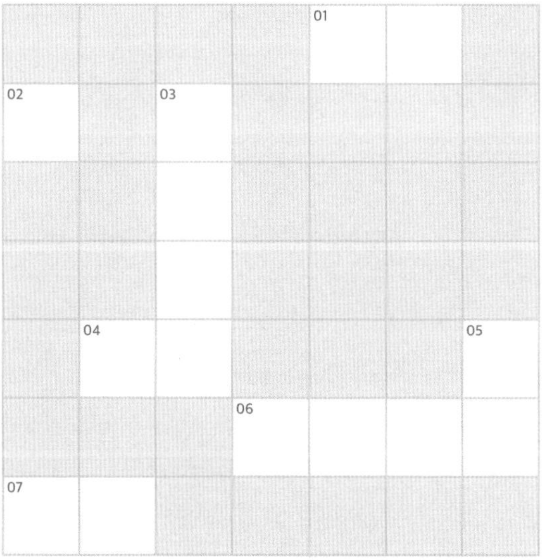

01 often
02 snow
03 to wait
04 to know
05 to be cold
06 to call, to telephone
07 wind

Fill in the blanks using one of the words that you learned in Day 28.
(Please refer to page 017 to review how to conjugate verbs/adjectives.)

01 친구를 ( ) 있어요. I am waiting for a friend.

02 그런데 갑자기 ( )이 와요. But it suddenly snows.

03 ( )도 불어요. The wind blows, too.

04 너무 ( ). It is so cold.

05 ( ) 가는 카페에 들어갔어요. I went into a café that I go to often.

06 ( )에서 기다릴 거예요. I will wait inside.

07 친구한테 ( ). I called my friend.

08 친구도 이 카페를 ( ). My friend also knows this café.

09 ( )이랑 목도리를 살 거예요. I am going to buy gloves and a scarf.

10 장갑이랑 ( )를 살 거예요. I am going to buy gloves and a scarf.

Day 29

- 잘하다
- 맛
- 못하다
- 사랑
- 양파
- 감자
- 칼
- 썰다
- 손가락
- 배달

Day 29 LET'S WARM UP!

Imagine the situation in the story below to help you remember the ten Korean words in context.

29

잘하다
My mom cooks well.

맛 못하다
All the food my mom makes is delicious. I can't cook.

사랑
But today, for my dear mom, I am going to cook.

양파
I peeled an onion.

썰다 감자 칼
I chopped a potato with a knife.

손가락 배달
I hurt my finger. In the end, I ordered delivery food.

LET'S KEEP THE BALL ROLLING!

Word	Meaning	Related Words	Meaning
잘하다 *jal-ha-da*	to do well, to be good at something, to be skillful	요리를 잘하다 *yo-ri-reul jal-ha-da*	to cook well
		공부를 잘하다 *gong-bu-reul jal-ha-da*	to be good in school
		잘하는 운동 *jal-ha-neun un-dong*	a sport that one is good at
		못하다 *mo-ta-da*	to be bad at
맛 *mat*	taste	무슨 맛 *mu-seun mat*	what flavor
		맛있다 *ma-sit-tta*	to be delicious
		맛없다 *ma-deop-tta*	to not be tasty
		맛보다 *mat-ppo-da*	to taste
못하다 *mo-ta-da*	to not do well, to be bad at something, to be unskillful	노래를 못하다 *no-rae-reul mo-ta-da*	to sing terribly, to not sing well
		운전을 못하다 *un-jeo-neul mo-ta-da*	to be terrible at driving
		못하는 것 *mo-ta-neun geot*	something that one is not good at
		잘하다 *jal-ha-da*	to do well

사랑 *sa-rang*	love	짝사랑 *jjak-ssa-rang*	unrequited love, crush
		사랑하다 *sa-rang-ha-da*	to love
		사랑하는 엄마 *sa-rang-ha-neun eom-ma*	one's dear mom
		사랑스럽다 *sa-rang-seu-reop-tta*	to be lovely
양파 *yang-pa*	onion	양파를 까다 *yang-pa-reul kka-da*	to peel an onion
		양파 껍질 *yang-pa kkeop-jjil*	skin of an onion
		양파 냄새 *yang-pa naem-sae*	smell of an onion
감자 *gam-ja*	potato	감자가 익다 *gam-ja-ga ik-tta*	the potato is cooked
		찐 감자 *jjin gam-ja*	steamed potato
		고구마 *go-gu-ma*	sweet potato
칼 *kal*	knife	칼로 자르다 *kal-lo ja-reu-da*	to cut with a knife
		칼에 베이다 *ka-re be-i-da*	to get a cut from a knife
		칼 한 자루 *kal han ja-ru*	one knife
		부엌칼 *bu-eok-kal*	kitchen knife

썰다 *sseol-da*	to chop, to cut	양파를 썰다 *yang-pa-reul sseol-da*	to chop an onion
		칼로 썰다 *kal-lo sseol-da*	to chop with a knife
		자르다 *ja-reu-da*	to cut

손가락 *son-kka-rak*	finger	손가락이 길다 *son-kka-ra-gi gil-da*	one's finger is long
		손가락이 두껍다 *son-kka-ra-gi du-kkeop-tta*	one's finger is thick
		엄지손가락 *eom-ji-son-kka-rak*	thumb
		새끼손가락 *sae-kki-son-kka-rak*	pinky finger

배달 *bae-dal*	delivery	배달 음식 *bae-dal eum-sik*	delivery food
		우유 배달 *u-yu bae-dal*	milk delivery
		신문 배달 *sin-mun bae-dal*	newspaper delivery
		배달하다 *bae-dal-ha-da*	to deliver

LET'S REVIEW!

Read the story again, but this time in Korean!

엄마는 요리를 **잘해요.**

엄마가 만든 음식은 다 **맛**있어요. 저는 요리를 **못해요.**

하지만 오늘은 **사랑**하는 엄마를 위해서 요리를 할 거예요.

양파를 깠어요.

감자를 **칼**로 **썰었어요.**

손가락을 다쳤어요. 결국 **배달** 음식을 시켰어요.

Translation

My mom cooks well. All the food my mom makes is delicious.
I can't cook. But today, for my dear mom, I am going to cook.
I peeled an onion. I chopped a potato with a knife. I hurt my finger.
In the end, I ordered delivery food.

Match each Korean word to its English translation.

못하다 ·	· potato
양파 ·	· knife
칼 ·	· to do well, to be skillful
썰다 ·	· taste
맛 ·	· love
배달 ·	· onion
잘하다 ·	· to not do well, to be unskillful
손가락 ·	· delivery
감자 ·	· finger
사랑 ·	· to chop, to cut

Crossword Puzzle

01 knife
02 to do well
03 to not do well
04 taste
05 potato
06 delivery
07 finger

Fill in the blanks using one of the words that you learned in Day 29.
(Please refer to page 017 to review how to conjugate verbs/adjectives.)

01 엄마는 요리를 ( ). — My mom cooks well.

02 엄마가 만든 음식은 다 ( )있어요. — All the food my mom makes is delicious.

03 저는 요리를 ( ). — I can't cook.

04 하지만 오늘은 ( )하는 엄마를 위해서 요리를 할 거예요. — But today, for my dear mom, I am going to cook.

05 ( )를 깠어요. — I peeled an onion.

06 ( )를 칼로 썰었어요. — I chopped a potato with a knife.

07 감자를 ( )로 썰었어요. — I chopped a potato with a knife.

08 감자를 칼로 ( ). — I chopped a potato with a knife.

09 ( )을 다쳤어요. — I hurt my finger.

10 결국 ( ) 음식을 시켰어요. — In the end, I ordered delivery food.

Day 30

- 손님
- 빨래
- 설거지
- 이불
- 베개
- 쓰레기
- 버리다
- 시장
- 과자
- 준비하다

Day 30 LET'S WARM UP!

Imagine the situation in the story below to help you remember the ten Korean words in context.

30

손님
Tonight, guests will come to my house.

빨래 설거지
I washed my clothes and did the dishes.

이불 베개
I tidied up the blankets and pillows.

버리다 쓰레기
I threw away the trash.

시장
I went to the market and did some grocery shopping.

과자
I bought some snacks for the kids.

준비하다
Now I am going to prepare food.

LET'S KEEP THE BALL ROLLING!

Word	Meaning	Related Words	Meaning
손님 *son-nim*	guest	손님이 오다 *son-ni-mi o-da*	a guest comes
		손님이 많다 *son-ni-mi man-ta*	there are many guests
		손님들 *son-nim-deul*	guests
빨래 *ppal-lae*	laundry	빨래를 널다 *ppal-lae-reul neol-da*	to hang up the laundry
		빨래를 개다 *ppal-lae-reul gae-da*	to fold the laundry
		빨래하다 *ppal-lae-ha-da*	to wash clothes
		세탁기 *se-tak-kki*	washing machine
설거지 *seol-geo-ji*	doing the dishes	설거지하다 *seol-geo-ji-ha-da*	to do the dishes
		부엌 *bu-eok*	kitchen
		싱크대 *sing-keu-dae*	sink
		그릇 *geu-reut*	dish, plate, bowl

이불 *i-bul*	blanket	**이불을 개다** *i-bu-reul gae-da*	to fold a blanket
		이불을 덮다 *i-bu-reul deop-tta*	to cover oneself with a blanket
		이불 빨래 *i-bul ppal-lae*	washing blankets
베개 *be-gae*	pillow	**베개를 베다** *be-gae-reul be-da*	to rest one's head on the pillow
		베개가 높다 *be-gae-ga nop-tta*	the pillow is big
		무릎베개 *mu-reup-ppe-gae*	resting one's head on someone's lap
쓰레기 *sseu-re-gi*	trash	**쓰레기를 버리다** *sseu-re-gi-reul beo-ri-da*	to throw away trash
		쓰레기를 치우다 *sseu-re-gi-reul chi-u-da*	to get rid of trash
		쓰레기봉투 *sseu-re-gi-bong-tu*	trash bag
		쓰레기통 *sseu-re-gi-tong*	trash bin
버리다 *beo-ri-da*	to throw away	**휴지를 버리다** *hyu-ji-reul beo-ri-da*	to throw away trash
		쓰레기통에 버리다 *sseu-re-gi-tong-e beo-ri-da*	to throw away in a trash bin
		아무 데나 버리다 *a-mu de-na beo-ri-da*	to litter
		버린 물건 *beo-rin mul-geon*	an object that has been thrown away

시장 *si-jang*	market	**시장에 가다** *si-jang-e ga-da*	to go to the market
		시장에서 사다 *si-jang-e-seo sa-da*	to buy at the market
		전통 시장 *jeon-tong si-jang*	traditional market
		장을 보다 *jang-eul bo-da*	to do grocery shopping

과자 *gwa-ja*	snack	**과자 한 봉지** *gwa-ja han bong-ji*	a bag of snacks
		맛있는 과자 *ma-sin-neun gwa-ja*	delicious snacks

준비하다 *jun-bi-ha-da*	to prepare	**선물을 준비하다** *seon-mu-reul jun-bi-ha-da*	to prepare a present
		식사를 준비하다 *sik-ssa-reul jun-bi-ha-da*	to prepare a meal
		준비 *jun-bi*	preparation

LET'S REVIEW!

Read the story again, but this time in Korean!

오늘 밤 저희 집에 **손님**들이 올 거예요.

빨래도 하고 **설거지**도 했어요.

이불과 **베개**를 정리했어요.

쓰레기를 **버렸어요.**

시장에 가서 장을 봤어요. 아이들을 위해 **과자**도 샀어요.

이제 음식을 **준비할 거예요.**

Translation

Tonight, guests will come to my house. I washed my clothes and did the dishes. I tidied up the blankets and pillows. I threw away the trash. I went to the market and did some grocery shopping. I bought some snacks for the kids. Now I am going to prepare food.

Match each Korean word to its English translation.

베개 ·	· laundry
쓰레기 ·	· doing the dishes
준비하다 ·	· blanket
손님 ·	· pillow
빨래 ·	· guest
버리다 ·	· trash
과자 ·	· market
설거지 ·	· snack
이불 ·	· to prepare
시장 ·	· to throw away

Crossword Puzzle

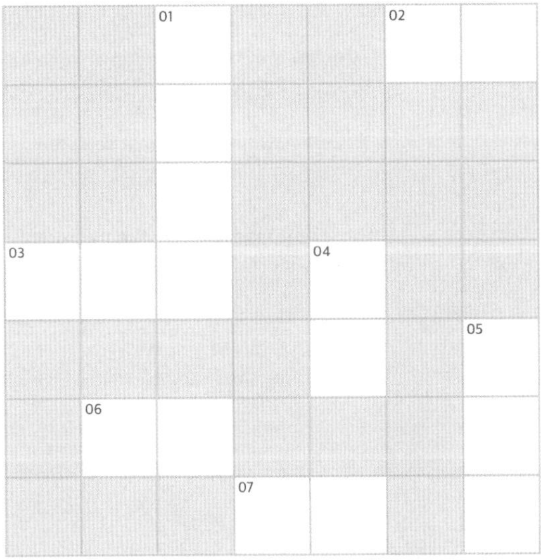

01 to prepare
02 laundry
03 to throw away
04 pillow
05 doing the dishes
06 market
07 snack

Fill in the blanks using one of the words that you learned in Day 30.
(Please refer to page 017 to review how to conjugate verbs/adjectives.)

01 오늘 밤 저희 집에 (　　　　　　　　)들이 올 거예요. — Tonight, guests will come to my house.

02 (　　　　　　　　)도 하고 설거지도 했어요. — I washed my clothes and did the dishes.

03 빨래도 하고 (　　　　　　　　)도 했어요. — I washed my clothes and did the dishes.

04 (　　　　　　　　)과 베개를 정리했어요. — I tidied up the blankets and pillows.

05 이불과 (　　　　　　　　)를 정리했어요. — I tidied up the blankets and pillows.

06 (　　　　　　　　)를 버렸어요. — I threw away the trash.

07 쓰레기를 (　　　　　　　　). — I threw away the trash.

08 (　　　　　　　　)에 가서 장을 봤어요. — I went to the market and did some grocery shopping.

09 아이들을 위해 (　　　　　　　　)도 샀어요. — I bought some snacks for the kids.

10 이제 음식을 (　　　　　　　　). — Now I am going to prepare food.

QUIZ
DAY 21-30

01 What is the Korean word for the item in the picture?

a. 캐메라
b. 캐머러
c. 캠러
d. 카메라

02 Besides **"eye"**, what does 눈 mean?

a. carrot b. mushroom c. snow d. rain

03 How can you say in Korean, the item that your head rests upon when you sleep?

a. 봄 b. 베개 c. 그림 d. 상자

04 Which item is 과일?

a. 버섯 b. 당근 c. 양파 d. 딸기

05 What color is 빨간색?

a. black b. yellow c. green d. red

06 What is the antonym of 잘하다?

a. 못하다 b. 멋있다 c. 비싸다 d. 배우다

07 Choose the noun-verb pair that is matched incorrectly.

a. 쓰레기 - 버리다 b. 감자 - 썰다
c. 사진 - 찍다 d. 빨래 - 좁다

08 Choose the word that is **NOT** a body part.

a. 다리 b. 창문 c. 손가락 d. 얼굴

09 Which of the following can you see when you look at the 하늘?

a. 장갑 b. 과일 c. 구름 d. 거실

10 What is the area in the house where you cook?

a. 부엌 b. 산책 c. 층 d. 손님

11 Choose the word pair that is matched incorrectly.

a. 자주 - often
b. 혼자 - alone
c. 누구 - where
d. 다 - all

12 What do you call the item you wrap around your neck to feel warm in the winter?

a. 시계 b. 이사 c. 목도리 d. 벽

13 Choose the term that has a kinship meaning.

a. 처음 b. 언니 c. 연예인 d. 시장

14 Choose the term that is the opposite of 넣다.

a. 빼다 b. 들다 c. 오다 d. 쓰다

15 Which of the following does **NOT** become a verb if you attach -하다?

a. 여행 b. 사랑 c. 꽃 d. 연락

16 Which of the following is **NOT** related to 날씨?

a. 바람 b. 춥다 c. 따뜻하다 d. 전화하다

17 With which item can you chop vegetables?

a. 꿈 b. 칼 c. 맛 d. 설거지

18 Which of the following refers to an action?

a. 앉다 b. 무겁다 c. 귀엽다 d. 좋아하다

19 How do you say **"to be tall"** in Korean?

a. 키가 길다 b. 키가 크다 c. 키가 웃다 d. 키가 씻다

20 What is the Korean word for the item in the picture?

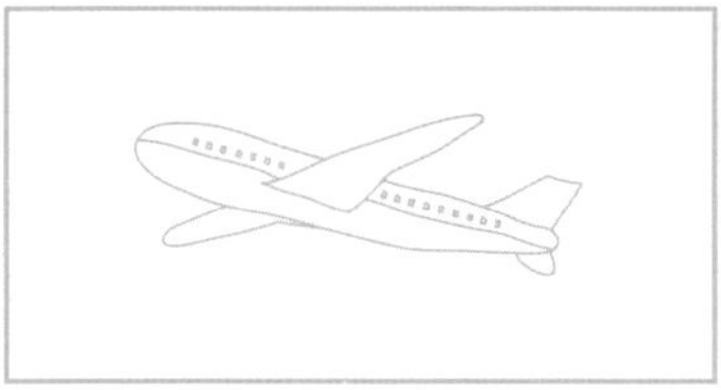

a. 비행기

b. 이불

c. 엘리베이터

d. 과자

QUIZ

DAY 21-30

Answers : d c b d d / a d b c a / c c b a c / d b a b a

Day 31

- 인터넷
- 치마
- 주문하다
- 실패
- 작다
- 쇼핑
- 어렵다
- 성공
- 다음
- 모자

Day 31 LET'S WARM UP!

Imagine the situation in the story below to help you remember the ten Korean words in context.

31

주문하다 치마 인터넷

I ordered a skirt on the Internet.

실패

This time was also a failure.

작다

The skirt is too small.

쇼핑 어렵다

Shopping online is too difficult.

성공

When will I succeed?

다음 모자

Next time, I will order a hat.

LET'S KEEP THE BALL ROLLING!

Word	Meaning	Related Words	Meaning
인터넷 *in-teo-net*	the Internet	인터넷 쇼핑 *in-teo-net syo-ping*	Internet shopping, online shopping
		인터넷에 연결하다 *in-teo-ne-se yeon-gyeol-ha-da*	to connect to the Internet
		인터넷으로 *in-teo-ne-seu-ro*	via the Internet
치마 *chi-ma*	skirt	치마를 입다 *chi-ma-reul ip-tta*	to put on a skirt, to wear a skirt
		치마를 벗다 *chi-ma-reul beot-tta*	to take off a skirt
		긴 치마 *gin chi-ma*	long skirt
		짧은 치마 *jjal-beun chi-ma*	short skirt
주문하다 *ju-mun-ha-da*	to order	옷을 주문하다 *o-seul ju-mun-ha-da*	to order clothes
		음식을 주문하다 *eum-si-geul ju-mun-ha-da*	to order food
		주문한 책 *ju-mun-han chaek*	a book that was ordered

실패
sil-pae

failure

실패하다 *sil-pae-ha-da*	to fail
실패 원인 *sil-pae wo-nin*	reason for failure, cause for failure
성공 *seong-gong*	success

작다
jak-tta

to be small

치마가 작다 *chi-ma-ga jak-tta*	the skirt is small
키가 작다 *ki-ga jak-tta*	to be short (height)
작은 집 *ja-geun jip*	small house

쇼핑
syo-ping

shopping

쇼핑을 좋아하다 *syo-ping-eul jo-a-ha-da*	to like shopping
쇼핑하다 *syo-ping-ha-da*	to shop
쇼핑몰 *syo-ping-mol*	shopping mall
백화점 *bae-kwa-jeom*	department store

어렵다
eo-ryeop-tta

to be difficult,
to be hard

문제가 어렵다 *mun-je-ga eo-ryeop-tta*	the question is difficult
어려운 시험 *eo-ryeo-un si-heom*	difficult test
어려운 일 *eo-ryeo-un il*	difficult thing to do, difficult task, difficult work

성공 *seong-gong*	success	**성공하다** *seong-gong-ha-da*	to succeed
		실패 *sil-pae*	fail, failure
다음 *da-eum*	next	**다음 날** *da-eum nal*	next day
		다음 역 *da-eum yeok*	next stop, next station
		다음 페이지 *da-eum pe-i-ji*	next page
		다음에 *da-eu-me*	next time
모자 *mo-ja*	hat, cap	**모자를 쓰다** *mo-ja-reul sseu-da*	to put on a hat, to wear a hat
		모자를 벗다 *mo-ja-reul beot-tta*	to take off a hat
		야구 모자 *ya-gu mo-ja*	baseball cap

LET'S REVIEW!

Read the story again, but this time in Korean!

인터넷으로 **치마**를 **주문했어요.**

이번에도 **실패**예요.

치마가 너무 **작아요.**

인터넷 **쇼핑**은 너무 **어려워요.**

언제 **성공**할까요?

다음에는 **모자**를 주문할 거예요.

Translation

I ordered a skirt on the Internet. This time was also a failure.
The skirt is too small. Shopping online is too difficult.
When will I succeed? Next time, I will order a hat.

Match each Korean word to its English translation.

실패 ·	· to order
쇼핑 ·	· the Internet
어렵다 ·	· to be small
모자 ·	· to be difficult, to be hard
치마 ·	· success
인터넷 ·	· shopping
주문하다 ·	· next
다음 ·	· hat, cap
성공 ·	· skirt
작다 ·	· failure

Crossword Puzzle

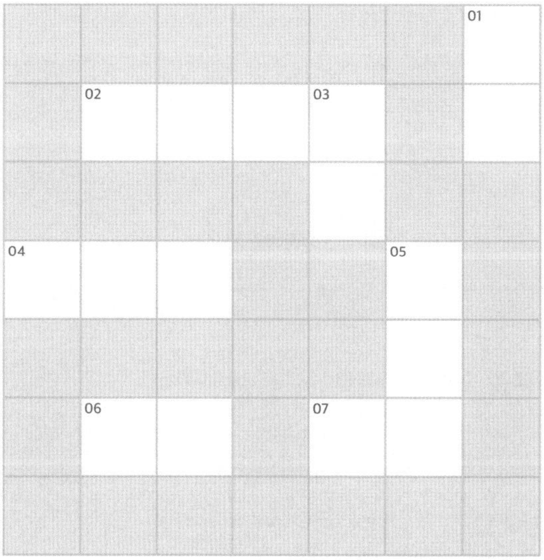

01 failure
02 to order
03 next
04 the Internet
05 to be difficult, to be hard
06 hat, cap
07 to be small

Fill in the blanks using one of the words that you learned in Day 31.
(Please refer to page 017 to review how to conjugate verbs/adjectives.)

01 (   )으로 치마를 주문했어요. I ordered a skirt on the Internet.

02 인터넷으로 (   )를 주문했어요. I ordered a skirt on the Internet.

03 인터넷으로 치마를 (   ). I ordered a skirt on the Internet.

04 이번에도 (   )예요. This time was also a failure.

05 치마가 너무 (   ). The skirt is too small.

06 인터넷 (   )은 너무 어려워요. Shopping online is too difficult.

07 인터넷 쇼핑은 너무 (   ). Shopping online is too difficult.

08 언제 (   )할까요? When will I succeed?

09 (   )에는 모자를 주문할 거예요. Next time, I will order a hat.

10 다음에는 (   )를 주문할 거예요. Next time, I will order a hat.

Day 32

- 약속
- 늦다
- 택시
- 오토바이
- 사고
- 경찰
- 문자
- 보내다
- 허리
- 조금

Day 32 LET'S WARM UP!

Imagine the situation in the story below to help you remember the ten Korean words in context.

32

약속 늦다
I had plans to meet a friend, but I was late.

택시
I took a taxi.

오토바이
But a motorcycle suddenly cut us off.

사고
So, we got into an accident.

경찰
The police came.

보내다 문자
I sent a text message to my friend.

허리 조금
I think I hurt my lower back a little.

LET'S KEEP THE BALL ROLLING!

Word	Meaning	Related Words	Meaning
약속 *yak-ssok*	promise, plan, appointment	약속이 있다 *yak-sso-gi it-tta*	to have an appointment
		약속 시간 *yak-ssok si-gan*	appointment time
		약속 장소 *yak-ssok jang-so*	appointment place
		약속하다 *yak-sso-ka-da*	to promise
늦다 *neut-tta*	to be late	많이 늦다 *ma-ni neut-tta*	to be very late
		늦은 점심 *neu-jeun jeom-sim*	late lunch
		늦게 오다 *neut-kke o-da*	to come late
		지각 *ji-gak*	being late
택시 *taek-ssi*	taxi, cab	택시를 타다 *taek-ssi-reul ta-da*	to ride in a taxi
		택시를 잡다 *taek-ssi-reul jap-tta*	to catch a taxi
		택시 한 대 *taek-ssi han dae*	one taxi
		택시 기사 *taek-ssi gi-sa*	taxi driver

오토바이 *o-to-ba-i*	motorcycle	오토바이를 타다 *o-to-ba-i-reul ta-da*	to ride a motorcycle
		오토바이 두 대 *o-to-ba-i du dae*	two motorcycles
		헬멧 *hel-met*	helmet
사고 *sa-go*	accident	큰 사고 *keun sa-go*	big accident
		자동차 사고 *ja-dong-cha sa-go*	car accident
		사고가 나다 *sa-go-ga na-da*	to have an accident
		사고를 당하다 *sa-go-reul dang-ha-da*	to get into an accident
경찰 *gyeong-chal*	police	경찰관 *gyeong-chal-gwan*	police officer
		경찰이 오다 *gyeong-cha-ri o-da*	the police come
		경찰에 신고하다 *gyeong-cha-re sin-go-ha-da*	to report to the police
		경찰차 *gyeong-chal-cha*	police car

문자 *mun-jja*	text message	**문자 메시지** *mun-jja me-ssi-ji*	text message
		문자를 보내다 *mun-jja-reul bo-nae-da*	to send a text message
		문자를 받다 *mun-jja-reul bat-tta*	to receive a text message
		답장하다 *dap-jjang-ha-da*	to reply
보내다 *bo-nae-da*	to send, to spend	**편지를 보내다** *pyeon-ji-reul bo-nae-da*	to send a letter
		답장을 보내다 *dap-jjang-eul bo-nae-da*	to send a reply
		시간을 보내다 *si-ga-neul bo-nae-da*	to spend time
허리 *heo-ri*	lower back, waist, the small of one's back	**허리를 다치다** *heo-ri-reul da-chi-da*	to hurt one's lower back
		허리가 아프다 *heo-ri-ga a-peu-da*	one's lower back hurts
		날씬한 허리 *nal-ssi-nan heo-ri*	slim waist
조금 *jo-geum*	a little, a bit	**조금 늦다** *jo-geum neut-tta*	to be a little late
		조금씩 *jo-geum-ssik*	little by little
		조금밖에 없다 *jo-geum-ba-kke eop-tta*	to only have a little

LET'S REVIEW!

Read the story again, but this time in Korean!

친구와 **약속**이 있는데 **늦었어요.**

택시를 탔어요.

그런데 **오토바이**가 갑자기 끼어들었어요.

그래서 **사고**가 났어요. **경찰**이 왔어요.

친구한테 **문자**를 **보냈어요.**

허리를 **조금** 다친 것 같아요.

Translation

I had plans to meet a friend, but I was late. I took a taxi.
But a motorcycle suddenly cut us off. So, we got into an accident.
The police came. I sent a text message to my friend.
I think I hurt my lower back a little.

Match each Korean word to its English translation.

허리 ·	· police
문자 ·	· to be late
늦다 ·	· accident
경찰 ·	· text message
보내다 ·	· promise, plan, appointment
약속 ·	· motorcycle
조금 ·	· lower back, waist
택시 ·	· to send, to spend
사고 ·	· taxi
오토바이 ·	· a little, a bit

Crossword Puzzle

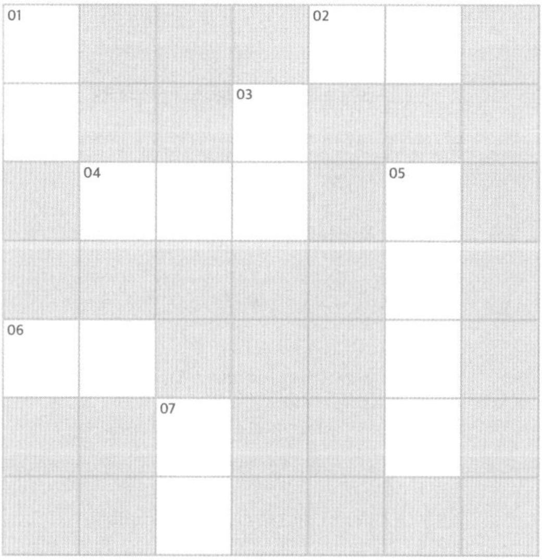

01 accident
02 text message
03 to be late
04 to send, to spend
05 motorcycle
06 a little, a bit
07 promise, plan

Fill in the blanks using one of the words that you learned in Day 32.
(Please refer to page 017 to review how to conjugate verbs/adjectives.)

01 친구와 (   )이 있는데 늦었어요. I had plans to meet a friend, but I was late.

02 친구와 약속이 있는데 (   ). I had plans to meet a friend, but I was late.

03 (   )를 탔어요. I took a taxi.

04 그런데 (   )가 갑자기 끼어들었어요. But a motorcycle suddenly cut us off.

05 그래서 (   )가 났어요. So, we got into an accident.

06 (   )이 왔어요. The police came.

07 친구한테 (   )를 보냈어요. I sent a text message to my friend.

08 친구한테 문자를 (   ). I sent a text message to my friend.

09 (   )를 조금 다친 것 같아요. I think I hurt my lower back a little.

10 허리를 (   ) 다친 것 같아요. I think I hurt my lower back a little.

Day 33

- 가수
- 인기
- 나라
- 한국어
- 필요하다
- 단어
- 귀
- 지도
- 주소
- 궁금하다

Day 33 LET'S WARM UP!

Imagine the situation in the story below to help you remember the ten Korean words in context.

33

가수 인기
These days, Korean singers are popular.

나라
They are more popular than singers from other countries.

한국어 필요하다
Studying Korean is necessary in order to listen to Korean songs.

귀 단어
I pay close attention and listen to the pronunciation of the words.

지도
I look up Korea on a map.

궁금하다 주소
I am curious to know the address of the company of the singer that I like.

LET'S KEEP THE BALL ROLLING!

Word	Meaning	Related Words	Meaning
가수 *ga-su*	singer	인기 있는 가수 *in-kki in-neun ga-su*	popular singer
		가수가 되다 *ga-su-ga doe-da*	to become a singer
		가수들 *ga-su-deul*	singers
		노래 *no-rae*	song
인기 *in-kki*	popularity	인기가 많다 *in-kki-ga man-ta*	to be popular
		인기가 있다 *in-kki-ga it-tta*	to be popular
		인기 가요 *in-kki ga-yo*	popular pop song
		인기 상품 *in-kki sang-pum*	popular product
나라 *na-ra*	country, nation	우리나라 *u-ri-na-ra*	our country, my country
		다른 나라 *da-reun na-ra*	other country, foreign country
		어느 나라 *eo-neu na-ra*	which country

한국어 *han-gu-geo*	Korean (language)	한국어 공부 *han-gu-geo gong-bu*	Korean studies
		한국어 선생님 *han-gu-geo seon-saeng-nim*	Korean teacher
		한국어 시험 *han-gu-geo si-heom*	Korean test
필요하다 *pi-ryo-ha-da*	to need, to be necessary	나에게 필요하다 *na-e-ge pi-ryo-ha-da*	to be necessary to me
		돈이 필요하다 *do-ni pi-ryo-ha-da*	to need money
		필요한 것 *pi-ryo-han geot*	necessary things
단어 *da-neo*	word	영어 단어 *yeong-eo da-neo*	English word
		단어를 외우다 *da-neo-reul oe-u-da*	to memorize words
		단어를 찾다 *da-neo-reul chat-tta*	to look up a word
		사전 *sa-jeon*	dictionary
귀 *gwi*	ear	귀를 막다 *gwi-reul mak-tta*	to block one's ears
		귀 기울이다 *gwi gi-u-ri-da*	to pay attention to
		귀가 잘 안 들리다 *gwi-ga jal an deul-li-da*	can't hear well
		귀가 아프다 *gwi-ga a-peu-da*	one's ear hurts

지도 *ji-do*	map	**서울 지도** *seo-ul ji-do*	Seoul map
		세계 지도 *se-gye ji-do*	world map
		지도를 보다 *ji-do-reul bo-da*	to see on a map
		지도에서 찾다 *ji-do-e-seo chat-tta*	to look up on a map
주소 *ju-so*	address	**집 주소** *jip ju-so*	home address
		주소가 잘못되다 *ju-so-ga jal-mot-ttoe-da*	the address is wrong
		틀린 주소 *teul-lin ju-so*	wrong address
		주소를 쓰다 *ju-so-reul sseu-da*	to write down an address
궁금하다 *gung-geu-ma-da*	to be curious	**이유가 궁금하다** *i-yu-ga gung-geu-ma-da*	to be curious about the reason
		궁금한 것 *gung-geu-man geot*	something that one is curious about
		궁금해하다 *gung-geu-mae-ha-da*	to feel curious
		물어보다 *mu-reo-bo-da*	to ask

LET'S REVIEW!

Read the story again, but this time in Korean!

요즘 한국 **가수**들이 **인기**가 많아요.

다른 **나라** 가수들보다 인기가 많아요.

한국 노래를 듣기 위해서 **한국어** 공부가 **필요해요.**

단어 발음을 **귀** 기울여 들어요.

지도에서 한국을 찾아 봐요.

제가 좋아하는 가수 회사 **주소**가 **궁금해요.**

Translation

These days, Korean singers are popular. They are more popular than singers from other countries. Studying Korean is necessary in order to listen to Korean songs. I pay close attention and listen to the pronunciation of the words. I look up Korea on a map. I am curious to know the address of the company of the singer that I like.

Match each Korean word to its English translation.

나라 ·	· popularity
가수 ·	· map
지도 ·	· singer
궁금하다 ·	· to need, to be necessary
단어 ·	· ear
인기 ·	· Korean (language)
필요하다 ·	· address
귀 ·	· to be curious
주소 ·	· country, nation
한국어 ·	· word

Crossword Puzzle

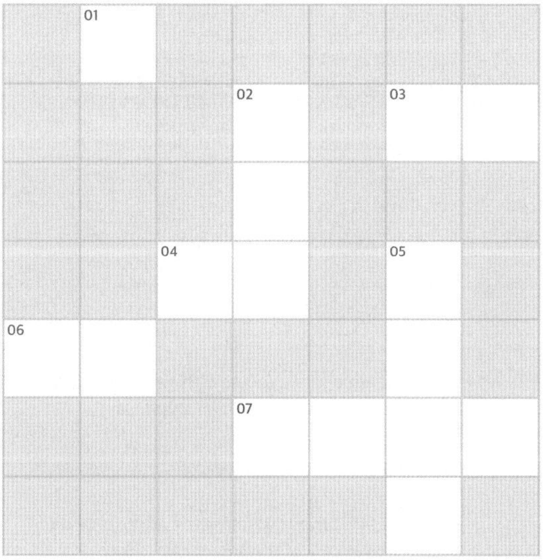

01 ear
02 Korean (language)
03 country, nation
04 word
05 to need, to be necessary
06 popularity
07 to be curious

Fill in the blanks using one of the words that you learned in Day 33.
(Please refer to page 017 to review how to conjugate verbs/adjectives.)

01 요즘 한국 ( )들이 인기가 많아요.
These days, Korean singers are popular.

02 요즘 한국 가수들이 ( )가 많아요.
These days, Korean singers are popular.

03 다른 ( ) 가수들보다 인기가 많아요.
They are more popular than singers from other countries.

04 한국 노래를 듣기 위해서 ( ) 공부가 필요해요.
Studying Korean is necessary in order to listen to Korean songs.

05 한국 노래를 듣기 위해서 한국어 공부가 ( ).
Studying Korean is necessary in order to listen to Korean songs.

06 ( ) 발음을 귀 기울여 들어요.
I pay close attention and listen to the pronunciation of the words.

07 단어 발음을 ( ) 기울여 들어요.
I pay close attention and listen to the pronunciation of the words.

08 ( )에서 한국을 찾아 봐요.
I look up Korea on a map.

09 제가 좋아하는 가수 회사 ( )가 궁금해요.
I am curious to know the address of the company of the singer that I like.

10 제가 좋아하는 가수 회사 주소가 ( ).
I am curious to know the address of the company of the singer that I like.

Day 34

- 문
- 열다
- 감기
- 열
- 코
- 나오다
- 약국
- 약
- 차
- 건강

Day 34 LET'S WARM UP!

Imagine the situation in the story below to help you remember the ten Korean words in context.

34

문 열다
Yesterday I slept with the door open.

감기 열
So, I caught a cold. I had a fever.

나오다 코
I had a runny nose.

약국 약
I went to the pharmacy and bought medicine.

차
I will drink hot tea and rest at home.

건강
I think health is really important.

LET'S KEEP THE BALL ROLLING!

Word	Meaning	Related Words	Meaning
문 *mun*	door	문을 열다 *mu-neul yeol-da*	to open the door
		문을 닫다 *mu-neul dat-tta*	to close the door
		문을 잠그다 *mu-neul jam-geu-da*	to lock the door
열다 *yeol-da*	to open	뚜껑을 열다 *ttu-kkeong-eul yeol-da*	to open the lid, to lift the cover
		창문을 열다 *chang-mu-neul yeol-da*	to open the window
		열리다 *yeol-li-da*	to be opened, to get opened
		닫다 *dat-tta*	to close
감기 *gam-gi*	cold	감기에 걸리다 *gam-gi-e geol-li-da*	to catch a cold
		감기가 낫다 *gam-gi-ga nat-tta*	to recover from a cold
		감기약 *gam-gi-yak*	cold medicine

열 *yeol*	fever	열이 나다 *yeo-ri na-da*	to have a fever
		열이 있다 *yeo-ri it-tta*	to have a fever
		열이 내려가다 *yeo-ri nae-ryeo-ga-da*	a fever breaks, a fever subsides
코 *ko*	nose	콧물 *kon-mul*	nasal discharge, snot
		코가 막히다 *ko-ga ma-ki-da*	one's nose is stuffy
		코가 높다 *ko-ga nop-tta*	to have a high nose, to have high standards
		코가 낮다 *ko-ga nat-tta*	to have a low nose
나오다 *na-o-da*	to come out	밖에 나오다 *ba-kke na-o-da*	to come outside
		물이 나오다 *mu-ri na-o-da*	the water comes out, the water runs (from the tap)
약국 *yak-kkuk*	pharmacy	약국에 가다 *yak-kku-ge ga-da*	to go to the pharmacy
		약사 *yak-ssa*	pharmacist
		병원 *byeong-won*	hospital

약 *yak*	medicine	약을 먹다 *ya-geul meok-tta*	to take medicine
		약이 쓰다 *ya-gi sseu-da*	the medicine is bitter
		약을 바르다 *ya-geul ba-reu-da*	to apply medicine, to apply ointment

차 *cha*	tea	차를 마시다 *cha-reul ma-si-da*	to drink tea
		녹차 *nok-cha*	green tea
		홍차 *hong-cha*	black tea

건강 *geon-gang*	health	건강하다 *geon-gang-ha-da*	to be healthy
		건강에 좋다 *geong-gang-e jo-ta*	to be good for health
		건강이 안 좋다 *geon-gang-i an jo-ta*	to not be healthy

LET'S REVIEW!

Read the story again, but this time in Korean!

어제 **문**을 **열고** 잤어요.

그래서 **감기**에 걸렸어요. **열**이 났어요.

코에서 콧물이 **나왔어요.**

약국에 가서 **약**을 샀어요.

따뜻한 **차**를 마시고 집에서 푹 쉴 거예요.

건강은 정말 중요한 것 같아요.

Translation

Yesterday I slept with the door open. So, I caught a cold. I had a fever. I had a runny nose. I went to the pharmacy and bought medicine. I will drink hot tea and rest at home. I think health is really important.

Match each Korean word to its English translation.

열 ·	· to come out
열다 ·	· pharmacy
약국 ·	· nose
건강 ·	· to open
문 ·	· cold
차 ·	· door
약 ·	· fever
감기 ·	· medicine
나오다 ·	· tea
코 ·	· health

Crossword Puzzle

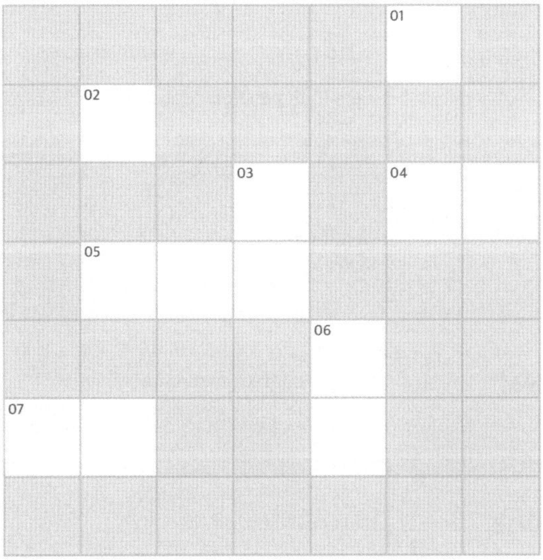

01 tea
02 door
03 to open
04 health
05 to come out
06 pharmacy
07 cold

Fill in the blanks using one of the words that you learned in Day 34.
(Please refer to page 017 to review how to conjugate verbs/adjectives.)

01	어제 (　　　　　)을 열고 잤어요.	Yesterday I slept with the door open.
02	어제 문을 (　　　　　) 잤어요.	Yesterday I slept with the door open.
03	그래서 (　　　　　)에 걸렸어요.	So, I caught a cold.
04	(　　　　　)이 났어요.	I had a fever.
05	(　　　　　)에서 콧물이 나왔어요.	I had a runny nose.
06	코에서 콧물이 (　　　　　).	I had a runny nose.
07	(　　　　　)에 가서 약을 샀어요.	I went to the pharmacy and bought medicine.
08	약국에 가서 (　　　　　)을 샀어요.	I went to the pharmacy and bought medicine.
09	따뜻한 (　　　　　)를 마시고 집에서 푹 쉴 거예요.	I will drink hot tea and rest at home.
10	(　　　　　)은 정말 중요한 것 같아요.	I think health is really important.

Day 35

- 사과
- 바나나
- 일하다
- 오이
- 토마토
- 배
- 마음
- 약하다
- 몸무게
- 절대

Day 35 LET'S WARM UP!

Imagine the situation in the story below to help you remember the ten Korean words in context.

35

I am on a diet these days.

사과 바나나
This morning, I ate an **apple**, **banana** and some potatoes.

일하다 오이 토마토
I **worked** hard. At lunch, I ate a **cucumber** and a **tomato**.

배 약하다 마음
In the evening, I became so **hungry** and **weak-hearted**.

So, I ate a lot for dinner.

몸무게
I weighed myself. I gained **weight**.

절대
I will **never** be weak-hearted again.

LET'S KEEP THE BALL ROLLING!

Word	Meaning	Related Words	Meaning
사과 *sa-gwa*	apple	사과를 깎다 *sa-gwa-reul kkak-tta*	to peel an apple
		빨간 사과 *ppal-gan sa-gwa*	red apple
		사과 나무 *sa-gwa na-mu*	apple tree
		과일 *gwa-il*	fruit
바나나 *ba-na-na*	banana	바나나 한 송이 *ba-na-na han song-i*	one bunch of bananas
		바나나를 먹다 *ba-na-na-reul meok-tta*	to eat a banana
일하다 *il-ha-da*	to work	열심히 일하다 *yeol-ssi-mi il-ha-da*	to work hard
		일하는 날 *il-ha-neun nal*	working day
		일 *il*	work
		쉬다 *swi-da*	to rest

오이 *o-i*	cucumber	**오이 한 개** *o-i han gae*	one cucumber
		오이를 먹다 *o-i-reul meok-tta*	to eat a cucumber
		오이를 썰다 *o-i-reul sseol-da*	to chop a cucumber
토마토 *to-ma-to*	tomato	**방울토마토** *bang-ul-to-ma-to*	cherry tomato
		토마토 소스 *to-ma-to sso-sseu*	tomato sauce
		토마토 스파게티 *to-ma-to seu-pa-ge-ti*	tomato spaghetti
배 *bae*	belly, stomach	**배가 고프다** *bae-ga go-peu-da*	to be hungry
		배가 아프다 *bae-ga a-peu-da*	to have a stomachache
		배가 나오다 *bae-ga na-o-da*	to have a fat belly
		배꼽 *bae-kkop*	belly button
마음 *ma-eum*	mind, heart	**마음에 들다** *ma-eu-me deul-da*	to like
		마음대로 *ma-eum-dae-ro*	as one pleases, as one wants
		마음껏 *ma-eum-kkeot*	as much as one wants
		속마음 *song-ma-eum*	true feeling, honest feeling

약하다 *ya-ka-da*	to be weak	**힘이 약하다** *hi-mi ya-ka-da*	to be weak, to be feeble
		몸이 약하다 *mo-mi ya-ka-da*	to have a weak body
		약한 마음 *ya-kan ma-eum*	weak-hearted
		약해지다 *ya-kae-ji-da*	to become weak

몸무게 *mom-mu-ge*	body weight, one's weight	**몸무게를 재다** *mom-mu-ge-reul jae-da*	to measure one's weight
		몸무게가 늘다 *mom-mu-ge-ga neul-da*	to gain weight
		몸무게가 줄다 *mom-mu-ge-ga jul-da*	to lose weight
		체중계 *che-jung-gye*	scale

절대 *jeol-ttae*	absolutely	**절대로** *jeol-ttae-ro*	absolutely (not)
		절대 안 되다 *jeol-ttae an doe-da*	absolutely cannot happen

LET'S REVIEW!

Read the story again, but this time in Korean!

요즘 다이어트를 하고 있어요.

오늘 아침에는 **사과**랑 **바나나**랑 감자를 먹었어요.

그리고 열심히 **일했어요.**

점심에는 **오이**랑 **토마토**를 먹었어요.

저녁에는 너무 **배**가 고파서 **마음**이 **약해졌어요.**

그래서 저녁을 많이 먹었어요. 몸무게를 잿어요. **몸무게**가

늘었어요. **절대**로 다시는 마음 약해지지 않을 거예요.

Translation

I am on a diet these days. This morning, I ate an apple, banana and some potatoes. I worked hard. At lunch, I ate a cucumber and a tomato. In the evening, I became so hungry and weak-hearted. So, I ate a lot for dinner. I weighed myself. I gained weight.
I will never be weak-hearted again.

Match each Korean word to its English translation.

오이 ·	· to work
마음 ·	· apple
바나나 ·	· belly, stomach
절대 ·	· absolutely
사과 ·	· mind, heart
몸무게 ·	· banana
토마토 ·	· body weight, one's weight
일하다 ·	· to be weak
약하다 ·	· tomato
배 ·	· cucumber

Crossword Puzzle

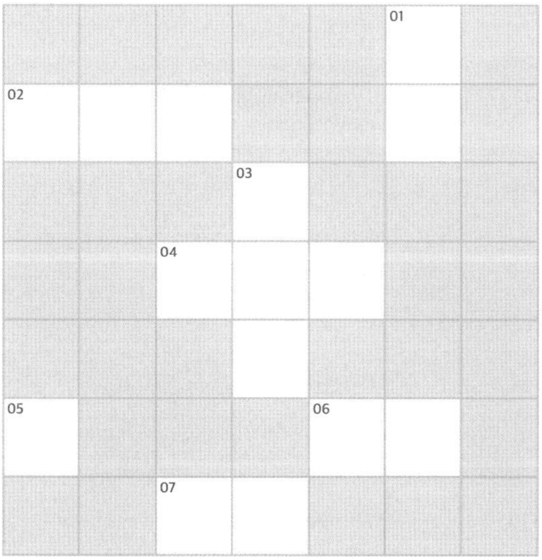

01 apple
02 banana
03 to work
04 to be weak
05 belly, stomach
06 absolutely
07 mind, heart

Fill in the blanks using one of the words that you learned in Day 35.
(Please refer to page 017 to review how to conjugate verbs/adjectives.)

01 오늘 아침에는 (   )랑 바나나랑 감자를 먹었어요.
This morning, I ate an apple, banana and some potatoes.

02 오늘 아침에는 사과랑 (   )랑 감자를 먹었어요.
This morning, I ate an apple, banana and some potatoes.

03 그리고 열심히 (   ).
I worked hard.

04 점심에는 (   )랑 토마토를 먹었어요.
At lunch, I ate a cucumber and a tomato.

05 점심에는 오이랑 (   )를 먹었어요.
At lunch, I ate a cucumber and a tomato.

06 저녁에는 너무 (   )가 고파서 마음이 약해졌어요.
In the evening, I became so hungry and weak-hearted.

07 저녁에는 너무 배가 고파서 (   )이 약해졌어요.
In the evening, I became so hungry and weak-hearted.

08 저녁에는 너무 배가 고파서 마음이 (   ).
In the evening, I became so hungry and weak-hearted.

09 (   )가 늘었어요.
I gained weight.

10 (   )로 다시는 마음 약해지지 않을 거예요.
I will never be weak-hearted again.

Day 36

- 어제
- 운동
- 넘어지다
- 손
- 다치다
- 아프다
- 병원
- 의사
- 쉬다
- 힘들다

Day 36 LET'S WARM UP!

Imagine the situation in the story below to help you remember the ten Korean words in context.

넘어지다 운동 어제

I **fell down** while **working out** **yesterday**.

다치다 손

I **hurt** my **hand**.

아프다

It **hurt** so much.

병원

I went to the **hospital**.

의사

I received medical treatment from the **doctor**.

쉬다

I laid on the bed and **rested**.

힘들다

Because I hurt my hand, it is so **hard** to eat.

LET'S KEEP THE BALL ROLLING!

Word	Meaning	Related Words	Meaning
어제 *eo-je*	yesterday	어젯밤 *eo-jet-ppam*	last night
		어제 아침 *eo-je a-chim*	yesterday morning
		그제 *geu-je*	the day before yesterday
		전날 *jeon-nal*	the previous day
운동 *un-dong*	exercise	운동하다 *un-dong-ha-da*	to exercise
		운동장 *un-dong-jang*	field, playing field
		운동선수 *un-dong-seon-su*	athlete
넘어지다 *neo-meo-ji-da*	to fall down	뒤로 넘어지다 *dwi-ro neo-meo-ji-da*	to fall backwards
		미끄러지다 *mi-kkeu-reo-ji-da*	to slip

손 *son*	hand	손을 들다 *so-neul deul-da*	to raise one's hand
		손을 잡다 *so-neul jap-tta*	to hold someone's hand
		손가락 *son-kka-rak*	finger
		악수하다 *ak-ssu-ha-da*	to shake hands
다치다 *da-chi-da*	to get hurt	크게 다치다 *keu-ge da-chi-da*	to get seriously hurt
		많이 다치다 *ma-ni da-chi-da*	to get hurt a lot
		허리를 다치다 *heo-ri-reul da-chi-da*	to hurt one's back
		상처 *sang-cheo*	wound
아프다 *a-peu-da*	to be sick, to hurt	배가 아프다 *bae-ga a-peu-da*	to have a stomachache
		마음이 아프다 *ma-eu-mi a-peu-da*	to feel sad, to be heartbroken
		머리가 아프다 *meo-ri-ga a-peu-da*	to have a headache
병원 *byeong-won*	hospital	병원에 가다 *byeong-wo-ne ga-da*	to go to the hospital, to go see a doctor
		동물 병원 *dong-mul byeong-won*	animal hospital, vet, veterinary clinic
		주사 *ju-sa*	shot, injection

의사 *ui-sa*	doctor	**의사 선생님** *ui-sa seon-saeng-nim*	doctor
		치과 의사 *chi-kkwa ui-sa*	dentist
		간호사 *ga-no-sa*	nurse

쉬다 *swi-da*	to rest	**푹 쉬다** *puk swi-da*	to rest up, to rest a lot
		집에서 쉬다 *ji-be-seo swi-da*	to rest at home
		쉬는 날 *swi-neun nal*	day off
		쉬는 시간 *swi-neun si-gan*	break, recess, break time

힘들다 *him-deul-da*	to be difficult, to be tiring, to be hard	**먹기 힘들다** *meok-kki him-deul-da*	to be hard to eat
		일이 힘들다 *i-ri him-deul-da*	the work is hard
		힘든 *him-deun*	hard, difficult, tiring
		힘들게 *him-deul-ge*	in a difficult manner, in a tiring manner

LET'S REVIEW!

Read the story again, but this time in Korean!

어제 운동을 하다가 넘어졌어요.

손을 다쳤어요. 너무 아팠어요.

병원에 갔어요.

의사 선생님에게 진료를 받았어요.

침대에 누워서 쉬었어요.

손을 다쳐서 밥 먹기가 너무 힘들어요.

Translation

I fell down while working out yesterday. I hurt my hand. It hurt so much. I went to the hospital. I received medical treatment from the doctor. I laid on the bed and rested. Because I hurt my hand, it is so hard to eat.

Match each Korean word to its English translation.

의사 ·	· to get hurt
아프다 ·	· to rest
힘들다 ·	· hospital
어제 ·	· exercise
병원 ·	· yesterday
운동 ·	· doctor
손 ·	· to fall down
쉬다 ·	· to be difficult, to be tiring
다치다 ·	· to be sick, to hurt
넘어지다 ·	· hand

Crossword Puzzle

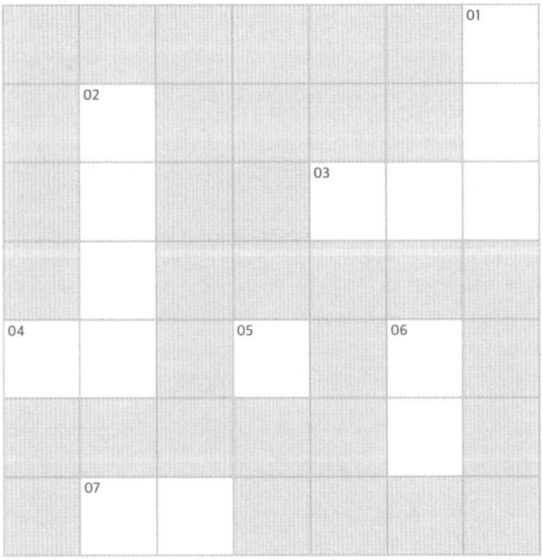

01 to get hurt
02 to fall down
03 to be difficult, to be hard
04 to rest
05 hand
06 yesterday
07 hospital

Fill in the blanks using one of the words that you learned in Day 36.
(Please refer to page 017 to review how to conjugate verbs/adjectives.)

01 ( ) 운동을 하다가 넘어졌어요. I fell down while working out yesterday.

02 어제 ( )을 하다가 넘어졌어요. I fell down while working out yesterday.

03 어제 운동을 하다가 ( ). I fell down while working out yesterday.

04 ( )을 다쳤어요. I hurt my hand.

05 손을 ( ). I hurt my hand.

06 너무 ( ). It hurt so much.

07 ( )에 갔어요. I went to the hospital.

08 ( ) 선생님에게 진료를 받았어요. I received medical treatment from the doctor.

09 침대에 누워서 ( ). I laid on the bed and rested.

10 손을 다쳐서 밥 먹기가 너무 ( ). Because I hurt my hand, it is so hard to eat.

Day 37

- 학생
- 자전거
- 다니다
- 비
- 우산
- 없다
- 신발
- 벗다
- 발
- 목욕

Day 37 LET'S WARM UP!

Imagine the situation in the story below to help you remember the ten Korean words in context.

37

학생 다니다 자전거

I am a student. I go to school on my bike.

비

Today on my way home, it rained.

없다 우산

I did not have an umbrella.

Therefore, my clothes got wet in the rain.

신발

My shoes got wet, too.

벗다

As soon as I came home, I took off my shoes.

발 목욕

My feet smelled. So, I took a bath.

LET'S KEEP THE BALL ROLLING!

Word	Meaning	Related Words	Meaning
학생 *hak-ssaeng*	student	초등학생 *cho-deung-hak-ssaeng*	elementary school student
		중학생 *jung-hak-ssaeng*	middle school student
		고등학생 *go-deung-hak-ssaeng*	high school student
		학생들 *hak-ssaeng-deul*	students
자전거 *ja-jeon-geo*	bicycle	자전거를 타다 *ja-jeon-geo-reul ta-da*	to ride a bicycle
		자전거를 타고 가다 *ja-jeon-geo-reul ta-go ga-da*	to go by bicycle
		자전거 바퀴 *ja-jeon-geo ba-kwi*	bicycle wheel
		자전거 한 대 *ja-jeon-geo han dae*	one bicycle
다니다 *da-ni-da*	to attend, to go to (regularly)	학교에 다니다 *hak-kkyo-e da-ni-da*	to go to school
		병원에 다니다 *byeong-wo-ne da-ni-da*	to go to the hospital (regularly)
		가지고 다니다 *ga-ji-go da-ni-da*	to carry with
		타고 다니다 *ta-go da-ni-da*	to go around (in a vehicle)

비 *bi*	rain	**비를 맞다** *bi-reul mat-tta*	to get rained on
		비가 내리다 *bi-ga nae-ri-da*	it rains, to rain
		비가 오다 *bi-ga o-da*	it rains, to rain
		비에 젖다 *bi-e jeot-tta*	to get wet in the rain
우산 *u-san*	umbrella	**우산을 쓰다** *u-sa-neul sseu-da*	to use an umbrella
		우산을 펴다 *u-sa-neul pyeo-da*	to open an umbrella
		우산을 접다 *u-sa-neul jeop-tta*	to fold up an umbrella
없다 *eop-tta*	to not have, to not be, to not exist	**아무도 없다** *a-mu-do eop-tta*	there is no one
		여기 없다 *yeo-gi eop-tta*	to not be here
		없어지다 *eop-sseo-ji-da*	to disappear, to not be anymore
		있다 *it-tta*	to be, to have, to exist

신발 *sin-bal*	shoe	신발을 신다 *sin-ba-reul sin-tta*	to put on shoes, to wear shoes
		새 신발 *sae sin-bal*	new shoes
		신발장 *sin-bal-jjang*	shoe rack
		신발 끈 *sin-bal kkeun*	shoestring, shoe lace
벗다 *beot-tta*	to take off (clothing)	신발을 벗다 *sin-ba-reul beot-tta*	to take off one's shoes
		옷을 벗다 *o-seul beot-tta*	to take off one's clothes
발 *bal*	foot	발이 크다 *ba-ri keu-da*	to have big feet
		발 냄새 *bal naem-sae*	foot smell
		발바닥 *bal-ppa-dak*	sole of one's foot
		손 *son*	hand
목욕 *mo-gyok*	bath	목욕하다 *mo-gyo-ka-da*	to take a bath, to bathe
		목욕탕 *mo-gyok-tang*	bathhouse
		욕조 *yok-jjo*	bathtub

LET'S REVIEW!

Read the story again, but this time in Korean!

저는 **학생**이에요. 학교에 **자전거**를 타고 **다녀요.**

오늘 집에 가는데 **비**가 왔어요.

우산이 **없었어요.**

그래서 옷이 비에 젖었어요. **신발**도 젖었어요.

집에 오자마자 신발을 **벗었어요.**

발에서 냄새가 났어요. 그래서 **목욕**을 했어요.

Translation

I am a student. I go to school on my bike. Today on my way home, it rained. I did not have an umbrella. Therefore, my clothes got wet in the rain. My shoes got wet, too. As soon as I came home, I took off my shoes. My feet smelled. So, I took a bath.

Match each Korean word to its English translation.

다니다 ·	· umbrella
비 ·	· to take off (clothing)
우산 ·	· student
목욕 ·	· shoe
학생 ·	· bath
벗다 ·	· rain
자전거 ·	· foot
발 ·	· bicycle
신발 ·	· to not have, to not be, to not exist
없다 ·	· to attend, to go to (regularly)

Crossword Puzzle

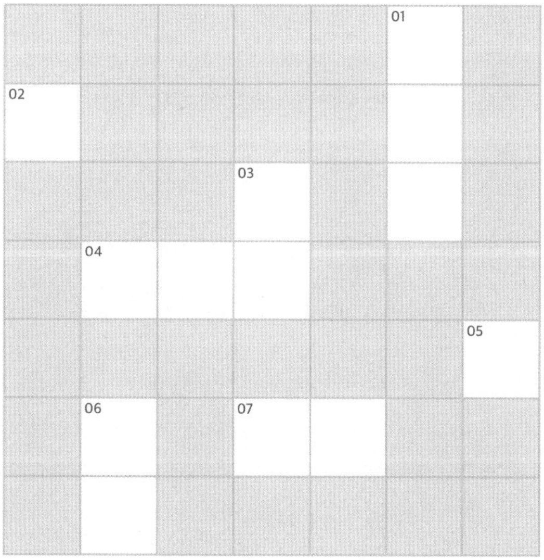

01 bicycle
02 foot
03 to take off (clothing)
04 to attend, to go to (regularly)
05 rain
06 umbrella
07 bath

Fill in the blanks using one of the words that you learned in Day 37.
(Please refer to page 017 to review how to conjugate verbs/adjectives.)

01 저는 ( )이에요. I am a student.

02 학교에 ( )를 타고 다녀요. I go to school on my bike.

03 학교에 자전거를 타고 ( ). I go to school on my bike.

04 오늘 집에 가는데 ( )가 왔어요. Today on my way home, it rained.

05 ( )이 없었어요. I did not have an umbrella.

06 우산이 ( ). I did not have an umbrella.

07 ( )도 젖었어요. My shoes got wet, too.

08 집에 오자마자 신발을 ( ). As soon as I came home, I took off my shoes.

09 ( )에서 냄새가 났어요. My feet smelled.

10 그래서 ( )을 했어요. So, I took a bath.

Day 38

- 오빠
- 가끔
- 거짓말
- 짜증
- 오전
- 머리
- 벌레
- 놀라다
- 싫다
- 이상하다

Day 38 LET'S WARM UP!

Imagine the situation in the story below to help you remember the ten Korean words in context.

38

오빠 가끔 거짓말
My older brother sometimes lies.

짜증
So, it's very irritating.

오전 벌레 머리
This morning, he said that there was a bug on my head.

놀라다
I was really surprised.

싫다
I hate bugs so much.

이상하다
My brother is really weird.

LET'S KEEP THE BALL ROLLING!

Word	Meaning	Related Words	Meaning
오빠 *o-ppa*	older brother (for a girl)	친오빠 *chi-no-ppa*	real brother, biological brother
		아는 오빠 *a-neun o-ppa*	older man a girl knows
		첫째 오빠 *cheot-jjae o-ppa*	eldest brother (for a girl)
가끔 *ga-kkeum*	sometimes	가끔 만나다 *ga-kkeum man-na-da*	to meet sometimes
		가끔 생각하다 *ga-kkeum saeng-ga-ka-da*	to think of something sometimes
		항상 *hang-sang*	always
거짓말 *geo-jin-mal*	lie	거짓말을 하다 *geo-jin-ma-reul ha-da*	to lie, to tell a lie
		거짓말쟁이 *geo-jin-mal-jaeng-i*	liar
짜증 *jja-jeung*	frustration, anger, irritation	짜증이 나다 *jja-jeung-i na-da*	to be irritated, to be angry
		짜증을 내다 *jja-jeung-eul nae-da*	to show one's irritation, to show one's frustration

오전 *o-jeon*	morning, before noon	**오전에** *o-jeo-ne*	in the morning
		오전 10시 *o-jeon yeol-ssi*	10 o'clock in the morning, 10 a.m.
		오후 *o-hu*	afternoon
머리 *meo-ri*	head, hair	**머리가 아프다** *meo-ri-ga a-peu-da*	to have a headache, one's head hurts
		머리가 좋다 *meo-ri-ga jo-ta*	to be smart
		긴 머리 *gin meo-ri*	long hair
		머리카락 *meo-ri-ka-rak*	hair
벌레 *beol-le*	bug, worm	**벌레 한 마리** *beol-le han ma-ri*	one bug, one worm
		징그럽다 *jing-geu-reop-tta*	to be gross
		벌레를 잡다 *beol-le-reul jap-tta*	to catch a bug, to catch a worm
		기어가다 *gi-eo-ga-da*	to crawl
놀라다 *nol-la-da*	to be surprised	**깜짝 놀라다** *kkam-jjak nol-la-da*	to be surprised, to be startled
		놀라게 하다 *nol-la-ge ha-da*	to surprise
		놀란 얼굴 *nol-lan eol-gul*	surprised look on one's face

싫다 *sil-ta*	to hate, to dislike, to be displeasing	**너무 싫다** *neo-mu sil-ta*	to really hate
		싫은 사람 *si-reun sa-ram*	someone that one hates, a hated person
		싫지 않다 *sil-chi an-ta*	to not be averse to, to not be displeasing, to be alright
		싫어하다 *si-reo-ha-da*	to hate

이상하다 *i-sang-ha-da*	to be strange, to be weird	**목소리가 이상하다** *mok-sso-ri-ga i-sang-ha-da*	one's voice is strange, to have a strange voice
		성격이 이상하다 *seong-kkyeo-gi i-sang-ha-da*	one's personality is strange, to have a strange personality
		이상한 사람 *i-sang-han sa-ram*	strange person

LET'S REVIEW!

Read the story again, but this time in Korean!

오빠가 가끔 거짓말을 해요.

그래서 너무 짜증이 나요.

오늘 오전에는 제 머리에 벌레가 있다고 했어요.

정말 깜짝 놀랐어요.

저는 벌레가 너무 싫어요.

오빠는 정말 이상해요.

Translation

My older brother sometimes lies. So, it's very irritating. This morning, he said that there was a bug on my head. I was really surprised. I hate bugs so much. My brother is really weird.

Match each Korean word to its English translation.

오전 ·	· lie
놀라다 ·	· frustration, anger, irritation
이상하다 ·	· sometimes
거짓말 ·	· older brother (for a girl)
오빠 ·	· to be strange, to be weird
가끔 ·	· head, hair
벌레 ·	· morning, before noon
짜증 ·	· to hate, to dislike
싫다 ·	· to be surprised
머리 ·	· bug, worm

Crossword Puzzle

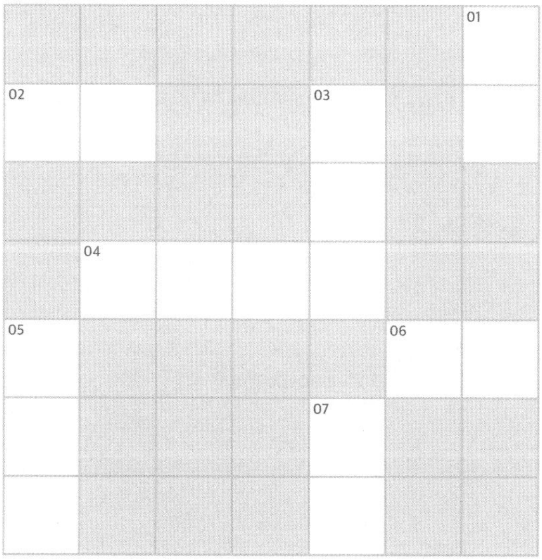

01 sometimes
02 frustration, anger
03 to be surprised
04 to be strange, to be weird
05 lie
06 bug, worm
07 head, hair

Fill in the blanks using one of the words that you learned in Day 38.
(Please refer to page 017 to review how to conjugate verbs/adjectives.)

01 (   )가 가끔 거짓말을 해요. My older brother sometimes lies.

02 오빠가 (   ) 거짓말을 해요. My older brother sometimes lies.

03 오빠가 가끔 (   )을 해요. My older brother sometimes lies.

04 그래서 너무 (   )이 나요. So, it's very irritating.

05 오늘 (   )에는 제 머리에 벌레가 있다고 했어요. This morning, he said that there was a bug on my head.

06 오늘 오전에는 제 (   )에 벌레가 있다고 했어요. This morning, he said that there was a bug on my head.

07 오늘 오전에는 제 머리에 (   )가 있다고 했어요. This morning, he said that there was a bug on my head.

08 정말 깜짝 (   ). I was really surprised.

09 저는 벌레가 너무 (   ). I hate bugs so much.

10 오빠는 정말 (   ). My brother is really weird.

Day 39

- 저녁
- 엄마
- 마트
- 고기
- 사다
- 생선
- 채소
- 말하다
- 달걀
- 요리

Day 39 LET'S WARM UP!

Imagine the situation in the story below to help you remember the ten Korean words in context.

39

마트 엄마 저녁

I went to the supermarket with my mom in the evening.

사다 고기

Mom bought some meat. I really like meat.

생선 채소

We also bought fish and vegetables.

I don't eat vegetables.

말하다

Mom said that I must also eat vegetables.

달걀

We also bought eggs. As for eggs, I like eating them.

요리

Mom will cook a delicious dish for me.

LET'S KEEP THE BALL ROLLING!

Word	Meaning	Related Words	Meaning
저녁 *jeo-nyeok*	evening	저녁에 *jeo-nyeo-ge*	in the evening
		저녁 식사 *jeo-nyeok sik-ssa*	supper, dinner
		저녁때 *jeo-nyeok-ttae*	at dinner, in the evening
		저녁을 먹다 *jeo-nyeo-geul meok-tta*	to have dinner
엄마 *eom-ma*	mom	우리 엄마 *u-ri eom-ma*	my mom
		새엄마 *sae-eom-ma*	stepmom
		부모 *bu-mo*	parents
마트 *ma-teu*	supermarket	마트에 가다 *ma-teu-e ga-da*	to go to the supermarket
		대형 마트 *dae-hyeong ma-teu*	big supermarket
		장을 보다 *jang-eul bo-da*	to go grocery shopping

고기 *go-gi*	meat	**돼지고기** *dwae-ji-go-gi*	pork
		소고기 *so-go-gi*	beef
		닭고기 *dak-kko-gi*	chicken
사다 *sa-da*	to buy	**밥을 사다** *ba-beul sa-da*	to buy someone a meal
		선물을 사다 *seon-mu-reul sa-da*	to buy a present
		싸게 사다 *ssa-ge sa-da*	to buy at a low price
		팔다 *pal-da*	to sell
생선 *saeng-seon*	fish	**생선 두 마리** *saeng-seon du ma-ri*	two fish
		생선 요리 *saeng-seon yo-ri*	fish dish
		물고기 *mul-kko-gi*	live fish
채소 *chae-so*	vegetable	**채소를 기르다** *chae-so-reul gi-reu-da*	to grow vegetables
		채소를 먹다 *chae-so-reul meok-tta*	to eat vegetables
		녹색 채소 *nok-ssaek chae-so*	green vegetables

말하다 *mal-ha-da*	to talk, to speak	**천천히 말하다** *cheon-cheo-ni mal-ha-da*	to talk slowly
		빨리 말하다 *ppal-li mal-ha-da*	to talk quickly
		말 *mal*	words, language
		이야기하다 *i-ya-gi-ha-da*	to talk, to chat

달걀 *dal-gyal*	egg	**달걀을 깨다** *dal-gya-reul kkae-da*	to break an egg
		삶은 달걀 *sal-meun dal-gyal*	boiled egg
		계란 *gye-ran*	egg

요리 *yo-ri*	cooking, food, dish	**요리사** *yo-ri-sa*	cook, chef
		요리하다 *yo-ri-ha-da*	to cook
		음식 *eum-sik*	dish, food

LET'S REVIEW!

Read the story again, but this time in Korean!

저녁에 **엄마**랑 **마트**에 갔어요.

엄마는 **고기**를 **샀어요.** 저는 고기를 정말 좋아해요.

그리고 **생선**이랑 **채소**도 샀어요. 저는 채소를 안 먹어요.

엄마는 채소도 꼭 먹어야 한다고 **말했어요.**

그리고 **달걀**도 샀어요. 저는 달걀은 잘 먹어요.

엄마가 맛있는 **요리**를 해 줄 거예요.

Translation

I went to the supermarket with my mom in the evening. Mom bought some meat. I really like meat. We also bought fish and vegetables. I don't eat vegetables. Mom said that I must also eat vegetables. We also bought eggs. As for eggs, I like eating them. Mom will cook a delicious dish for me.

Match each Korean word to its English translation.

마트 ·	· to buy
생선 ·	· meat
저녁 ·	· fish
채소 ·	· to talk, to speak
달걀 ·	· cooking, food, dish
요리 ·	· vegetable
엄마 ·	· supermarket
말하다 ·	· evening
사다 ·	· egg
고기 ·	· mom

Crossword Puzzle

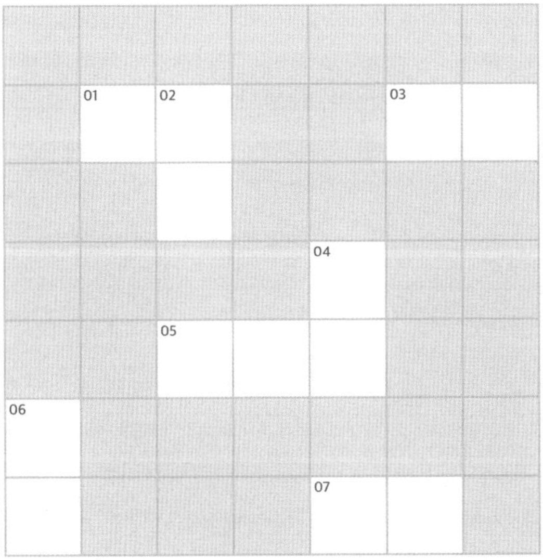

01 mom
02 supermarket
03 egg
04 to buy
05 to talk, to speak
06 evening
07 fish

Fill in the blanks using one of the words that you learned in Day 39.
(Please refer to page 017 to review how to conjugate verbs/adjectives.)

01 (   )에 엄마랑 마트에 갔어요.
I went to the supermarket with my mom in the evening.

02 저녁에 (   )랑 마트에 갔어요.
I went to the supermarket with my mom in the evening.

03 저녁에 엄마랑 (   )에 갔어요.
I went to the supermarket with my mom in the evening.

04 엄마는 (   )를 샀어요.
Mom bought some meat.

05 엄마는 고기를 (   ).
Mom bought some meat.

06 그리고 (   )이랑 채소도 샀어요.
We also bought fish and vegetables.

07 그리고 생선이랑 (   )도 샀어요.
We also bought fish and vegetables.

08 엄마는 채소도 꼭 먹어야 한다고 (   ).
Mom said that I must also eat vegetables.

09 그리고 (   )도 샀어요.
We also bought eggs.

10 엄마가 맛있는 (   )를 해 줄 거예요.
Mom will cook a delicious dish for me.

Day 40

- 할아버지
- 산
- 올라가다
- 믿다
- 사람
- 새
- 나무
- 냄새
- 몸
- 움직이다

Day 40 LET'S WARM UP!

Imagine the situation in the story below to help you remember the ten Korean words in context.

40

할아버지 올라가다 산

My **grandfather** **goes up** the **mountain** every day.

믿다

He **believes** that he will become healthy if he hikes up the mountain every day. I sometimes go with him, too.

사람

When we go to the mountain, there are a lot of **people**.

새 냄새 나무

There are a lot of **birds**, too. I like the **smell** of **trees**.

움직이다 몸

I also like **moving** my **body** a lot.

So, I also like hiking up the mountain.

LET'S KEEP THE BALL ROLLING!

Word	Meaning	Related Words	Meaning
할아버지 *ha-ra-beo-ji*	grandfather, old man	외할아버지 *oe-ha-ra-beo-ji*	maternal grandfather
		친할아버지 *chi-na-ra-beo-ji*	paternal grandfather
		할머니 *hal-meo-ni*	grandmother
산 *san*	mountain	산이 낮다 *sa-ni nat-tta*	the mountain is low
		높은 산 *no-peun san*	high mountain
		등산 *deung-san*	mountain hiking
올라가다 *ol-la-ga-da*	to go up	산에 올라가다 *sa-ne ol-la-ga-da*	to go up a mountain
		옥상에 올라가다 *ok-ssang-e ol-la-ga-da*	to go up to the roof
믿다 *mit-tta*	to trust, to believe	이야기를 믿다 *i-ya-gi-reul mit-tta*	to believe a story
		사람을 믿다 *sa-ra-meul mit-tta*	to believe a person, to trust a person
		믿음 *mi-deum*	belief, trust

사람 *sa-ram*	person, people	**미국 사람** *mi-guk sa-ram*	a person from the United States
		아는 사람 *a-neun sa-ram*	someone that one knows
		모르는 사람 *mo-reu-neun sa-ram*	someone that one doesn't know, a stranger
		사람들 *sa-ram-deul*	people
새 *sae*	bird	**새가 날다** *sae-ga nal-da*	a bird flies
		새 한 마리 *sae han ma-ri*	one bird
나무 *na-mu*	tree, wood	**나무 세 그루** *na-mu se geu-ru*	three trees
		나무를 심다 *na-mu-reul sim-tta*	to plant a tree
		나무 의자 *na-mu ui-ja*	wooden chair
냄새 *naem-sae*	smell	**냄새가 나다** *naem-sae-ga na-da*	to smell (lit. a smell grows/sprouts/happens)
		냄새가 좋다 *naem-sae-ga jo-ta*	to smell good
		이상한 냄새 *i-sang-han naem-sae*	strange smell
		향기 *hyang-gi*	scent, fragrance

몸 *mom*	body	**건강한 몸** *geon-gang-han mom*	healthy body
		몸이 아프다 *mo-mi a-peu-da*	to be sick
		몸이 힘들다 *mo-mi him-deul-da*	to be tired
		몸에 좋다 *mo-me jo-ta*	to be good for one's body, to be good for health

움직이다 *um-ji-gi-da*	to move	**천천히 움직이다** *cheon-cheo-ni um-ji-gi-da*	to move slowly
		몸을 움직이다 *mo-meul um-ji-gi-da*	to move one's body

LET'S REVIEW!

Read the story again, but this time in Korean!

저희 **할아버지**는 매일 **산**에 **올라가요.**

매일 산에 올라가면 건강해진다고 **믿어요.**

저도 가끔 같이 올라가요. 산에 가면 **사람**들이 많아요.

새들도 많아요. 저는 **나무 냄새**를 좋아해요.

몸을 많이 **움직이는** 것도 좋아해요.

그래서 저도 산에 올라가는 것을 좋아해요.

Translation

My grandfather goes up the mountain every day. He believes that he will become healthy if he hikes up the mountain every day. I sometimes go with him, too. When we go to the mountain, there are a lot of people. There are a lot of birds, too. I like the smell of trees. I also like moving my body a lot. So, I also like hiking up the mountain.

Match each Korean word to its English translation.

믿다 ·	· bird
냄새 ·	· tree, wood
새 ·	· mountain
산 ·	· to move
몸 ·	· to go up
움직이다 ·	· smell
나무 ·	· grandfather, old man
할아버지 ·	· person, people
올라가다 ·	· to trust, to believe
사람 ·	· body

Crossword Puzzle

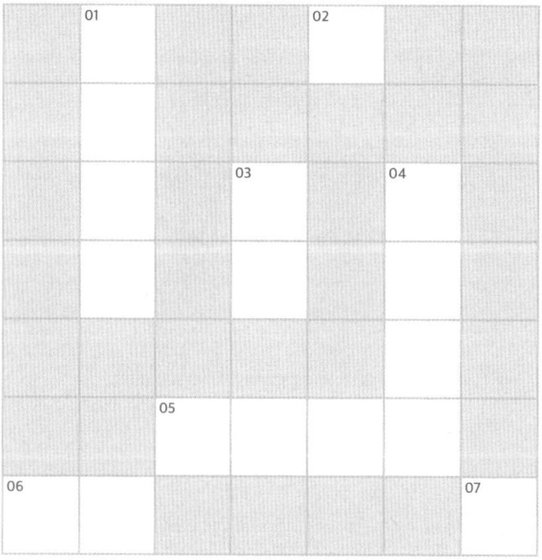

01 grandfather, old man
02 mountain
03 tree, wood
04 to go up
05 to move
06 person, people
07 bird

Fill in the blanks using one of the words that you learned in Day 40.
(Please refer to page 017 to review how to conjugate verbs/adjectives.)

01 저희 ( )는 매일 산에 올라가요. — My grandfather goes up the mountain every day.

02 저희 할아버지는 매일 ( )에 올라가요. — My grandfather goes up the mountain every day.

03 저희 할아버지는 매일 산에 ( ). — My grandfather goes up the mountain every day.

04 매일 산에 올라가면 건강해진다고 ( ). — He believes that he will become healthy if he hikes up the mountain every day.

05 산에 가면 ( )들이 많아요. — When we go to the mountain, there are a lot of people.

06 ( )들도 많아요. — There are a lot of birds, too.

07 저는 ( ) 냄새를 좋아해요. — I like the smell of trees.

08 저는 나무 ( )를 좋아해요. — I like the smell of trees.

09 ( )을 많이 움직이는 것도 좋아해요. — I also like moving my body a lot.

10 몸을 많이 ( ) 것도 좋아해요. — I also like moving my body a lot.

QUIZ

DAY 31-40

01 Choose the term that is an edible item.

a. 인기 b. 사과 c. 지도 d. 주소

02 Where do you go to buy medicine?

a. 약국 b. 나라 c. 가수 d. 발

03 Which one is **NOT** a mode of transportation?

a. 택시 b. 건강 c. 오토바이 d. 자전거

04 Which body part is 허리?

a. wrist b. ankle c. neck d. waist

05 Choose the term that is **NOT** a loanword from English.

a. 오이 b. 토마토 c. 바나나 d. 인터넷

06 Choose the word that is **NOT** a body part.

a. 배 b. 코 c. 손 d. 약

07 How do you address your father's father in Korean?

a. 할아버지 b. 할아버니 c. 할머니 d. 할머버지

08 Choose the item that you **CANNOT** wear.

a. 신발 b. 치마 c. 감기 d. 모자

09 Where can you go 쇼핑?

a. 마트 b. 달걀 c. 어제 d. 택시

10 Who do you most likely see when you go to the 병원?

a. 엄마 b. 경찰 c. 의사 d. 학생

11 Which of the following is something you can drink?

a. 고기 b. 생선 c. 차 d. 저녁

12 Which one syllable word means **"door"**?

a. 귀 b. 산 c. 비 d. 문

13 Which of the following means **"mind, heart"**?

a. 마음 b. 사고 c. 단어 d. 조금

14 How do you say **"to send a text message"** in Korean?

a. 약속을 보내다 b. 문자를 보내다

c. 문자를 주문하다 d. 약속을 주문하다

15 Which one of the following words is **NOT** related to time?

a. 어제 b. 머리 c. 오전 d. 가끔

16 Which of the following does **NOT** become a verb if you attach -하다?

a. 성공 b. 운동 c. 목욕 d. 벌레

17 What is the Korean word for the item in the picture?

a. 오빠

b. 요리

c. 우산

d. 채소

18 Which word is not related to the others?

a. 넘어지다 b. 다치다 c. 아프다 d. 필요하다

19 Choose the noun that refers to something you **CANNOT** see.

a. 새 b. 냄새 c. 나무 d. 사람

20 Choose the term that refers to the size of something.

a. 벗다 b. 이상하다 c. 작다 d. 늦다

Answers : b a b d a / d a c a c / c d a b b / d c d b c

Day 41

- 공항
- 넓다
- 길
- 잃어버리다
- 여기
- 어디
- 서점
- 들어가다
- 물어보다
- 찾다

Day 41

LET'S WARM UP!

Imagine the situation in the story below to help you remember the ten Korean words in context.

41

공항 넓다 잃어버리다 길

The airport is so big that I lost my way.

어디 여기

I don't know where this place is.

들어가다 서점

I went into the bookstore.

물어보다

I asked for directions.

찾다

Fortunately, I found my way.

LET'S KEEP THE BALL ROLLING!

Word	Meaning	Related Words	Meaning
공항 *gong-hang*	airport	공항버스 *gong-hang-ppeo-sseu*	airport shuttle bus
		비행기 *bi-haeng-gi*	airplane
		공항에 가다 *gong-hang-e ga-da*	to go to the airport
넓다 *neol-tta*	to be spacious, to be wide	공항이 넓다 *gong-hang-i neol-tta*	the airport is big
		넓은 집 *neol-beun jip*	spacious house
		좁다 *jop-tta*	to be narrow, to be small (in space)
길 *gil*	road, street	길가 *gil-kka*	roadside
		골목길 *gol-mok-kkil*	alley
		길이 막히다 *gi-ri ma-ki-da*	to be jammed with traffic
잃어버리다 *i-reo-beo-ri-da*	to lose, to misplace	길을 잃어버리다 *gi-reul i-reo-beo-ri-da*	to get lost
		돈을 잃어버리다 *do-neul i-reo-beo-ri-da*	to lose money
		잃어버린 지갑 *i-reo-beo-rin ji-gap*	lost wallet, misplaced wallet

여기 *yeo-gi*	here	**여기에서** *yeo-gi-e-seo*	from here
		여기까지 *yeo-gi-kka-ji*	to here, up to here
		여기저기 *yeo-gi-jeo-gi*	here and there

어디 *eo-di*	where	**어디에서** *eo-di-e-seo*	from where
		어디로 *eo-di-ro*	to where
		어디인지 모르다 *eo-di-in-ji mo-reu-da*	to not know where

서점 *seo-jeom*	bookstore	**책방** *chaek-ppang*	bookstore
		책 *chaek*	book
		동네 서점 *dong-ne seo-jeom*	local bookstore, bookstore in the neighborhood
		대형 서점 *dae-hyeong seo-jeom*	large-scale bookstore
		도서관 *do-seo-gwan*	library

들어가다 *deu-reo-ga-da*	to enter	서점에 들어가다 *seo-jeo-me deu-reo-ga-da*	to go into a bookstore
		교실로 들어가다 *gyo-sil-lo deu-reo-ga-da*	to go into a classroom
		들어오다 *deu-reo-o-da*	to come in
		나가다 *na-ga-da*	to go out

물어보다 *mu-reo-bo-da*	to ask	길을 물어보다 *gi-reul mu-reo-bo-da*	to ask for directions
		전화로 물어보다 *jeo-nwa-ro mu-reo-bo-da*	to ask over the phone
		대답하다 *dae-da-pa-da*	to answer

찾다 *chat-tta*	to find	길을 찾다 *gi-reul chat-tta*	to find one's way
		답을 찾다 *da-beul chat-tta*	to find the answer
		보물을 찾다 *bo-mu-reul chat-tta*	to find a treasure

LET'S REVIEW!

Read the story again, but this time in Korean!

공항이 너무 넓어서 길을 잃어버렸어요.

여기가 어디인지 모르겠어요.

서점에 들어갔어요.

길을 물어봤어요.

다행히 길을 찾았어요.

Translation

The airport is so big that I lost my way. I don't know where this place is. I went into the bookstore. I asked for directions. Fortunately, I found my way.

Match each Korean word to its English translation.

잃어버리다 ·	· to be spacious, to be wide
들어가다 ·	· bookstore
넓다 ·	· airport
어디 ·	· to ask
찾다 ·	· here
공항 ·	· to find
물어보다 ·	· to enter
길 ·	· where
서점 ·	· to lose, to misplace
여기 ·	· road, street

Crossword Puzzle

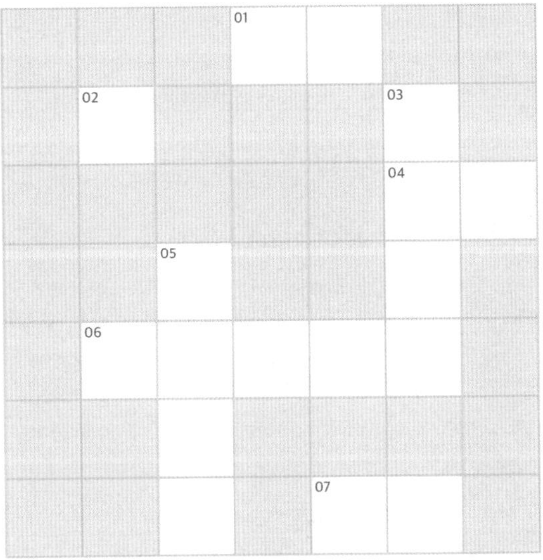

01 airport
02 road, street
03 to ask
04 where
05 to enter
06 to lose, to misplace
07 here

Fill in the blanks using one of the words that you learned in Day 41.
(Please refer to page 017 to review how to conjugate verbs/adjectives.)

01 (   )이 너무 넓어서 길을 잃어버렸어요. The airport is so big that I lost my way.

02 공항이 너무 (   ) 길을 잃어버렸어요. The airport is so big that I lost my way.

03 공항이 너무 넓어서 (   )을 잃어버렸어요. The airport is so big that I lost my way.

04 공항이 너무 넓어서 길을 (   ). The airport is so big that I lost my way.

05 (   )가 어디인지 모르겠어요. I don't know where this place is.

06 여기가 (   )인지 모르겠어요. I don't know where this place is.

07 (   )에 들어갔어요. I went into the bookstore.

08 서점에 (   ). I went into the bookstore.

09 길을 (   ). I asked for directions.

10 다행히 길을 (   ). Fortunately, I found my way.

Day 42

- 대학교
- 역
- 가깝다
- 오른쪽
- 은행
- 왼쪽
- 편의점
- 앞
- 건너다
- 다시

Day 42 LET'S WARM UP!

Imagine the situation in the story below to help you remember the ten Korean words in context.

42

대학교 가깝다 역
My university is very close to Sinchon station.

Come out from Exit 2 at Sinchon station.

오른쪽 은행 왼쪽
On your right, there is a bank, and on your left,

편의점
there is a convenience store.

앞 건너다
Walk straight. Cross the road.

다시
Go straight again. You will see the university soon.

LET'S KEEP THE BALL ROLLING!

Word	Meaning	Related Words	Meaning
대학교 *dae-hak-kkyo*	university, college	대학교 1학년 *dae-hak-kkyo i-rang-nyeon*	freshman, first year of university
		대학생 *dae-hak-ssaeng*	university student
		전공 *jeon-gong*	major
역 *yeok*	station	기차역 *gi-cha-yeok*	train station
		지하철역 *ji-ha-cheol yeok*	subway station
		신촌 역 *sin-chon yeok*	Sinchon station (name of a place in Seoul)
가깝다 *ga-kkap-tta*	to be close	아주 가깝다 *a-ju ga-kkap-tta*	to be very close
		더 가깝다 *deo ga-kkap-tta*	to be closer
		가까운 곳 *ga-kka-un got*	close place
		멀다 *meol-da*	to be far

오른쪽 *o-reun-jjok*	right side, right-hand side	오른쪽으로 가다 *o-reun-jjo-geu-ro ga-da*	to go to the right
		오른쪽 길 *o-reun-jjok gil*	path on the right-hand side
		오른 *o-reun*	right, right-sided
은행 *eu-naeng*	bank	은행 이자 *eu-naeng i-ja*	bank interest
		통장 *tong-jang*	bank book, account book
		저금하다 *jeo-geu-ma-da*	to save money, to deposit money
왼쪽 *oen-jjok*	left side, left-hand side	왼쪽에 있다 *oen-jjo-ge it-tta*	to be on the left-hand side
		왼쪽 다리 *oen-jjok da-ri*	left leg
		왼 *oen*	left, left-sided
편의점 *pyeo-nui-jeom*	convenience store	편의점에 가다 *pyeo-nui-jeo-me ga-da*	to go to the convenience store
		편의점에서 사다 *pyeo-nui-jeo-me-seo sa-da*	to buy (something) at a convenience store
		편의점이 열려 있다 *pyeo-nui-jeo-mi yeol-lyeo it-tta*	the convenience store is open

앞 *ap*	front	앞에 *a-pe*	in front
		앞으로 *a-peu-ro*	forward
건너다 *geon-neo-da*	to cross	길을 건너다 *gi-reul geon-neo-da*	to cross the road
		다리를 건너다 *da-ri-reul geon-neo-da*	to cross the bridge
		횡단보도 *hoeng-dan-bo-do*	crosswalk
다시 *da-si*	again	다시 하다 *da-si ha-da*	to do again
		또 *tto*	again

LET'S REVIEW!

Read the story again, but this time in Korean!

저희 **대학교**는 신촌 **역**에서 아주 **가까워요.**

신촌 역 2번 출구로 나와요.

오른쪽에 **은행**이 있고, **왼쪽**에 **편의점**이 있어요.

앞으로 걸어가요. 길을 **건너요.**

다시 앞으로 걸어가요.

곧 대학교가 보여요.

Translation

My university is very close to Sinchon station. Come out from Exit 2 at Sinchon station. On your right, there is a bank, and on your left, there is a convenience store. Walk straight. Cross the road.
Go straight again. You will see the university soon.

Match each Korean word to its English translation.

가깝다 ·	· university, college
은행 ·	· convenience store
역 ·	· right side, right-hand side
편의점 ·	· to cross
다시 ·	· station
대학교 ·	· to be close
앞 ·	· left side, left-hand side
건너다 ·	· front
왼쪽 ·	· again
오른쪽 ·	· bank

Crossword Puzzle

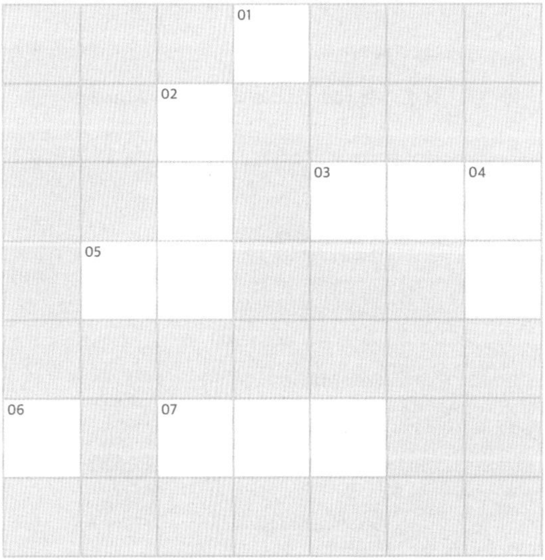

01 front
02 right side, right-hand side
03 to cross
04 again
05 left side, left-hand side
06 station
07 university, college

Fill in the blanks using one of the words that you learned in Day 42.
(Please refer to page 017 to review how to conjugate verbs/adjectives.)

01 저희 (   )는 신촌 역에서 아주 가까워요.
My university is very close to Sinchon station.

02 저희 대학교는 신촌 (   )에서 아주 가까워요.
My university is very close to Sinchon station.

03 저희 대학교는 신촌 역에서 아주 (   ).
My university is very close to Sinchon station.

04 (   )에 은행이 있고, 왼쪽에 편의점이 있어요.
On your right, there is a bank, and on your left, there is a convenience store.

05 오른쪽에 (   )이 있고, 왼쪽에 편의점이 있어요.
On your right, there is a bank, and on your left, there is a convenience store.

06 오른쪽에 은행이 있고, (   )에 편의점이 있어요.
On your right, there is a bank, and on your left, there is a convenience store.

07 오른쪽에 은행이 있고, 왼쪽에 (   )이 있어요.
On your right, there is a bank, and on your left, there is a convenience store.

08 (   )으로 걸어가요.
Walk straight.

09 길을 (   ).
Cross the road.

10 (   ) 앞으로 걸어가요.
Go straight again.

Day 43

- 색깔
- 검은색
- 지갑
- 자동차
- 가방
- 언제
- 모르다
- 형
- 하얀색
- 다르다

Day 43 LET'S WARM UP!

Imagine the situation in the story below to help you remember the ten Korean words in context.

43

색깔 검은색
My favorite color is black.

지갑
I have many things that are black, such as a black wallet,

자동차 가방
a black car, a black bag, and so on.

모르다 언제
I don't know when I started liking the color black.

형 하얀색
But my older brother likes the color white.

다르다
My personality and my brother's personality are very different.

LET'S KEEP THE BALL ROLLING!

Word	Meaning	Related Words	Meaning
색깔 *saek-kkal*	color	색 *saek*	color
		좋아하는 색깔 *jo-a-ha-neun saek-kkal*	color that one likes
		무슨 색깔 *mu-seun saek-kkal*	what color, which color
검은색 *geo-meun-saek*	black	검은색 자동차 *geo-meun-saek ja-dong-cha*	black car
		검은색 구두 *geo-meun-saek gu-du*	black shoes
		검정 *geom-jeong*	black
지갑 *ji-gap*	wallet	동전 지갑 *dong-jeon ji-gap*	coin wallet
		지갑을 열다 *ji-ga-beul yeol-da*	to open one's wallet
		지갑을 잃어버리다 *ji-ga-beul i-reo-beo-ri-da*	to lose one's wallet
자동차 *ja-dong-cha*	car	차 *cha*	car
		자동차 한 대 *ja-dong-cha han dae*	one car
		자동차를 타다 *ja-dong-cha-reul ta-da*	to ride in a car, to get in a car

가방 *ga-bang*	bag	가방이 무겁다 *ga-bang-i mu-geop-tta*	the bag is heavy
		가방을 메다 *ga-bang-eul me-da*	to carry a bag over one's shoulder
		책가방 *chaek-kka-bang*	book bag
		여행 가방 *yeo-haeng ga-bang*	suitcase, travel bag, luggage

언제 *eon-je*	when	언제부터 *eon-je-bu-teo*	since when, from when
		몇 시 *myeot si*	what time
		날짜 *nal-jja*	date
		며칠 *myeo-chil*	what date, how many days

모르다 *mo-reu-da*	to not know	아직 모르다 *a-jik mo-reu-da*	to still not know
		아무도 모르다 *a-mu-do mo-reu-da*	nobody knows
		모르는 사람 *mo-reu-neun sa-ram*	a stranger, someone one doesn't know
		알다 *al-da*	to know

형 *hyeong*	older brother (for a boy)	우리 형 *u-ri hyeong*	my older brother (for a boy)
		첫째 형 *cheot-jjae hyeong*	oldest brother (for a boy)
		사촌 형 *sa-chon hyeong*	older male cousin (for a boy)
하얀색 *ha-yan-saek*	white	흰색 *huin-saek*	white
		하얗다 *ha-ya-ta*	to be white
		하얀 *ha-yan*	white (adjective)
		하얀색 운동화 *ha-yan-saek un-dong-hwa*	white tennis shoes
다르다 *da-reu-da*	to be different	성격이 다르다 *seong-kkyeo-gi da-reu-da*	to have different personalities
		많이 다르다 *ma-ni da-reu-da*	to be very different
		다른 점 *da-reun jeom*	different point, difference
		달라지다 *dal-la-ji-da*	to become different
		같다 *gat-tta*	to be the same

LET'S REVIEW!

Read the story again, but this time in Korean!

제가 좋아하는 **색깔**은 **검은색**이에요.

검은색 **지갑**, 검은색 **자동차**, 검은색 **가방** 등등

검은색 물건이 많아요.

언제부터 검은색을 좋아했는지는 **몰라요.**

그런데 저희 **형**은 **하얀색**을 좋아해요.

저랑 저희 형은 성격이 많이 **달라요.**

Translation

My favorite color is black. I have many things that are black, such as a black wallet, a black car, a black bag, and so on. I don't know when I started liking the color black. But my older brother likes the color white. My personality and my brother's personality are very different.

Match each Korean word to its English translation.

검은색 ·	· when
가방 ·	· older brother (for a boy)
모르다 ·	· to be different
형 ·	· black
색깔 ·	· wallet
다르다 ·	· white
자동차 ·	· color
하얀색 ·	· to not know
지갑 ·	· bag
언제 ·	· car

Crossword Puzzle

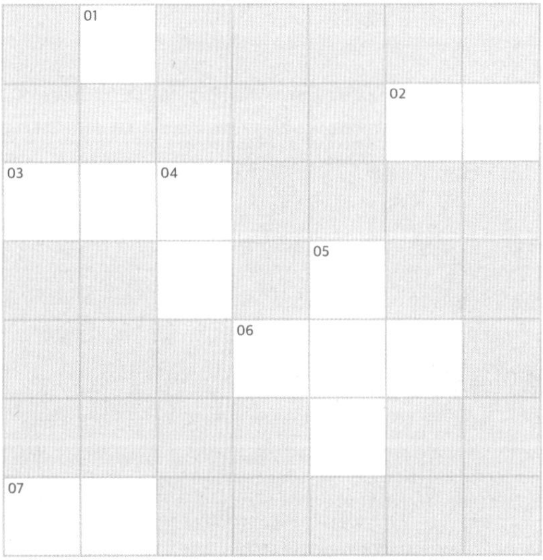

01 older brother (for a boy)
02 bag
03 black
04 color
05 to not know
06 to be different
07 when

Fill in the blanks using one of the words that you learned in Day 43.
(Please refer to page 017 to review how to conjugate verbs/adjectives.)

01 제가 좋아하는 (　　　　　　　)은 검은색이에요. My favorite color is black.

02 제가 좋아하는 색깔은 (　　　　　　　)이에요. My favorite color is black.

03 검은색 (　　　　　　　), 검은색 자동차, 검은색 가방 등등 검은색 물건이 많아요. I have many things that are black, such as a black wallet, a black car, a black bag, and so on.

04 검은색 지갑, 검은색 (　　　　　　　), 검은색 가방 등등 검은색 물건이 많아요. I have many things that are black, such as a black wallet, a black car, a black bag, and so on.

05 검은색 지갑, 검은색 자동차, 검은색 (　　　　　　　) 등등 검은색 물건이 많아요. I have many things that are black, such as a black wallet, a black car, a black bag, and so on.

06 (　　　　　　　)부터 검은색을 좋아했는지는 몰라요. I don't know when I started liking the color black.

07 언제부터 검은색을 좋아했는지는 (　　　　　　　). I don't know when I started liking the color black.

08 그런데 저희 (　　　　　　　)은 하얀색을 좋아해요. But my older brother likes the color white.

09 그런데 저희 형은 (　　　　　　　)을 좋아해요. But my older brother likes the color white.

10 저랑 저희 형은 성격이 많이 (　　　　　　　). My personality and my brother's personality are very different.

Day 44

- 착하다
- 문제
- 연필
- 빌려주다
- 펜
- 또
- 이유
- 미치다
- 나쁘다
- 아니다

Day 44 LET'S WARM UP!

Imagine the situation in the story below to help you remember the ten Korean words in context.

44

착하다
My friend is very kind-hearted.

문제
But there is one matter.

빌려주다 연필
When I lend him a pencil, he always loses them.

펜 또
Yesterday, I lent him a pen. He lost it again.

이유 미치다
I don't know why. It's driving me crazy.

아니다 나쁘다
He is not a bad person.

LET'S KEEP THE BALL ROLLING!

Word	Meaning	Related Words	Meaning
착하다 *cha-ka-da*	to be nice, to be kind-hearted	마음이 착하다 *ma-eu-mi cha-ka-da*	to be kind-hearted
		착한 일 *cha-kan il*	nice deed
		착한 사람 *cha-kan sa-ram*	nice person, kind-hearted person
문제 *mun-je*	problem, matter	문제가 있다 *mun-je-ga it-tta*	to have a problem
		문제가 생기다 *mun-je-ga saeng-gi-da*	a problem occurs, a problem happens
		중요한 문제 *jung-yo-han mun-je*	important problem, important matter
		문제없다 *mun-je-eop-tta*	to have no problem
연필 *yeon-pil*	pencil	연필 한 자루 *yeon-pil han ja-ru*	one pencil
		연필로 쓰다 *yeon-pil-lo sseu-da*	to write with a pencil
		연필을 깎다 *yeon-pi-reul kkak-tta*	to sharpen a pencil

빌려주다 *bil-lyeo-ju-da*	to lend	**펜을 빌려주다** *pe-neul bil-lyeo-ju-da*	to lend a pen
		빌려준 돈 *bil-lyeo-jun don*	money that one has lent
		돌려주다 *dol-lyeo-ju-da*	to return
		갚다 *gap-tta*	to pay back
펜 *pen*	pen	**펜이 잘 나오다** *pe-ni jal na-o-da*	the pen works well
		펜이 안 나오다 *pe-ni an na-o-da*	the pen doesn't work
		펜을 다 쓰다 *pe-neul da sseu-da*	to use up a pen
		검은색 펜 *geo-meun-saek pen*	black pen
또 *tto*	again	**또 잃어버리다** *tto i-reo-beo-ri-da*	to lose again
		또 있다 *tto it-tta*	to have another
		다시 *da-si*	again
이유 *i-yu*	reason	**이유를 모르다** *i-yu-reul mo-reu-da*	to not know the reason
		이유가 없다 *i-yu-ga eop-tta*	to have no reason
		이유를 물어보다 *i-yu-reul mu-reo-bo-da*	to ask the reason

미치다 *mi-chi-da*	to be crazy, to go crazy	**미치겠다** *mi-chi-get-tta*	something is driving me crazy
		미친 사람 *mi-chin sa-ram*	crazy person
		미친 듯이 *mi-chin deu-si*	like crazy
나쁘다 *na-ppeu-da*	to be bad	**나쁜 사람** *na-ppeun sa-ram*	bad person
		기분이 나쁘다 *gi-bu-ni na-ppeu-da*	to feel offended
		나쁘게 *na-ppeu-ge*	badly
아니다 *a-ni-da*	to not be	**사실이 아니다** *sa-si-ri a-ni-da*	to not be true
		사람이 아니다 *sa-ra-mi a-ni-da*	to not be human

LET'S REVIEW!

Read the story again, but this time in Korean!

제 친구는 정말 **착해요.**

그런데 한 가지 **문제**가 있어요.

제가 **연필**을 **빌려주면** 항상 잃어버려요.

어제는 **펜**을 빌려줬어요. **또** 잃어버렸어요.

이유를 모르겠어요. **미치겠어요.**

나쁜 아이는 **아니에요.**

Translation

My friend is very kind-hearted. But there is one matter.
When I lend him a pencil, he always loses them.
Yesterday, I lent him a pen. He lost it again. I don't know why.
It's driving me crazy. He is not a bad person.

Match each Korean word to its English translation.

연필 ·	· pen
펜 ·	· to be bad
이유 ·	· pencil
문제 ·	· to lend
아니다 ·	· to be nice, to be kind-hearted
빌려주다 ·	· to be crazy, to go crazy
착하다 ·	· problem, matter
나쁘다 ·	· reason
미치다 ·	· to not be
또 ·	· again

Crossword Puzzle

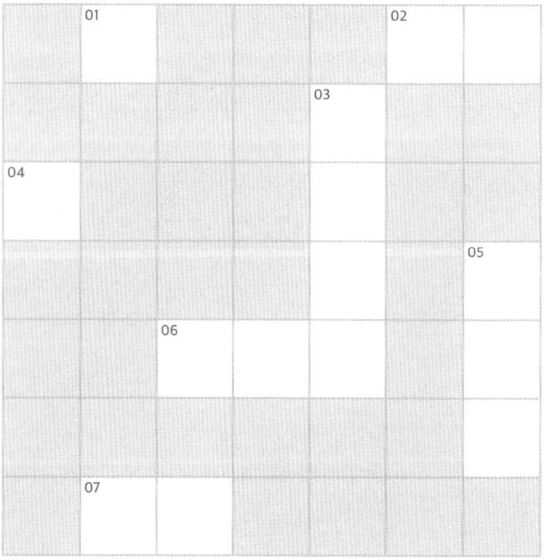

01 again
02 reason
03 to lend
04 pen
05 to be bad
06 to not be
07 problem, matter

Fill in the blanks using one of the words that you learned in Day 44.
(Please refer to page 017 to review how to conjugate verbs/adjectives.)

01 제 친구는 정말 (　　　　　　). My friend is very kind-hearted.

02 그런데 한 가지 (　　　　　　)가 있어요. But there is one matter.

03 제가 (　　　　　　)을 빌려주면 항상 잃어버려요. When I lend him a pencil, he always loses them.

04 제가 연필을 (　　　　　　) 항상 잃어버려요. When I lend him a pencil, he always loses them.

05 어제는 (　　　　　　)을 빌려줬어요. Yesterday, I lent him a pen.

06 (　　　　　　) 잃어버렸어요. He lost it again.

07 (　　　　　　)를 모르겠어요. I don't know why.

08 (　　　　　　). It's driving me crazy.

09 (　　　　　　) 아이는 아니에요. He is not a bad person.

10 나쁜 아이는 (　　　　　　). He is not a bad person.

Day 45

- 결혼
- 식물
- 카드
- 정하다
- 싸다
- 끓이다
- 달다
- 쓰다[03]
- 실망
- 계획

Day 45 LET'S WARM UP!

Imagine the situation in the story below to help you remember the ten Korean words in context.

45

결혼 식물
I changed a lot after **getting married**. I grow **plants** at home.

정하다 카드
I **decided** not to use credit **cards** and use cash (instead).

싸다
I go to the market where they sell stuff for **cheap**.

끓이다
I **boil** soup and cook rice.

But I am still not good at making other foods.

달다 쓰다 03
Some dishes are too **sweet**. Some dishes are too **bitter**.

실망 계획
But I don't get **disappointed**. I **plan** to practice more.

LET'S KEEP THE BALL ROLLING!

Word	Meaning	Related Words	Meaning
결혼 *gyeol-hon*	marriage, wedding	결혼하다 *gyeol-hon-ha-da*	to get married
		결혼식 *gyeol-hon-sik*	wedding ceremony
		결혼 생활 *gyeol-hon saeng-hwal*	married life
식물 *sing-mul*	plant	식물을 기르다 *sing-mu-reul gi-reu-da*	to grow a plant
		식물이 자라다 *sing-mu-ri ja-ra-da*	a plant grows
		동물 *dong-mul*	animal
카드 *ka-deu*	card	신용 카드 *si-nyong ka-deu*	credit card
		생일 카드 *saeng-il ka-deu*	birthday card
		카드를 쓰다 *ka-deu-reul sseu-da*	to use a card, to write a card

정하다 *jeong-ha-da*	to decide, to choose	하기로 정하다 *ha-gi-ro jeong-ha-da*	to decide to do
		장소를 정하다 *jang-so-reul jeong-ha-da*	to decide on a place
		정해지다 *jeong-hae-ji-da*	to be decided
		정한 날짜 *jeong-han nal-jja*	date that has been chosen
싸다 *ssa-da*	to be cheap, to be inexpensive	과일이 싸다 *gwa-i-ri ssa-da*	fruit is cheap
		싼 물건 *ssan mul-geon*	cheap things
		싸게 팔다 *ssa-ge pal-da*	to sell inexpensively
		비싸다 *bi-ssa-da*	to be expensive
끓이다 *kkeu-ri-da*	to boil	끓다 *kkeul-ta*	to boil
		국을 끓이다 *gu-geul kkeu-ri-da*	to boil soup
		차를 끓이다 *cha-reul kkeu-ri-da*	to boil tea
		끓여 먹다 *kkeu-ryeo meok-tta*	to boil and eat

달다 *dal-da*	to be sweet	**초콜릿이 달다** *cho-kol-li-si dal-da*	chocolate is sweet
		단 음식 *dan eum-sik*	sweet food
		단맛 *dan-mat*	sweet taste
쓰다 03 *sseu-da*	to be bitter	**커피가 쓰다** *keo-pi-ga sseu-da*	coffee is bitter
		쓴 약 *sseun yak*	bitter medicine
		쓴맛 *sseun-mat*	bitter taste
실망 *sil-mang*	disappointment	**실망하다** *sil-mang-ha-da*	to be disappointed
		실망이 크다 *sil-mang-i keu-da*	to be greatly disappointed
계획 *gye-hoek*	plan	**계획이 있다** *gye-hoe-gi it-tta*	to have a plan
		계획을 짜다 *gye-hoe-geul jja-da*	to make a plan
		할 계획이다 *hal gye-hoe-gi-da*	to be planning to
		계획하다 *gye-hoe-ka-da*	to plan

LET'S REVIEW!

Read the story again, but this time in Korean!

저는 **결혼**한 다음에 많이 달라졌어요. 집에서 **식물**을 길러요.

카드를 안 쓰고 현금을 쓰기로 **정했어요.**

물건을 **싸게** 파는 시장에 가요. 국을 **끓이고** 밥을 해요.

하지만 다른 음식은 아직 잘 못 해요.

어떤 음식은 너무 **달아요.** 어떤 음식은 너무 **써요.**

그래도 **실망**하지 않아요. 더 연습할 **계획**이에요.

Translation

I changed a lot after getting married. I grow plants at home.
I decided not to use credit cards and use cash (instead). I go to the market where they sell stuff for cheap. I boil soup and cook rice.
But I am still not good at making other foods. Some dishes are too sweet. Some dishes are too bitter. But I don't get disappointed.
I plan to practice more.

Match each Korean word to its English translation.

카드 ·	· to decide, to choose
달다 ·	· disappointment
계획 ·	· plant
결혼 ·	· to be bitter
실망 ·	· marriage, wedding
끓이다 ·	· card
식물 ·	· to boil
정하다 ·	· to be cheap, to be inexpensive
쓰다[03] ·	· to be sweet
싸다 ·	· plan

Crossword Puzzle

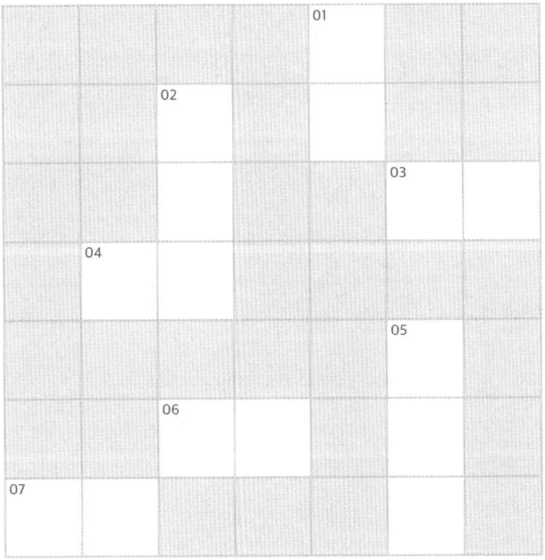

01 plant
02 to decide, to choose
03 disappointment
04 to be cheap, to be inexpensive
05 to boil
06 plan
07 card

Fill in the blanks using one of the words that you learned in Day 45.
(Please refer to page 017 to review how to conjugate verbs/adjectives.)

01 저는 ( )한 다음에 많이 달라졌어요. I changed a lot after getting married.

02 집에서 ( )을 길러요. I grow plants at home.

03 ( )를 안 쓰고 현금을 쓰기로 정했어요. I decided not to use credit cards and use cash (instead).

04 카드를 안 쓰고 현금을 쓰기로 ( ). I decided not to use credit cards and use cash (instead).

05 물건을 ( ) 파는 시장에 가요. I go to the market where they sell stuff for cheap.

06 국을 ( ) 밥을 해요. I boil soup and cook rice.

07 어떤 음식은 너무 ( ). Some dishes are too sweet.

08 어떤 음식은 너무 ( ). Some dishes are too bitter.

09 그래도 ( )하지 않아요. But I don't get disappointed.

10 더 연습할 ( )이에요. I plan to practice more.

Day 46

- 팔다
- 털
- 반지
- 짧다
- 때
- 라디오
- 유리
- 신문
- 종이
- 인사

Day 46 LET'S WARM UP!

Imagine the situation in the story below to help you remember the ten Korean words in context.

46

팔다
I run a clothing store. I sell women's clothes and men's clothes.

털 반지
In winter, I even sell woolen hats. I also sell rings and necklaces.

짧다
These days, short skirts sell well.

때 라디오
When there are no customers, I listen to the radio.

유리
I also wipe down the glass windows of the store.

신문 종이
I normally wipe the glass windows with newspaper or paper.

인사
When a customer comes, I greet them cheerfully.

LET'S KEEP THE BALL ROLLING!

Word	Meaning	Related Words	Meaning
팔다 *pal-da*	to sell	옷을 팔다 *o-seul pal-da*	to sell clothes
		파는 물건 *pa-neun mul-geon*	stuff that one sells
		팔리다 *pal-li-da*	to be sold, to get sold
		사다 *sa-da*	to buy
털 *teol*	fur, hair	털이 많다 *teo-ri man-ta*	to be furry, to have a lot of hair/fur
		털이 부드럽다 *teo-ri bu-deu-reop-tta*	the fur is soft
		털모자 *teol-mo-ja*	woolen hat
반지 *ban-ji*	ring	반지를 끼다 *ban-ji-reul kki-da*	to put on a ring
		반지를 빼다 *ban-ji-reul ppae-da*	to take off a ring
		금반지 *geum-ban-ji*	gold ring
		커플 반지 *keo-peul ban-ji*	couple ring (for boyfriends and girlfriends)

짧다 *jjal-tta*	to be short	다리가 짧다 *da-ri-ga jjal-tta*	one's legs are short
		밤이 짧다 *ba-mi jjal-tta*	the night is short
		짧은 치마 *jjal-beun chi-ma*	short skirt
		짧은 머리 *jjal-beun meo-ri*	short hair

때 *ttae*	time, when	때와 장소 *ttae-wa jang-so*	time and place
		손님이 없을 때 *son-ni-mi eop-sseul ttae*	when there are no customers
		방학 때 *bang-hak ttae*	during school break
		점심때 *jeom-sim-ttae*	at lunch

라디오 *ra-di-o*	radio	라디오를 듣다 *ra-di-o-reul deut-tta*	to listen to the radio
		라디오에 출연하다 *ra-di-o-e chu-ryeon-ha-da*	to appear on the radio
		라디오 주파수 *ra-di-o ju-pa-su*	radio frequency

유리 *yu-ri*	glass	유리가 깨지다 *yu-ri-ga kkae-ji-da*	the glass breaks
		유리로 만들다 *yu-ri-ro man-deul-da*	to make (something) with glass
		유리창 *yu-ri-chang*	glass window
		유리컵 *yu-ri-keop*	glass cup

신문 *sin-mun*	newspaper	**신문을 읽다** *sin-mu-neul ik-tta*	to read the newspaper
		신문에 나다 *sin-mu-ne na-da*	to be in the newspaper
		신문 기사 *sin-mun gi-sa*	newspaper article

종이 *jong-i*	paper	**종이를 찢다** *jong-i-reul jjit-tta*	to tear paper
		종이에 적다 *jong-i-e jeok-tta*	to write down on paper
		종이 한 장 *jong-i han jang*	a piece of paper
		종이컵 *jong-i-keop*	paper cup

인사 *in-sa*	greeting	**인사를 잘하다** *in-sa-reul jal-ha-da*	to greet people well, to be diligent in greeting people
		작별 인사 *jak-ppyeol in-sa*	farewell message, good-bye
		인사말 *in-sa-mal*	words of greeting
		인사하다 *in-sa-ha-da*	to greet

LET'S REVIEW!

Read the story again, but this time in Korean!

저는 옷 가게를 해요. 여자 옷이랑 남자 옷을 **팔아요.**

겨울에는 **털**모자도 팔아요. **반지**랑 목걸이도 팔아요.

요즘에는 **짧은** 치마가 잘 팔려요.

손님이 없을 **때**는 **라디오**를 들어요.

가게 **유리**창을 닦기도 해요.

유리창은 보통 **신문**이나 **종이**로 닦아요.

손님이 오면 밝게 **인사**해요.

Translation

I run a clothing store. I sell women's clothes and men's clothes. In winter, I even sell woolen hats. I also sell rings and necklaces. These days, short skirts sell well. When there are no customers, I listen to the radio. I also wipe down the glass windows of the store. I normally wipe the glass windows with newspaper or paper. When a customer comes, I greet them cheerfully.

Match each Korean word to its English translation.

때 ·	· greeting
짧다 ·	· to sell
인사 ·	· fur, hair
종이 ·	· ring
팔다 ·	· radio
신문 ·	· glass
털 ·	· to be short
유리 ·	· time, when
반지 ·	· paper
라디오 ·	· newspaper

Crossword Puzzle

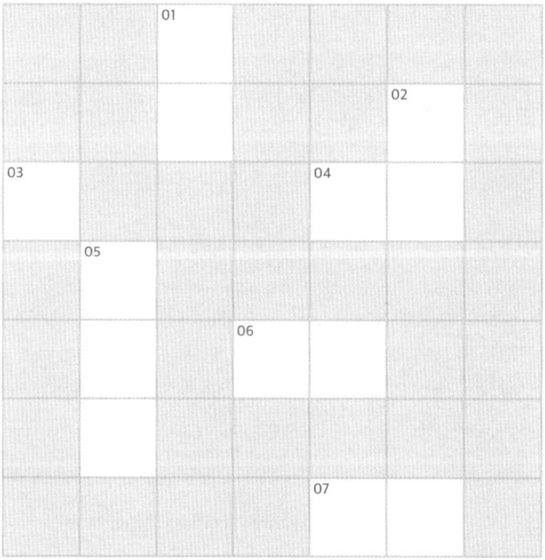

01 greeting
02 to be short
03 time, when
04 to sell
05 radio
06 newspaper
07 paper

Fill in the blanks using one of the words that you learned in Day 46.
(Please refer to page 017 to review how to conjugate verbs/adjectives.)

01 여자 옷이랑 남자 옷을 ( ). — I sell women's clothes and men's clothes.

02 겨울에는 ( )모자도 팔아요. — In winter, I even sell woolen hats.

03 ( )랑 목걸이도 팔아요. — I also sell rings and necklaces.

04 요즘에는 ( ) 치마가 잘 팔려요. — These days, short skirts sell well.

05 손님이 없을 ( )는 라디오를 들어요. — When there are no customers, I listen to the radio.

06 손님이 없을 때는 ( )를 들어요. — When there are no customers, I listen to the radio.

07 가게 ( )창을 닦기도 해요. — I also wipe down the glass windows of the store.

08 유리창은 보통 ( )이나 종이로 닦아요. — I normally wipe the glass windows with newspaper or paper.

09 유리창은 보통 신문이나 ( )로 닦아요. — I normally wipe the glass windows with newspaper or paper.

10 손님이 오면 밝게 ( )해요. — When a customer comes, I greet them cheerfully.

Day 47

- 쌍둥이
- 어리다
- 비슷하다
- 생각하다
- 쉽다
- 안경
- 입
- 멀다
- 뒤
- 실수

Day 47 LET'S WARM UP!

Imagine the situation in the story below to help you remember the ten Korean words in context.

47

쌍둥이 어리다
There are twin brothers at our school. When they were little, they

비슷하다
were very much the same. Now, they just look similar.

생각하다 쉽다
They think similarly, too. But you can easily distinguish them.

안경
The older brother wears glasses. The younger brother has a mole

입 멀다
next to his mouth. But, if you look from afar, you can't easily tell.

뒤
If you also look from behind, you can't know for sure.

실수
You might make a mistake.

LET'S KEEP THE BALL ROLLING!

Word	Meaning	Related Words	Meaning
쌍둥이 *ssang-dung-i*	twin	쌍둥이 형제 *ssang-dung-i hyeong-je*	twin brother
		쌍둥이를 낳다 *ssang-dung-i-reul na-ta*	to give birth to twins
		세쌍둥이 *se-ssang-dung-i*	triplets
어리다 *eo-ri-da*	to be young	나이가 어리다 *na-i-ga eo-ri-da*	to be young
		세 살 어리다 *se sal eo-ri-da*	to be three years younger
		어렸을 때 *eo-ryeo-sseul ttae*	when one was young
		어린 시절 *eo-rin si-jeol*	one's childhood
비슷하다 *bi-seu-ta-da*	to be similar	많이 비슷하다 *ma-ni bi-seu-ta-da*	to be quite similar
		친구랑 비슷하다 *chin-gu-rang bi-seu-ta-da*	to be similar to a friend
		비슷한 노래 *bi-seu-tan no-rae*	similar song
		비슷하게 생기다 *bi-seu-ta-ge saeng-gi-da*	to look similar

생각하다 *saeng-ga-ka-da*	to think	쉽게 생각하다 *swip-kke saeng-ga-ka-da*	to think easily, to think lightly of something
		잘 생각하다 *jal saeng-ga-ka-da*	to think well
		생각 *saeng-gak*	thought
		생각 중이다 *saeng-gak jung-i-da*	to be thinking
쉽다 *swip-tta*	to be easy	시험이 쉽다 *si-heo-mi swip-tta*	the exam is easy
		쉬운 문제 *swi-un mun-je*	easy question
		쉽게 구별하다 *swip-kke gu-byeol-ha-da*	to easily distinguish
안경 *an-gyeong*	glasses	안경을 쓰다 *an-gyeong-eul sseu-da*	to put on one's glasses
		안경을 벗다 *an-gyeong-eul beot-tta*	to take off one's glasses
		안경테 *an-gyeong-te*	eyeglass frames
		동그란 안경 *dong-geu-ran an-gyeong*	round glasses
입 *ip*	mouth	입을 벌리다 *i-beul beol-li-da*	to open one's mouth
		입을 다물다 *i-beul da-mul-da*	to close one's mouth
		입 냄새 *ip naem-sae*	breath smell
		입술 *ip-ssul*	lips

# 멀다 *meol-da*	to be far	집이 멀다 *ji-bi meol-da*	one's house is far away
		거리가 멀다 *geo-ri-ga meol-da*	the distance is far
		멀리 *meol-li*	far away
		멀리서 보다 *meol-li-seo bo-da*	to see from far away

# 뒤 *dwi*	behind, after	뒤에 있다 *dwi-e it-tta*	to be behind
		뒤에서 보다 *dwi-e-seo bo-da*	to look from behind
		며칠 뒤 *myeo-chil dwi*	a few days after
		앞 *ap*	front

# 실수 *sil-ssu*	mistake	작은 실수 *ja-geun sil-ssu*	small mistake
		말실수 *mal-sil-ssu*	slip of the tongue
		실수하다 *sil-ssu-ha-da*	to make a mistake
		실수로 *sil-ssu-ro*	by mistake

LET'S REVIEW!

Read the story again, but this time in Korean!

저희 학교에는 **쌍둥이** 형제가 있어요.

어렸을 때는 아주 똑같았어요. 지금은 **비슷하게** 생겼어요.

생각하는 것도 비슷해요. 하지만 **쉽게** 구별할 수 있어요.

형은 **안경**을 썼어요. 동생은 **입** 옆에 점이 있어요.

그런데 **멀리서** 보면 잘 몰라요. **뒤**에서 봐도 잘 몰라요.

실수할 수도 있어요.

Translation

There are twin brothers at our school. When they were little, they were very much the same. Now, they just look similar. They think similarly, too. But you can easily distinguish them. The older brother wears glasses. The younger brother has a mole next to his mouth. But, if you look from afar, you can't easily tell. If you also look from behind, you can't know for sure. You might make a mistake.

Match each Korean word to its English translation.

비슷하다 ·	· to be far
입 ·	· glasses
실수 ·	· to think
쌍둥이 ·	· to be young
뒤 ·	· twin
쉽다 ·	· mistake
멀다 ·	· behind, after
어리다 ·	· to be similar
안경 ·	· to be easy
생각하다 ·	· mouth

Crossword Puzzle

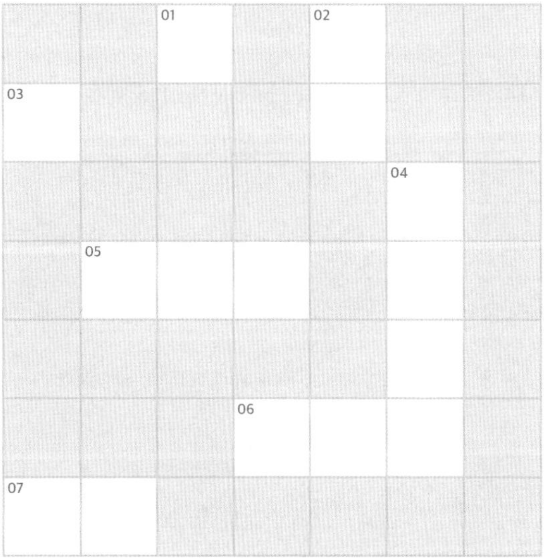

01 behind, after
02 mistake
03 mouth
04 to be similar
05 twin
06 to be young
07 to be easy

Fill in the blanks using one of the words that you learned in Day 47.
(Please refer to page 017 to review how to conjugate verbs/adjectives.)

01 저희 학교에는 ( ) 형제가 있어요. There are twin brothers at our school.

02 ( ) 때는 아주 똑같았어요. When they were little, they were very much the same.

03 지금은 ( ) 생겼어요. Now, they just look similar.

04 ( ) 것도 비슷해요. They think similarly, too.

05 하지만 ( ) 구별할 수 있어요. But you can easily distinguish them.

06 형은 ( )을 썼어요. The older brother wears glasses.

07 동생은 ( ) 옆에 점이 있어요. The younger brother has a mole next to his mouth.

08 그런데 ( ) 보면 잘 몰라요. But, if you look from afar, you can't easily tell.

09 ( )에서 봐도 잘 몰라요. If you also look from behind, you can't know for sure.

10 ( )할 수도 있어요. You might make a mistake.

Day 48

- 축구
- 농구
- 야구
- 지나다
- 이기다
- 팔
- 비밀
- 발가락
- 영어
- 사전

Day 48 LET'S WARM UP!

Imagine the situation in the story below to help you remember the ten Korean words in context.

48

축구 농구 야구

I like all kinds of sports. I like soccer, basketball, baseball,

지나다 이기다

all of them! I played basketball last weekend. My team won.

팔 비밀

But I hurt my arm. I kept it a secret from my mom.

발가락

When I was little, I liked playing soccer, but I hurt my toes often.

So, my mom didn't like me playing sports.

영어

My mom likes it the most when I study English.

사전

I received an English dictionary as my birthday present.

LET'S KEEP THE BALL ROLLING!

Word	Meaning	Related Words	Meaning
축구 *chuk-kku*	soccer	축구를 하다 *chuk-kku-reul ha-da*	to play soccer
		축구 선수 *chuk-kku seon-su*	soccer player
		축구팀 *chuk-kku-tim*	soccer team
농구 *nong-gu*	basketball	농구를 하다 *nong-gu-reul ha-da*	to play basketball
		농구공 *nong-gu-gong*	basketball ball
		농구장 *nong-gu-jang*	basketball court
야구 *ya-gu*	baseball	야구를 하다 *ya-gu-reul ha-da*	to play baseball
		야구 경기 *ya-gu gyeong-gi*	baseball game
		야구 시즌 *ya-gu si-jeun*	baseball season
		프로 야구 *peu-ro ya-gu*	professional baseball

지나다 *ji-na-da*	to pass	**시간이 지나다** *si-ga-ni ji-na-da*	time passes
		날짜가 지나다 *nal-jja-ga ji-na-da*	dates pass
		지난 주말 *ji-nan ju-mal*	past weekend
		지난달 *ji-nan-dal*	past month
		지난주 *ji-nan-ju*	past week
이기다 *i-gi-da*	to win	**쉽게 이기다** *swip-kke i-gi-da*	to win easily
		겨우 이기다 *gyeo-u i-gi-da*	to barely manage to win
		이긴 팀 *i-gin tim*	winning team, team that won
		지다 *ji-da*	to lose
팔 *pal*	arm	**팔을 다치다** *pa-reul da-chi-da*	to hurt one's arm
		왼팔 *oen-pal*	left arm
		오른팔 *o-reun-pal*	right arm
		팔꿈치 *pal-kkum-chi*	elbow

비밀 *bi-mil*	secret	**비밀번호** *bi-mil-beo-no*	password
		비밀 이야기 *bi-mil i-ya-gi*	secret, secret story
		비밀을 지키다 *bi-mi-reul ji-ki-da*	to keep a secret
		비밀로 하다 *bi-mil-lo ha-da*	to keep as a secret
발가락 *bal-kka-rak*	toe	**엄지 발가락** *eom-ji bal-kka-rak*	big toe
		발가락을 다치다 *bal-kka-ra-geul da-chi-da*	to hurt one's toe
영어 *yeong-eo*	English (language)	**영어를 배우다** *yeong-eo-reul bae-u-da*	to learn English
		영어를 잘하다 *yeong-eo-reul jal-ha-da*	to be good at English
		영어로 말하다 *yeong-eo-ro mal-ha-da*	to speak in English
		영어 사전 *yeong-eo sa-jeon*	English dictionary
사전 *sa-jeon*	dictionary	**사전에서 찾다** *sa-jeo-ne-seo chat-tta*	to look up in a dictionary
		한영사전 *ha-nyeong-sa-jeon*	Korean-English dictionary
		전자사전 *jeon-ja-sa-jeon*	electronic dictionary

LET'S REVIEW!

Read the story again, but this time in Korean!

저는 운동을 좋아해요. **축구, 농구, 야구** 다 좋아해요.

지난 주말에 농구를 했어요. 저희 팀이 **이겼어요.**

하지만 **팔**을 다쳤어요. 엄마한테는 **비밀**이에요.

어렸을 때는 축구를 좋아해서 **발가락**을 자주 다쳤어요.

그래서 엄마는 제가 운동하는 것을 싫어해요.

엄마는 제가 **영어** 공부하는 것을 제일 좋아해요.

엄마한테 생일 선물로 영어 **사전**을 받았어요.

Translation

I like all kinds of sports. I like soccer, basketball, baseball, all of them! I played basketball last weekend. My team won. But I hurt my arm. I kept it a secret from my mom. When I was little, I liked playing soccer, but I hurt my toes often. So, my mom didn't like me playing sports. My mom likes it the most when I study English.
I received an English dictionary as my birthday present.

Match each Korean word to its English translation.

이기다 ·	· toe
지나다 ·	· secret
사전 ·	· arm
축구 ·	· basketball
영어 ·	· dictionary
발가락 ·	· baseball
비밀 ·	· to pass
농구 ·	· English (language)
야구 ·	· soccer
팔 ·	· to win

Crossword Puzzle

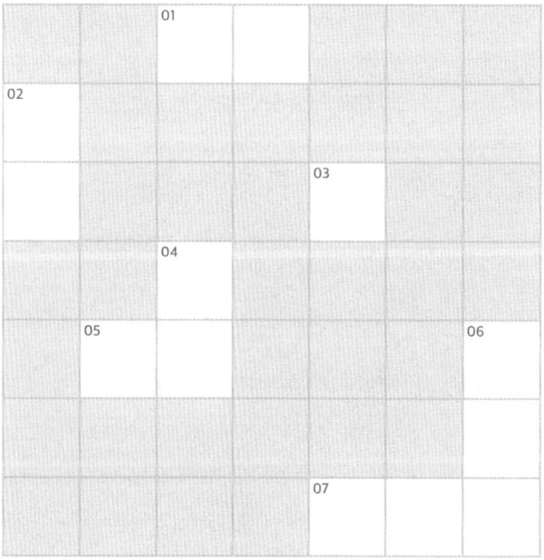

01 secret
02 dictionary
03 arm
04 baseball
05 soccer
06 to pass
07 to win

Fill in the blanks using one of the words that you learned in Day 48.
(Please refer to page 017 to review how to conjugate verbs/adjectives.)

01 (   ), 농구, 야구 다 좋아해요. — I like soccer, basketball, baseball, all of them!

02 축구, (   ), 야구 다 좋아해요. — I like soccer, basketball, baseball, all of them!

03 축구, 농구, (   ) 다 좋아해요. — I like soccer, basketball, baseball, all of them!

04 (   ) 주말에 농구를 했어요. — I played basketball last weekend.

05 저희 팀이 (   ). — My team won.

06 하지만 (   )을 다쳤어요. — But I hurt my arm.

07 엄마한테는 (   )이에요. — I kept it a secret from my mom.

08 어렸을 때는 축구를 좋아해서 (   )을 자주 다쳤어요. — When I was little, I liked playing soccer, but I hurt my toes often.

09 엄마는 제가 (   ) 공부하는 것을 제일 좋아해요. — My mom likes it the most when I study English.

10 엄마한테 생일 선물로 영어 (   )을 받았어요. — I received an English dictionary as my birthday present.

Day 49

- 주차장
- 고르다
- 표
- 세다
- 불
- 날다
- 지구
- 우주
- 알아듣다
- 바꾸다

Day 49 LET'S WAIRM UP!

Imagine the situation in the story below to help you remember the ten Korean words in context.

I got out of the car in the parking lot (주차장) of the movie theater. I went up to the ticket counter and chose (고르다) a movie. I bought a ticket (표).

I went inside. There were not that many people. I counted (세다) the number of people. There were ten people. The lights (불) went out and the movie started. The main character flew (날다) around the sky. He left Earth (지구) and went to space (우주). But the person next to me was loud, so it was hard to understand (알아듣다). So, I changed (바꾸다) seats.

LET'S KEEP THE BALL ROLLING!

Word	Meaning	Related Words	Meaning
주차장 *ju-cha-jang*	parking lot	주차장이 넓다 *ju-cha-jang-i neol-tta*	the parking lot is big
		무료 주차장 *mu-ryo ju-cha-jang*	free parking lot
		유료 주차장 *yu-ryo ju-cha-jang*	paid parking lot
		지하 주차장 *ji-ha ju-cha-jang*	underground parking lot
고르다 *go-reu-da*	to pick, to choose	세 개 중에서 고르다 *se gae jung-e-seo go-reu-da*	to choose out of three
		하나를 고르다 *ha-na-reul go-reu-da*	to choose one
		고르기 어렵다 *go-reu-gi eo-ryeop-tta*	to be hard to pick
표 *pyo*	ticket	표를 사다 *pyo-reul sa-da*	to buy a ticket
		표가 다 팔리다 *pyo-ga da pal-li-da*	the tickets are sold out
		표 두 장 *pyo du jang*	two tickets

세다 *se-da*	to count	숫자를 세다 *sut-jja-reul se-da*	to count numbers
		돈을 세다 *do-neul se-da*	to count money
		사람 수를 세다 *sa-ram su-reul se-da*	to count the number of people
		세어 보다 *se-eo bo-da*	to count

불 *bul*	fire, light	불을 켜다 *bu-reul kyeo-da*	to turn on the light
		불을 끄다 *bu-reul kkeu-da*	to turn off the light
		산불 *san-ppul*	forest fire, wildfire
		뜨거운 불 *tteu-geo-un bul*	hot fire

날다 *nal-da*	to fly	하늘을 날다 *ha-neu-reul nal-da*	to fly in the sky
		새가 날다 *sae-ga nal-da*	a bird flies
		날아가다 *na-ra-ga-da*	to fly somewhere
		날개 *nal-gae*	wing

지구 *ji-gu*	Earth	**지구에 살다** *ji-gu-e sal-da*	to live on Earth
		지구가 돌다 *ji-gu-ga dol-da*	the Earth rotates
		태양 *tae-yang*	the Sun
우주 *u-ju*	cosmos, universe, space	**우주에 가다** *u-ju-e ga-da*	to go to space
		우주여행 *u-ju-yeo-haeng*	space travel
		우주선 *u-ju-seon*	spaceship
알아듣다 *a-ra-deut-tta*	to understand	**알아들을 수 없다** *a-ra-deu-reul su eop-tta*	to not be able to understand
		못 알아듣다 *mot a-ra-deut-tta*	to not understand
		잘 알아듣다 *jal a-ra-deut-tta*	to understand well
		알아듣기 힘들다 *a-ra-deut-kki him-deul-da*	to be hard to understand
바꾸다 *ba-kku-da*	to change	**표를 바꾸다** *pyo-reul ba-kku-da*	to change tickets
		이름을 바꾸다 *i-reu-meul ba-kku-da*	to change one's name
		바꾼 자리 *ba-kkun ja-ri*	seats that have been switched

LET'S REVIEW!

Read the story again, but this time in Korean!

영화관 **주차장**에 내렸어요.

매표소로 올라가서 영화를 **골랐어요.**

표를 샀어요. 안으로 들어갔어요. 사람들이 별로 없었어요.

사람 수를 **세어** 봤어요. 열 명 있었어요.

불이 꺼지고 영화가 시작됐어요. 주인공이 하늘을 **날았어요.**

지구를 떠나서 **우주**로 갔어요. 그런데 옆 사람이 시끄러워서

알아듣기 힘들었어요. 그래서 자리를 **바꿨어요.**

Translation

I got out of the car in the parking lot of the movie theater. I went up to the ticket counter and chose a movie. I bought a ticket. I went inside. There were not that many people. I counted the number of people. There were ten people. The lights went out and the movie started. The main character flew around the sky. He left Earth and went to space. But the person next to me was loud, so it was hard to understand. So, I changed seats.

Match each Korean word to its English translation.

불 ·	· to count
날다 ·	· to understand
바꾸다 ·	· cosmos, universe, space
우주 ·	· parking lot
주차장 ·	· to pick, to choose
세다 ·	· Earth
알아듣다 ·	· fire, light
고르다 ·	· ticket
지구 ·	· to fly
표 ·	· to change

Crossword Puzzle

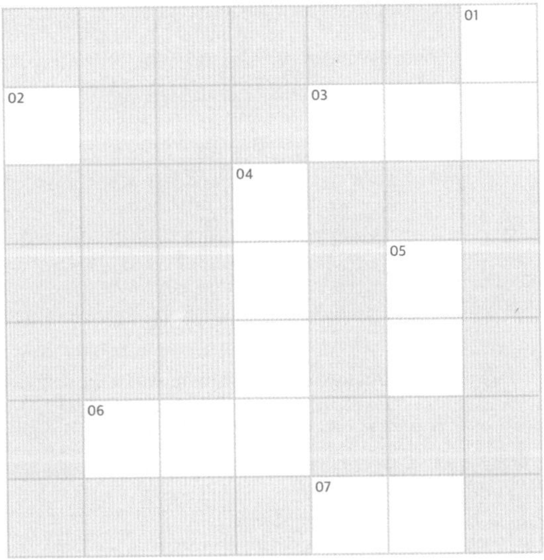

01 to count
02 ticket
03 to pick, to choose
04 to understand
05 Earth
06 to change
07 cosmos, universe, space

Fill in the blanks using one of the words that you learned in Day 49.
(Please refer to page 017 to review how to conjugate verbs/adjectives.)

01 영화관 (   )에 내렸어요. — I got out of the car in the parking lot of the movie theater.

02 매표소로 올라가서 영화를 (   ). — I went up to the ticket counter and chose a movie.

03 (   )를 샀어요. — I bought a ticket.

04 사람 수를 (   ) 봤어요. — I counted the number of people.

05 (   )이 꺼지고 영화가 시작됐어요. — The lights went out and the movie started.

06 주인공이 하늘을 (   ). — The main character flew around the sky.

07 (   )를 떠나서 우주로 갔어요. — He left Earth and went to space.

08 지구를 떠나서 (   )로 갔어요. — He left Earth and went to space.

09 그런데 옆 사람이 시끄러워서 (   ) 힘들었어요. — But the person next to me was loud, so it was hard to understand.

10 그래서 자리를 (   ). — So, I changed seats.

Day 50

- 운전
- 느리다
- 내리다
- 열쇠
- 잡다
- 그것
- 가볍다
- 휴지
- 맞다
- 서다

Day 50 LET'S WARM UP!

Imagine the situation in the story below to help you remember the ten Korean words in context.

운전

I drove to the supermarket.

느리다 내리다

I slowly parked and got out of the car.

열쇠

I dropped my key. The key went under the car.

잡다

I reached down and grabbed the key.

그것 가볍다 휴지

But, it (what I picked up) was too light. It was trash.

맞다

I reached down again. This time, it was heavy. It was indeed a key.

서다

People who were standing around were looking at me.

LET'S KEEP THE BALL ROLLING!

Word	Meaning	Related Words	Meaning
운전 *un-jeon*	driving	운전을 배우다 *un-jeo-neul bae-u-da*	to learn to drive
		운전하다 *un-jeon-ha-da*	to drive
		차를 운전하다 *cha-reul un-jeon-ha-da*	to drive a car
		운전면허 *un-jeon-myeon-heo*	driver's license
느리다 *neu-ri-da*	to be slow	말이 느리다 *ma-ri neu-ri-da*	to speak slowly
		시계가 느리다 *si-gye-ga neu-ri-da*	the clock is slow
		느리게 *neu-ri-ge*	slowly
		느리게 기어가다 *neu-ri-ge gi-eo-ga-da*	to crawl slowly
내리다 *nae-ri-da*	to get off/out of (a vehicle)	차에서 내리다 *cha-e-seo nae-ri-da*	to get out of a car
		서울에 내리다 *seo-u-re nae-ri-da*	to get off in Seoul
		타다 *ta-da*	to ride, to get in a vehicle

열쇠 *yeol-ssoe*	key	열쇠를 잃어버리다 *yeol-ssoe-reul i-reo-beo-ri-da*	to lose a key
		열쇠를 떨어뜨리다 *yeol-ssoe-reul tteo-reo-tteu-ri-da*	to drop a key
		집 열쇠 *jip yeol-ssoe*	house key
		열쇠고리 *yeol-ssoe-go-ri*	keychain
잡다 *jap-tta*	to grab, to hold	손을 잡다 *so-neul jap-tta*	to hold someone's hand
		손잡이를 잡다 *son-ja-bi-reul jap-tta*	to hold a handle/knob
		꼭 잡다 *kkok jap-tta*	to hold firmly
		놓다 *no-ta*	to let go
그것 *geu-geot*	it, that	그거 *geu-geo*	that, that thing
		그게 *geu-ge*	that is
		그 *geu*	the, that
		이것 *i-geot*	this thing
		저것 *jeo-geot*	that thing

가볍다 *ga-byeop-tta*	to be light	가방이 가볍다 *ga-bang-i ga-byeop-tta*	the bag is light
		몸이 가볍다 *mo-mi ga-byeop-tta*	one's body is light
		가벼운 짐 *ga-byeo-un jim*	light luggage
		무겁다 *mu-geop-tta*	to be heavy

휴지 *hyu-ji*	tissue, toilet paper, trash	휴지 한 장 *hyu-ji han jang*	one tissue
		휴지통 *hyu-ji-tong*	trash can, rubbish bin
		화장실 *hwa-jang-sil*	bathroom

맞다 *mat-tta*	to be correct, to be right	답이 맞다 *da-bi mat-tta*	the answer is correct
		맞는 말 *man-neun mal*	words that are right/true
		틀리다 *teul-li-da*	to be wrong

서다 *seo-da*	to stand	서 있다 *seo it-tta*	to be standing
		일어서다 *i-reo-seo-da*	to stand up
		앉다 *an-tta*	to sit

LET'S REVIEW!

Read the story again, but this time in Korean!

운전을 해서 마트에 갔어요.

느리게 주차를 하고 차에서 **내렸어요.**

열쇠를 떨어뜨렸어요. 열쇠가 차 아래로 들어갔어요.

손을 넣어서 열쇠를 **잡았어요.**

그런데 **그것**은 너무 **가벼웠어요.**

휴지였어요. 다시 손을 넣었어요. 이번에는 무거웠어요.

열쇠가 **맞았어요. 서** 있는 사람들이 저를 쳐다봤어요.

Translation

I drove to the supermarket. I slowly parked and got out of the car. I dropped my key. The key went under the car. I reached down and grabbed the key. But, it (what I picked up) was too light. It was trash. I reached down again. This time, it was heavy. It was indeed a key. People who were standing around were looking at me.

Match each Korean word to its English translation.

열쇠 ·	· to be correct, to be right
서다 ·	· to be light
가볍다 ·	· to get off/out of (a vehicle)
운전 ·	· it, that
맞다 ·	· key
느리다 ·	· driving
그것 ·	· to stand
내리다 ·	· to grab, to hold
휴지 ·	· to be slow
잡다 ·	· tissue, toilet paper, trash

Crossword Puzzle

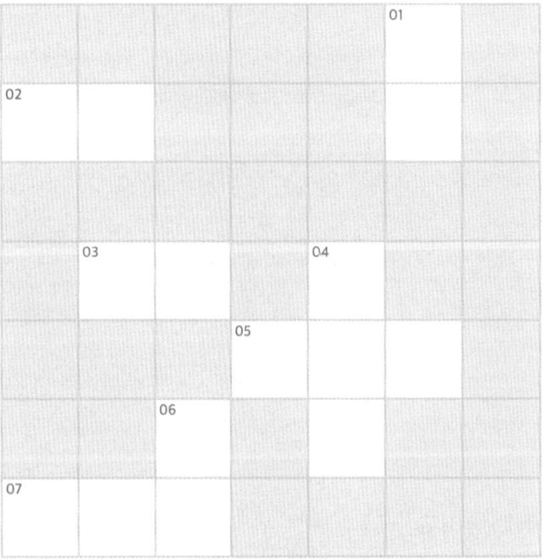

01 tissue, toilet paper, trash
02 it, that
03 key
04 to get off/out of (a vehicle)
05 to be slow
06 to grab, to hold
07 to be light

Fill in the blanks using one of the words that you learned in Day 50.
(Please refer to page 017 to review how to conjugate verbs/adjectives.)

01 (   )을 해서 마트에 갔어요. I drove to the supermarket.

02 (   ) 주차를 하고 차에서 내렸어요. I slowly parked and got out of the car.

03 느리게 주차를 하고
차에서 (   ). I slowly parked and got out of the car.

04 (   )를 떨어뜨렸어요. I dropped my key.

05 손을 넣어서 열쇠를 (   ). I reached down and grabbed the key.

06 그런데 (   )은 너무 가벼웠어요. But, it (what I picked up) was too light.

07 그런데 그것은 너무 (   ). But, it (what I picked up) was too light.

08 (   )였어요. It was trash.

09 열쇠가 (   ). It was indeed a key.

10 (   ) 있는 사람들이 저를 쳐다봤어요. People who were standing around were looking at me.

QUIZ
DAY 41-50

01 What is **"airport"** in Korean?

a. 궁항 b. 공항 c. 공헝 d. 공향

02 What does 대학교 mean in English?

a. high school b. elementary school
c. university d. middle school

03 What is the antonym of 가깝다?

a. 말다 b. 멀다 c. 몰다 d. 물다

04 How do you say **"English (language)"** in Korean?

a. 영어 b. 식물 c. 안경 d. 이유

05 Which of the following words is a place?

a. 비밀 b. 실수 c. 결혼 d. 편의점

06 Which word is most related to age?

a. 아니다 b. 고르다 c. 어리다 d. 모르다

07 Besides "to write" or "to use", what other meaning does 쓰다 have?

a. to be easy b. to be cheap

c. to be bitter d. to be sweet

08 Choose the item that refers to a direction.

a. 은행 b. 왼쪽 c. 지갑 d. 짧다

09 Choose the word that best replaces ○.

축○ = soccer 농○ = basketball 야○ = baseball

a. 구 b. 고 c. 그 d. 가

10 Choose the word that best replaces ○.

기차○ = train station 지하철○ = subway station

a. 뒤 b. 또 c. 역 d. 털

11 "[something] boils" is 끓다 in Korean. What is **"to boil [something]"** in Korean?

a. 끓히다 b. 끓이다 c. 끓리다 d. 끓기다

12 Choose the term that is **NOT** a loanword from English.

a. 팔 b. 펜 c. 라디오 d. 카드

13 How do Korean boys address an older brother?

a. 입 b. 표 c. 불 d. 형

14 What is 신문 made of?

a. 가방 b. 종이 c. 열쇠 d. 반지

15 Which of the following does **NOT** refer to an action?

a. 들어가다 b. 내리다 c. 건너다 d. 나쁘다

16 Where do you park your car?

a. 오른쪽 b. 서점 c. 주차장 d. 발가락

17 Which of the following terms becomes a noun and keeps the same meaning if you dettach 하다?

a. 생각하다 b. 비슷하다 c. 정하다 d. 착하다

18 Which of the following does **NOT** become a verb if you attach -하다?

a. 운전 b. 실망 c. 계획 d. 연필

19 What does 길을 잃어버리다 mean in English?

a. to find the way b. to throw away

c. to lose money d. to get lost

20 What 색깔 is the 자동차 in the picture?

a. 검은색

b. 하얀색

c. 빨간색

d. none of the above

QUIZ
DAY 41-50

Answers : b c b a d / c c b a c / b a d b d / c a d d a

ANTONYMS

ANSWERS

INDEX

ANTONYMS

Here is a compilation of words that have the opposite meaning from one another.
All of these words appear in this book.

I, me	나	↔	너	you
busy	바쁘다	↔	한가하다	to be free, to not be busy
weekend	주말	↔	평일	weekday
to wear, to put on	입다	↔	벗다	to take off clothes
to be dirty	더럽다	↔	깨끗하다	to be clean
up	위	↔	아래	down
to be hungry	배고프다	↔	배부르다	to be full
to give	주다	↔	받다	to receive
teacher	선생님	↔	학생	student
to be a lot	많다	↔	적다	to be few, to be little
winter	겨울	↔	여름	summer
grandmother	할머니	↔	할아버지	grandfather
to go	가다	↔	오다	to come
to ride, to get on/in (a vehicle)	타다	↔	내리다	to get off/out of (a vehicle)
man	남자	↔	여자	woman
to fight, to argue	싸우다	↔	화해하다	to make up (with), to reconcile (with)

to lose	지다	↔	이기다	to win
to close	닫다	↔	열다	to open
to listen, to hear	듣다	↔	말하다	to talk, to tell
to exist, to have, to be	있다	↔	없다	to not have, to not be, to not exist
to live	살다	↔	죽다	to die
to be sad	슬프다	↔	기쁘다	to be glad, to be happy
younger brother/sister	동생	↔	형	older brother (for a boy)
to cry	울다	↔	웃다	to laugh, to smile
to borrow, to rent	빌리다	↔	빌려주다	to lend
to be cold	차갑다	↔	뜨겁다	to be hot
to teach	가르치다	↔	배우다	to learn
to write	쓰다	↔	지우다	to erase
to be good	좋다	↔	나쁘다	to be bad
to like	좋다	↔	싫다	to hate, to dislike, to be displeasing
to be fun	재미있다	↔	재미없다	to be boring
dad	아빠	↔	엄마	mom
to be delicious	맛있다	↔	맛없다	to be not tasty
to dislike, to hate	싫어하다	↔	좋아하다	to like

to be hot (temperature)	**덥다**	↔	**춥다**	to be cold
outside	**밖**	↔	**안**	inside
to go out	**나가다**	↔	**들어오다**	to come in
to turn on	**켜다**	↔	**끄다**	to turn off
to be cool (temperature)	**시원하다**	↔	**따뜻하다**	to be warm
night	**밤**	↔	**낮**	day, daytime
to lie down	**눕다**	↔	**일어나다**	to get up
afternoon	**오후**	↔	**오전**	morning
arrival	**도착**	↔	**출발**	departure
daughter	**딸**	↔	**아들**	son
to be the same	**같다**	↔	**다르다**	to be different
morning	**아침**	↔	**저녁**	evening
to forget	**잊어버리다**	↔	**기억하다**	to remember
to depart	**출발하다**	↔	**도착하다**	to arrive
countryside	**시골**	↔	**도시**	city
to be noisy	**시끄럽다**	↔	**조용하다**	to be quiet
to be high	**높다**	↔	**낮다**	to be low
to be dark	**어둡다**	↔	**밝다**	to be bright
to go down	**내려가다**	↔	**올라가다**	to go up

to be big	크다	↔	작다	to be small
to be long	길다	↔	짧다	to be short
to sit	앉다	↔	서다	to stand
to be heavy	무겁다	↔	가볍다	to be light
to put in	넣다	↔	빼다	to take out, to pull out
to be narrow	좁다	↔	넓다	to be wide
to be comfortable	편하다	↔	힘들다	to be difficult, to be tiring, to be hard
to be expensive	비싸다	↔	싸다	to be cheap
spring (season)	봄	↔	가을	fall, autumn
to know	알다	↔	모르다	to not know
to do well, to be good at	잘하다	↔	못하다	to not do well, to be bad at
failure	실패	↔	성공	success
to be difficult, to be hard	어렵다	↔	쉽다	to be easy
to send	보내다	↔	받다	to receive
to come out	나오다	↔	들어가다	to go in, to enter
to work	일하다	↔	쉬다	to rest
hand	손	↔	발	foot
to be difficult, to be tiring, to be hard	힘들다	↔	쉽다	to be easy

to buy	**사다**	↔	**팔다**	to sell
to lose, to misplace	**잃어버리다**	↔	**찾다**	to find
to ask	**물어보다**	↔	**대답하다**	to answer
to be close	**가깝다**	↔	**멀다**	to be far
right side, right-hand side	**오른쪽**	↔	**왼쪽**	left side, left-hand side
front	**앞**	↔	**뒤**	behind, after
black	**검은색**	↔	**하얀색**	white
to be sweet	**달다**	↔	**쓰다**	to be bitter
to be slow	**느리다**	↔	**빠르다**	to be quick
to grab, to hold	**잡다**	↔	**놓다**	to let go
to be correct, to be right	**맞다**	↔	**틀리다**	to be wrong

ANSWERS

Day 01 page 047

Match

주말	I, me
만나다	to meet
보통	movie
카페	to be busy
너무	café
바쁘다	we, our
나	usually, usual
회사원	weekend
영화	company employee
우리	too, very

Crossword Puzzle

			만			
			나		주	말
	바	쁘	다			
나					회	
		우	리		사	
					원	
	보	통				

Fill in the blanks

01 제
02 회사원
03 너무
04 바빠요
05 저희
06 보통
07 주말
08 만나요
09 영화
10 카페

Day 02 page 055

Match

회사	make-up
물	to wear, to put on
일찍	clothes
세수	to drink
일어나다	water
마시다	every day
매일	company
옷	early
입다	to get up
화장	washing one's face

Crossword Puzzle

	물					입
			일	어	나	다
화	장		찍			
					마	
	회	사			시	
					다	

Fill in the blanks

01 매일
02 일찍
03 일어나요
04 물
05 마시고
06 세수
07 옷
08 입고
09 화장
10 회사

Day 03

page 063

Match

공책	pencil case
더럽다	up, top
청소	notebook
깨끗하다	desk
시험	to begin, to start
시작하다	to be clean
필통	text, exam
의자	chair
책상	to be dirty
위	cleaning

Crossword Puzzle

				필	통	
	공	책				위
		상				
깨					더	
끗					럽	
하		시	작	하	다	
다						

Fill in the blanks

01 시험
02 의자
03 책상
04 더러워요
05 위
06 청소
07 깨끗해요
08 공책
09 필통
10 시작해요

Day 04

page 071

Match

졸다	to be full
무섭다	to doze
배고프다	teacher
아까	to be scary
빵	to give
선생님	now
음료수	earlier
주다	bread
지금	beverage
배부르다	to be hungry

Crossword Puzzle

	빵		주	다		
					배	
음	료	수			부	
					르	
		배	고	프	다	
	아					
	까			지	금	

Fill in the blanks

01 배고파요
02 아까
03 빵
04 음료수
05 줬어요
06 지금
07 배불러요
08 졸면
09 선생님
10 무서워요

Day 05

page 079

Match

어른	to be a lot
공원	adult, grown-up
아기	child
신기하다	to be few, to be little
어떻게	park
학교	family
적다	baby
어린이	school
가족	to be interesting
많다	how

Crossword Puzzle

					학	
	어	린	이		교	
	른					적
			신	기	하	다
어	떻	게				
		가	족			

Fill in the blanks

01 어린이
02 학교
03 가족
04 공원
05 많았어요
06 어른
07 아기
08 적었어요
09 신기했어요
10 어떻게

Day 06 page 087

Match

동물	bus
가다	subway
겨울	to ride
타다	school vacation
놀다	winter
할머니	cat
방학	animal
지하철	to hang out
고양이	grandmother
버스	to go

Crossword Puzzle

					동	물
		놀				
	가	다				
지				할	머	니
하		방				
철		학		겨		
				울		

Fill in the blanks

01 겨울
02 방학
03 할머니
04 가요
05 버스
06 지하철
07 타요
08 고양이
09 동물
10 놀고

Day 07 page 095

Match

샴푸	underwear
티셔츠	socks
속옷	hairdryer
휴가	t-shirt
남자	vacation, leave
양말	pants
드라이기	man
바지	shampoo
린스	woman
여자	hair conditioner

Crossword Puzzle

				양	말	
드	라	이	기			
						여
	린				남	자
	스					
			티	셔	츠	
샴	푸					

Fill in the blanks

01 휴가
02 남자
03 여자
04 샴푸
05 린스
06 속옷
07 양말
08 드라이기
09 바지
10 티셔츠

Day 08 page 103

Match

닫다	TV drama
싸우다	news
음악	to lose
듣다	music
뉴스	to listen, to hear
방	older sister
누나	room
텔레비전	to fight, to argue
드라마	television
지다	to close

Crossword Puzzle

			텔	레	비	전
	드					
	라		싸			
	마		우		누	나
		닫	다			
					듣	
				지	다	

Fill in the blanks

01 누나
02 텔레비전
03 드라마
04 뉴스
05 싸웠어요
06 져요
07 방
08 닫고
09 음악
10 들었어요

Day 09 page 111

Match

죽다	name
슬프다	time
동생	to live
개	tear
시간	younger sibling
있다	dog
살다	to cry
이름	to exist, to have
눈물	to be sad
울다	to die

Crossword Puzzle

					개	
			울			
	슬	프	다			
				있		
	이		살	다		
	름					
				시	간	

Fill in the blanks

01 개
02 있었어요
03 이름
04 시간
05 살았어요
06 죽었어요
07 슬퍼요
08 동생
09 울었어요
10 눈물

Day 10 page 119

Match

수영	store
수건	soap
차갑다	to teach
돈	strength, power
어깨	swimming
빌리다	to be cold
비누	towel
가게	money
가르치다	shoulder
힘	to borrow, to rent

Crossword Puzzle

			가	게		
	힘		르			
			치			
	빌	리	다		수	건
					영	
		차	갑	다		

Fill in the blanks

01 수영
02 수건
03 가게
04 돈
05 빌렸어요
06 비누
07 차가웠어요
08 어깨
09 힘
10 가르쳐

Day 11 page 131

Match

쓰다 **01**	to receive
기쁘다	to be good
받다	earrings
무엇	necklace
목걸이	to write
좋다	tomorrow
선물	to be close
친하다	present, gift
귀고리	to be glad
내일	what

Crossword Puzzle

		기				
		쁘		내	일	
친	하	다				
	귀		선	물		좋
	고				받	다
	리					

Fill in the blanks

01 내일
02 친한
03 쓸
04 받으면
05 기뻐할까요
06 선물
07 뭐
08 좋을까요
09 귀고리
10 목걸이

Day 12 page 139

Match

친구	to congratulate
축하하다	birthday
춤	friend
오늘	day, one day
먹다	song
생일	today
하루	classroom
재미있다	to eat
교실	dance
노래	to be fun

Crossword Puzzle

		오	늘			
먹						
다				축		
	노	래		하	루	
				하		
	재	미	있	다		친
						구

Fill in the blanks

01 오늘
02 생일
03 교실
04 먹었어요
05 친구
06 노래
07 춤
08 축하해
09 재미있는
10 하루

Day 13 page 147

Match

보다	restaurant
커피	to walk
음식	to see, to watch
식당	dad
아빠	to be happy
행복하다	sea, ocean
바다	coffee
별	to be delicious
맛있다	star
걷다	food

Crossword Puzzle

		커				
별		피				맛
						있
			행	복	하	다
	보					
바	다			음		
				식		

Fill in the blanks

01 아빠
02 바다
03 걸었어요
04 식당
05 맛있는
06 음식
07 커피
08 별
09 봤어요
10 행복했어요

Day 14 page 155

Match

집	to be hot
나가다	summer
얼음	to be cool
에어컨	to turn on
여름	to dislike, to hate
시원하다	outside
덥다	to go out
싫어하다	ice
켜다	house, home
밖	air conditioner

Crossword Puzzle

		싫				
		어			여	름
시	원	하	다			
		다				
	밖				켜	
			나	가	다	
		집				

Fill in the blanks

01 여름
02 싫어해요
03 더워요
04 밖
05 나가요
06 집
07 에어컨
08 켜요
09 시원한
10 얼음

Day 15 page 163

Match

눕다	bed
벌써	book
읽다	milk
냉장고	already
침대	bathroom
잠	to read
화장실	night
우유	to lie down
밤	sleep
책	refrigerator

Crossword Puzzle

			침			
	냉		대		우	유
	장					
	고			밤		
		눕		화	장	실
	읽	다				

Fill in the blanks

01 벌써
02 밤
03 침대
04 누워요
05 잠
06 화장실
07 책
08 읽어요
09 냉장고
10 우유

Day 16 page 171

Match

뜨겁다	computer
이메일	to charge
중요하다	to be hot
컵	e-mail
바르다	make-up product
컴퓨터	cup
충전하다	to be important
화장품	to apply, to put on
거울	laptop computer
노트북	mirror

Crossword Puzzle

	거					
	울		컵		충	
					전	
			중	요	하	다
		바			다	
		르				
뜨	겁	다		노	트	북

Fill in the blanks

01 컵
02 뜨거운
03 컴퓨터
04 이메일
05 노트북
06 충전해요
07 중요한
08 거울
09 화장품
10 발라요

Day 17 page 179

Match

부부	invitation
오후	arrival
딸	side, next to
같다	age
사이	kindergarten
옆	married couple
유치원	relationship
초대	afternoon
나이	daughter
도착	to be the same

Crossword Puzzle

	오	후				
					부	
			나		부	
		사	이			
딸				유		
				치		
	초	대		원		

Fill in the blanks

01 옆
02 부부
03 초대
04 오후
05 도착
06 딸
07 나이
08 같아요
09 유치원
10 사이

Day 18 page 187

Match

아침	game
점심	rice, food, meal
아들	to feel angry
화나다	morning
걱정	son
공부	why
밥	lunch
게임	study
왜	day of the week
요일	worry, concern

Crossword Puzzle

				밥		
	아	침				
	들				요	
			화		일	
걱	정		나			
			다			
					왜	

Fill in the blanks

01 아들
02 게임
03 토요일
04 아침
05 점심
06 밥
07 화났어요
08 걱정
09 왜
10 공부

Day 19 page 195

Match

날짜	feeling
전화번호	calendar
빨리	to forget
느낌	shape
아래	date
출발하다	phone number
잊어버리다	reservation
달력	to depart
예약	fast, quickly
모양	down, below

Crossword Puzzle

아				모	양	
래		잊				
		어			달	력
		버		느		
	빨	리		낌		
		다				
			전	화	번	호

Fill in the blanks

01 느낌
02 달력
03 날짜
04 모양
05 아래
06 전화번호
07 잊어버렸어요
08 빨리
09 예약
10 출발해요

Day 20 page 203

Match

도시	to be quiet
등산	the sun
낮다	to be noisy
내려가다	to be high
어둡다	to go down
시골	hiking
시끄럽다	city
해	to be dark
높다	to be low
조용하다	countryside

Crossword Puzzle

			도			
	내		시			해
	려				시	
	가				끄	
낮	다				럽	
		조	용	하	다	
등	산					

Fill in the blanks

01 시골
02 도시
03 시끄러워요
04 조용해요
05 등산
06 높은
07 낮은
08 해
09 어두워요
10 내려가요

Day 21 page 215

Match

키	eye
얼굴	to be big
웃다	entertainer
귀엽다	who
연예인	one's height
눈 **01**	to be long
길다	face
다리	to laugh, to smile
크다	to be cute
누구	leg

Crossword Puzzle

	키					
					길	
누			귀	엽	다	
구						
					눈	
	연	예	인			
					다	리

Fill in the blanks

01 연예인
02 누구
03 키
04 커요
05 웃는
06 얼굴
07 귀여워요
08 눈
09 다리
10 길어요

Day 22 page 223

Match

비행기	beginning
창문	together
이따가	to sit
구름	later
앉다	older sister
여행	sky
언니	travel
하늘	cloud
처음	window
같이	airplane

Crossword Puzzle

					언	
	같	이			니	
		따				
처		가		구	름	
음						
	하		비	행	기	
	늘					

Fill in the blanks

01 언니
02 같이
03 여행
04 비행기
05 처음
06 창문
07 앉았어요
08 이따가
09 하늘
10 구름

Day 23 page 231

Match

넣다	to be heavy
엘리베이터	to lift, to carry
무겁다	to be narrow
빼다	floor
들다	contact
좁다	to help
상자	elevator
도와주다	to put in
연락	to take out
층	box

Crossword Puzzle

	층					엘
			들			리
도	와	주	다			베
						이
	상	자			무	터
					겁	
			넣		다	

Fill in the blanks

01 연락
02 도와줄
03 층
04 엘리베이터
05 무거운
06 상자
07 들고
08 넣어요
09 좁아요
10 빼요

Day 24 page 239

Match

거실	clock
그림	to be cool
혼자	wall
시계	alone
부엌	to make
쓰다 **02**	moving
이사	living room
벽	painting, drawing
만들다	to use
멋있다	kitchen

Crossword Puzzle

				혼		
		만		자		
		들				
	쓰	다			벽	
						거
멋	있	다				실
			이	사		

Fill in the blanks

01 이사
02 혼자
03 멋있게
04 거실
05 벽
06 그림
07 시계
08 부엌
09 만들
10 쓸

Day 25 page 247

Match

부르다	to wash
편하다	all, every
버섯	to call
산책	mushroom
감사	gratitude
지우다	to be comfortable
씻다	to erase, to wash off
당근	walk
밝다	carrot
다	to be bright

Crossword Puzzle

				버	섯	
		씻				
부	르	다		감		
				사		
						편
	당	근				하
					밝	다

Fill in the blanks

01 지워요
02 씻어요
03 버섯
04 당근
05 불러요
06 다
07 산책
08 밝아요
09 편해요
10 감사

Day 26 page 255

Match

사진	camera
비싸다	price
휴대폰	to be famous
연습하다	dream
유명하다	to learn
찍다	to be expensive
꿈	photo
가격	to practice
카메라	to take, to film
배우다	mobile phone

Crossword Puzzle

			유		가	격
꿈			명			
	연	습	하	다		
			다			
	카				찍	
	메		배	우	다	
	라					

Fill in the blanks

01 꿈
02 사진
03 배우고
04 카메라
05 가격
06 비싸요
07 휴대폰
08 찍어요
09 연습할
10 유명한

Day 27 page 263

Match

오다	weather
예쁘다	to be warm
딸기	flower
빨간색	to come
과일	strawberry
봄	to be pretty
날씨	red (color)
좋아하다	fruit
꽃	spring (season)
따뜻하다	to like

Crossword Puzzle

				오		
	따	뜻	하	다		
					꽃	
딸	기		좋			
			아			봄
			하			
	예	쁘	다			

Fill in the blanks

01 봄
02 왔어요
03 날씨
04 따뜻해요
05 예쁜
06 꽃
07 딸기
08 빨간색
09 좋아하는
10 과일

Day 28 page 271

Match

눈 **02**	to be cold
자주	inside
전화하다	wind
목도리	to wait
장갑	scarf
기다리다	snow
알다	glove
바람	often
안	to know
춥다	to call

Crossword Puzzle

				자	주	
눈		기				
		다				
		리				
	알	다				춥
			전	화	하	다
바	람					

Fill in the blanks

01 기다리고
02 눈
03 바람
04 추워요
05 자주
06 안
07 전화했어요
08 알아요
09 장갑
10 목도리

Day 29 page 279

Match

못하다	potato
양파	knife
칼	to do well
썰다	taste
맛	love
배달	onion
잘하다	to not do well
손가락	delivery
감자	finger
사랑	to chop, to cut

Crossword Puzzle

	칼					
				잘		
			못	하	다	
				다		맛
	감	자			배	
					달	
		손	가	락		

Fill in the blanks

01 잘해요
02 맛
03 못해요
04 사랑
05 양파
06 감자
07 칼
08 썰었어요
09 손가락
10 배달

Day 30 page 287

Match

베개	laundry
쓰레기	doing the dishes
준비하다	blanket
손님	pillow
빨래	guest
버리다	trash
과자	market
설거지	snack
이불	to prepare
시장	to throw away

Crossword Puzzle

		준			빨	래
		비				
		하				
버	리	다		베		
				개		설
	시	장				거
			과	자		지

Fill in the blanks

01 손님
02 빨래
03 설거지
04 이불
05 베개
06 쓰레기
07 버렸어요
08 시장
09 과자
10 준비할 거예요

Day 31 page 299

Match

실패	to order
쇼핑	the Internet
어렵다	to be small
모자	to be difficult
치마	success
인터넷	shopping
주문하다	next
다음	hat, cap
성공	skirt
작다	failure

Crossword Puzzle

						실
	주	문	하	다		패
				음		
인	터	넷			어	
					렵	
	모	자		작	다	

Fill in the blanks

01 인터넷
02 치마
03 주문했어요
04 실패
05 작아요
06 쇼핑
07 어려워요
08 성공
09 다음
10 모자

Day 32 page 307

Match

허리	police
문자	to be late
늦다	accident
경찰	text message
보내다	promise, plan
약속	motorcycle
조금	lower back
택시	to send, to spend
사고	taxi, cab
오토바이	a little, a bit

Crossword Puzzle

사				문	자	
고			늦			
	보	내	다		오	
					토	
조	금				바	
		약			이	
		속				

Fill in the blanks

01 약속
02 늦었어요
03 택시
04 오토바이
05 사고
06 경찰
07 문자
08 보냈어요
09 허리
10 조금

Day 33 page 315

Match

나라	popularity
가수	map
지도	singer
궁금하다	to need
단어	ear
인기	Korean (language)
필요하다	address
귀	to be curious
주소	country, nation
한국어	word

Crossword Puzzle

	귀					
			한		나	라
			국			
		단	어		필	
인	기				요	
			궁	금	하	다
					다	

Fill in the blanks

01 가수
02 인기
03 나라
04 한국어
05 필요해요
06 단어
07 귀
08 지도
09 주소
10 궁금해요

Day 34 page 323

Match

열	to come out
열다	pharmacy
약국	nose
건강	to open
문	cold
차	door
약	fever
감기	medicine
나오다	tea
코	health

Crossword Puzzle

					차	
	문					
			열		건	강
	나	오	다			
				약		
감	기			국		

Fill in the blanks

01 문
02 열고
03 감기
04 열
05 코
06 나왔어요
07 약국
08 약
09 차
10 건강

Day 35 page 331

Match

오이	to work
마음	apple
바나나	belly, stomach
절대	absolutely
사과	mind, heart
몸무게	banana
토마토	body weight
일하다	to be weak
약하다	tomato
배	cucumber

Crossword Puzzle

					사	
바	나	나			과	
			일			
		약	하	다		
			다			
배				절	대	
		마	음			

Fill in the blanks

01 사과
02 바나나
03 일했어요
04 오이
05 토마토
06 배
07 마음
08 약해졌어요
09 몸무게
10 절대

Day 36 page 339

Match

의사	to get hurt
아프다	to rest
힘들다	hospital
어제	exercise
병원	yesterday
운동	doctor
손	to fall down
쉬다	to be difficult
다치다	to be sick, to hurt
넘어지다	hand

Crossword Puzzle

						다
	넘					치
	어			힘	들	다
	지					
쉬	다		손		어	
					제	
	병	원				

Fill in the blanks

01 어제
02 운동
03 넘어졌어요
04 손
05 다쳤어요
06 아팠어요
07 병원
08 의사
09 쉬었어요
10 힘들어요

Day 37 page 347

Match

다니다	umbrella
비	to take off
우산	student
목욕	shoe
학생	bath
벗다	rain
자전거	foot
발	bicycle
신발	to not have
없다	to attend

Crossword Puzzle

					자	
발					전	
			벗		거	
	다	니	다			
						비
	우		목	욕		
	산					

Fill in the blanks

01 학생
02 자전거
03 다녀요
04 비
05 우산
06 없었어요
07 신발
08 벗었어요
09 발
10 목욕

Day 38 page 355

Match

오전	lie
놀라다	frustration, anger
이상하다	sometimes
거짓말	older brother
오빠	to be strange
가끔	head, hair
벌레	morning
짜증	to hate
싫다	to be surprised
머리	bug, worm

Crossword Puzzle

						가
짜	증			놀		끔
				라		
	이	상	하	다		
거					벌	레
짓				머		
말				리		

Fill in the blanks

01 오빠
02 가끔
03 거짓말
04 짜증
05 오전
06 머리
07 벌레
08 놀랐어요
09 싫어요
10 이상해요

Day 39 page 363

Match

마트	to buy
생선	meat
저녁	fish
채소	to talk, to speak
달걀	cooking, food
요리	vegetable
엄마	supermarket
말하다	evening
사다	egg
고기	mom

Crossword Puzzle

	엄	마			달	걀
		트				
				사		
		말	하	다		
저						
녁				생	선	

Fill in the blanks

01 저녁
02 엄마
03 마트
04 고기
05 샀어요
06 생선
07 채소
08 말했어요
09 달걀
10 요리

Day 40 page 371

Match

믿다	bird
냄새	tree, wood
새	mountain
산	to move
몸	to go up
움직이다	smell
나무	grandfather
할아버지	person, people
올라가다	to trust
사람	body

Crossword Puzzle

	할			산		
	아					
	버		나		올	
	지		무		라	
					가	
		움	직	이	다	
사	람					새

Fill in the blanks

01 할아버지
02 산
03 올라가요
04 믿어요
05 사람
06 새
07 나무
08 냄새
09 몸
10 움직이는

Day 41 page 383

Match

잃어버리다	to be spacious
들어가다	bookstore
넓다	airport
어디	to ask
찾다	here
공항	to find
물어보다	to enter
길	where
서점	to lose
여기	road, street

Crossword Puzzle

			공	항		
	길				물	
					어	디
		들			보	
	잃	어	버	리	다	
		가				
		다		여	기	

Fill in the blanks

01 공항
02 넓어서
03 길
04 잃어버렸어요
05 여기
06 어디
07 서점
08 들어갔어요
09 물어봤어요
10 찾았어요

Day 42 page 391

Match

가깝다	university, college
은행	convenience store
역	right side
편의점	to cross
다시	station
대학교	to be close
앞	left side
건너다	front
왼쪽	again
오른쪽	bank

Crossword Puzzle

			앞			
		오				
		른		건	너	다
	왼	쪽				시
역		대	학	교		

Fill in the blanks

01 대학교
02 역
03 가까워요
04 오른쪽
05 은행
06 왼쪽
07 편의점
08 앞
09 건너요
10 다시

Day 43 page 399

Match

검은색	when
가방	older brother
모르다	to be different
형	black
색깔	wallet
다르다	white
자동차	color
하얀색	to not know
지갑	bag
언제	car

Crossword Puzzle

	형					
					가	방
검	은	색				
		깔		모		
			다	르	다	
				다		
언	제					

Fill in the blanks

01 색깔
02 검은색
03 지갑
04 자동차
05 가방
06 언제
07 몰라요
08 형
09 하얀색
10 달라요

Day 44 page 407

Match

연필	pen
펜	to be bad
이유	pencil
문제	to lend
아니다	to be nice
빌려주다	to be crazy
착하다	problem
나쁘다	reason
미치다	to not be
또	again

Crossword Puzzle

	또				이	유
				빌		
펜				려		
				주		나
		아	니	다		쁘
						다
	문	제				

Fill in the blanks

01 착해요
02 문제
03 연필
04 빌려주면
05 펜
06 또
07 이유
08 미치겠어요
09 나쁜
10 아니에요

Day 45 page 415

Match

카드	to decide, to choose
달다	disappointment
계획	plant
결혼	to be bitter
실망	marriage, wedding
끓이다	card
식물	to boil
정하다	to be cheap
쓰다 **03**	to be sweet
싸다	plan

Crossword Puzzle

				식		
		정		물		
		하			실	망
	싸	다				
					끓	
		계	획		이	
카	드				다	

Fill in the blanks

01 결혼
02 식물
03 카드
04 정했어요
05 싸게
06 끓이고
07 달아요
08 써요
09 실망
10 계획

Day 46 page 423

Match

때	greeting
짧다	to sell
인사	fur, hair
종이	ring
팔다	radio
신문	glass
털	to be short
유리	time, when
반지	paper
라디오	newspaper

Crossword Puzzle

		인				
		사			짧	
때				팔	다	
	라					
	디		신	문		
	오					
				종	이	

Fill in the blanks

01 팔아요
02 털
03 반지
04 짧은
05 때
06 라디오
07 유리
08 신문
09 종이
10 인사

Day 47 page 431

Match

비슷하다	to be far
입	glasses
실수	to think
쌍둥이	to be young
뒤	twin
쉽다	mistake
멀다	behind, after
어리다	to be similar
안경	to be easy
생각하다	mouth

Crossword Puzzle

		뒤		실		
입				수		
					비	
	쌍	둥	이		슷	
					하	
			어	리	다	
쉽	다					

Fill in the blanks

01 쌍둥이
02 어렸을
03 비슷하게
04 생각하는
05 쉽게
06 안경
07 입
08 멀리서
09 뒤
10 실수

Day 48 page 439

Match

이기다	toe
지나다	secret
사전	arm
축구	basketball
영어	dictionary
발가락	baseball
비밀	to pass
농구	English
야구	soccer
팔	to win

Crossword Puzzle

		비	밀			
사						
전				팔		
		야				
	축	구				지
						나
				이	기	다

Fill in the blanks

01 축구
02 농구
03 야구
04 지난
05 이겼어요
06 팔
07 비밀
08 발가락
09 영어
10 사전

Day 49 page 447

Match

불	to count
날다	to understand
바꾸다	cosmos, universe
우주	parking lot
주차장	to pick, to choose
세다	Earth
알아듣다	fire, light
고르다	ticket
지구	to fly
표	to change

Crossword Puzzle

						세
표				고	르	다
			알			
			아		지	
			듣		구	
	바	꾸	다			
				우	주	

Fill in the blanks

01 주차장
02 골랐어요
03 표
04 세어
05 불
06 날았어요
07 지구
08 우주
09 알아듣기
10 바꿨어요

Day 50 page 455

Match

열쇠	to be correct
서다	to be light
가볍다	to get off/out of
운전	it, that
맞다	key
느리다	driving
그것	to stand
내리다	to grab, to hold
휴지	to be slow
잡다	tissue

Crossword Puzzle

					휴	
그	것				지	
	열	쇠		내		
			느	리	다	
		잡		다		
가	볍	다				

Fill in the blanks

01 운전
02 느리게
03 내렸어요
04 열쇠
05 잡았어요
06 그것
07 가벼웠어요
08 휴지
09 맞았어요
10 서

INDEX listed in Korean dictionary order

ㄱ

ㄴ

ㄷ

ㅂ

ㅇ

ㅊ

ㅋ

ㅌ

MP3 audio files can be downloaded at
https://talktomeinkorean.com/audio.